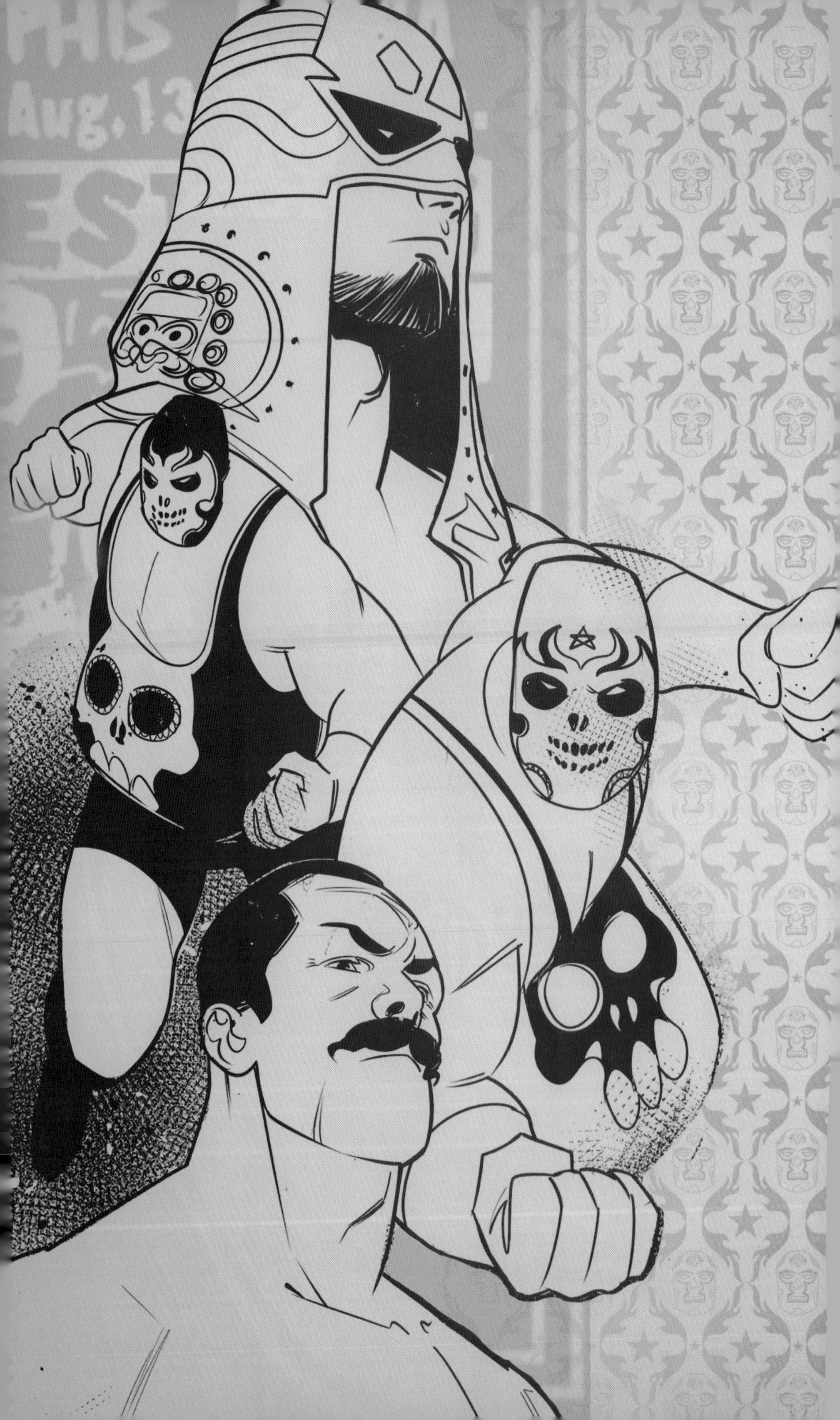

I WILL RISE!

OVER THE ROPES™

STLING
ANDRE THE
GIANT
ARCHIE GOULDIE THE
STOMPER

JAY SANDLIN
WRITER

ARTIST
ANTONELLO COSENTINO

STEFANO SEGALA
COLORIST

LETTERER
JUSTIN BIRCH

EDITORS
GIOVANNA T. OROZCO
CHRIS FERNANDEZ

DIANA BERMÚDEZ
BOOK DESIGNER

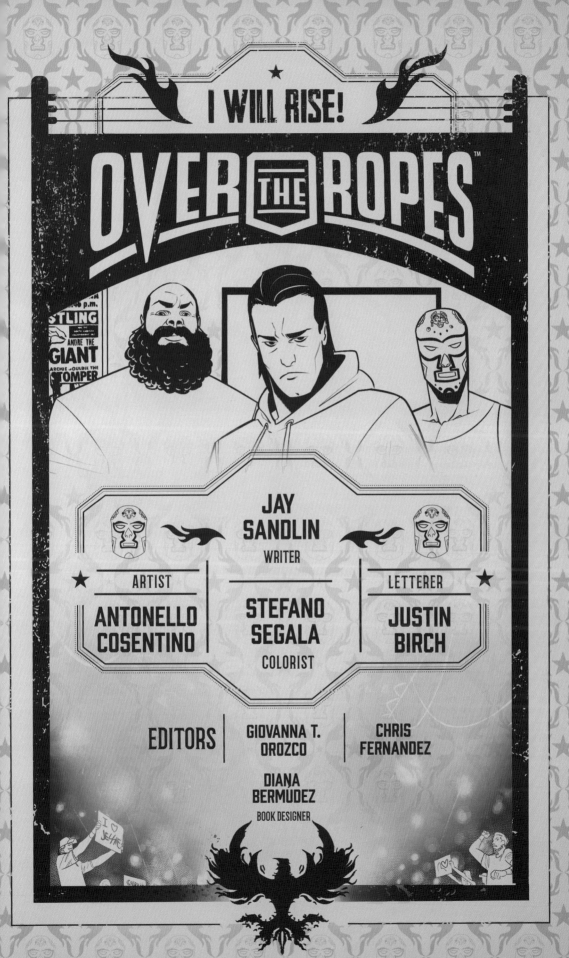

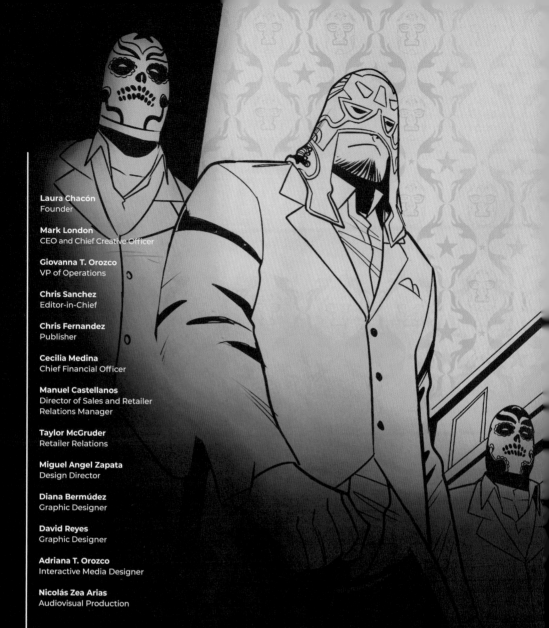

Laura Chacón
Founder

Mark London
CEO and Chief Creative Officer

Giovanna T. Orozco
VP of Operations

Chris Sanchez
Editor-in-Chief

Chris Fernandez
Publisher

Cecilia Medina
Chief Financial Officer

Manuel Castellanos
Director of Sales and Retailer
Relations Manager

Taylor McGruder
Retailer Relations

Miguel Angel Zapata
Design Director

Diana Bermúdez
Graphic Designer

David Reyes
Graphic Designer

Adriana T. Orozco
Interactive Media Designer

Nicolás Zea Arias
Audiovisual Production

FOR MAD CAVE COMICS, INC.

Over the ropes™ Trade Paperback

Published by Mad Cave Studios, Inc. 8838 SW 129 St. Miami, FL 33176 © 2020 Mad Cave
Studios, Inc. All rights reserved. Contains materials originally published in single magazine
form as Over the ropes™ #1-5.

Printed in Canada
ISBN: 978-1-952303-00-5

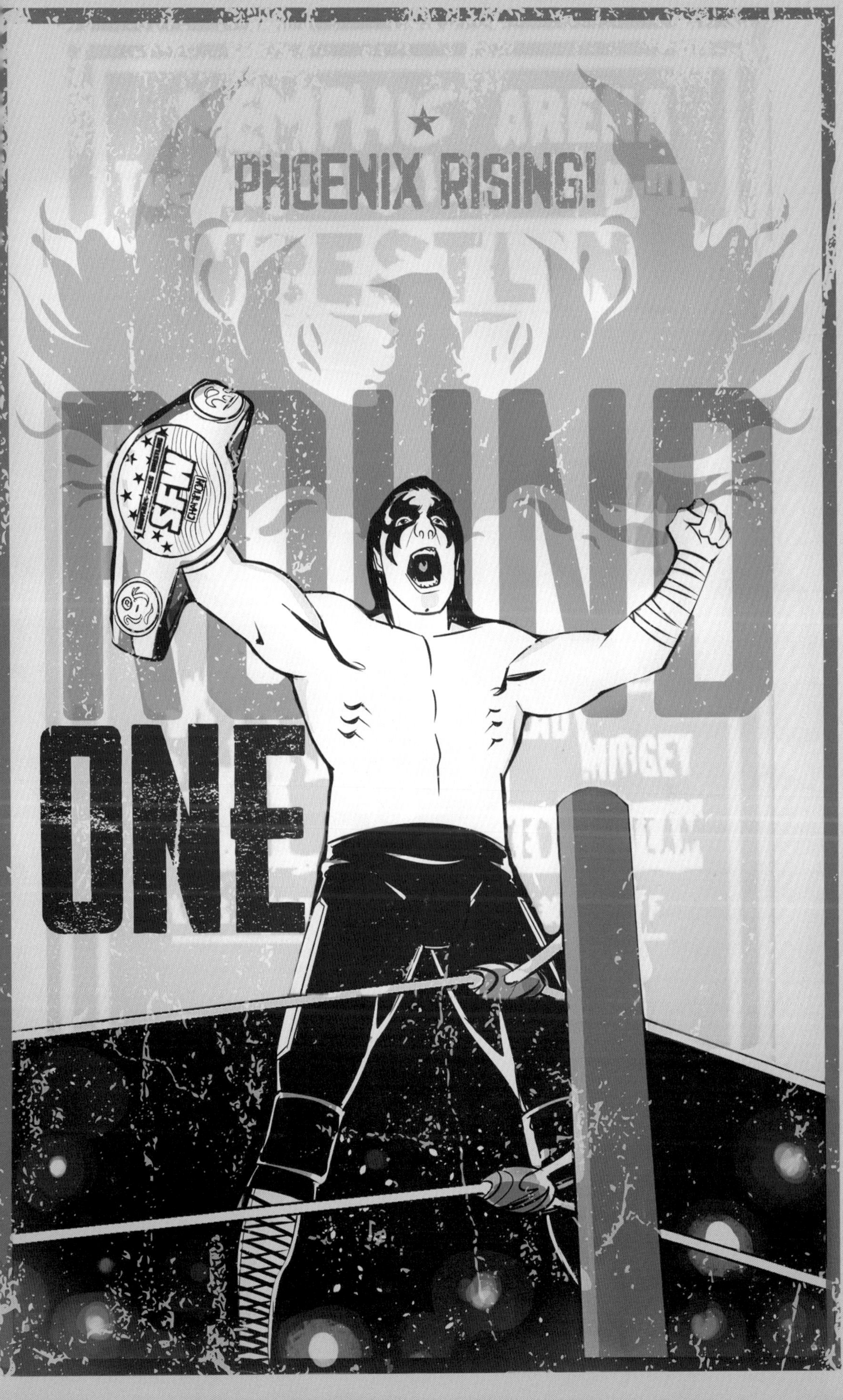
PHOENIX RISING!
ROUND
ONE

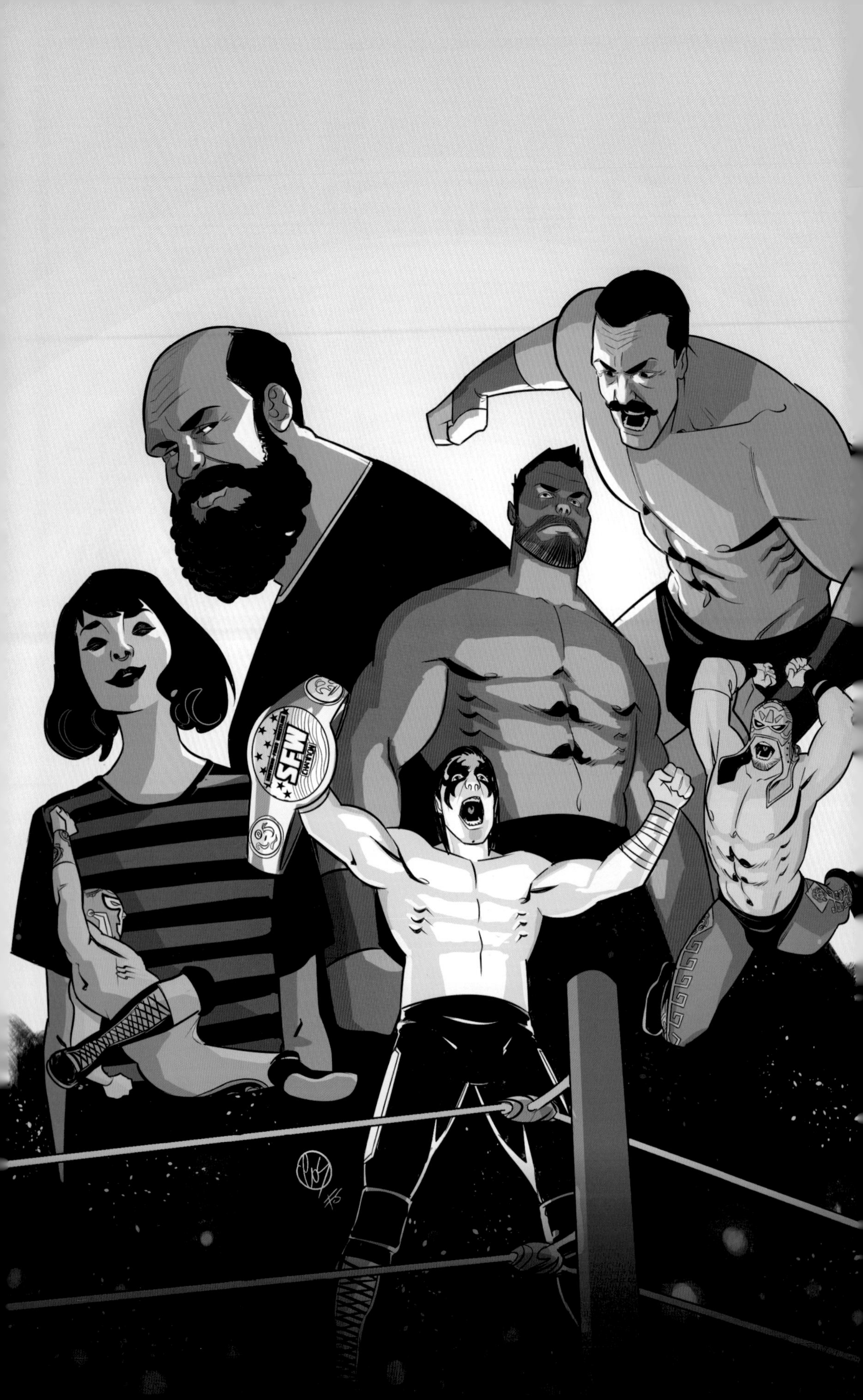
SFW
CHAMPION

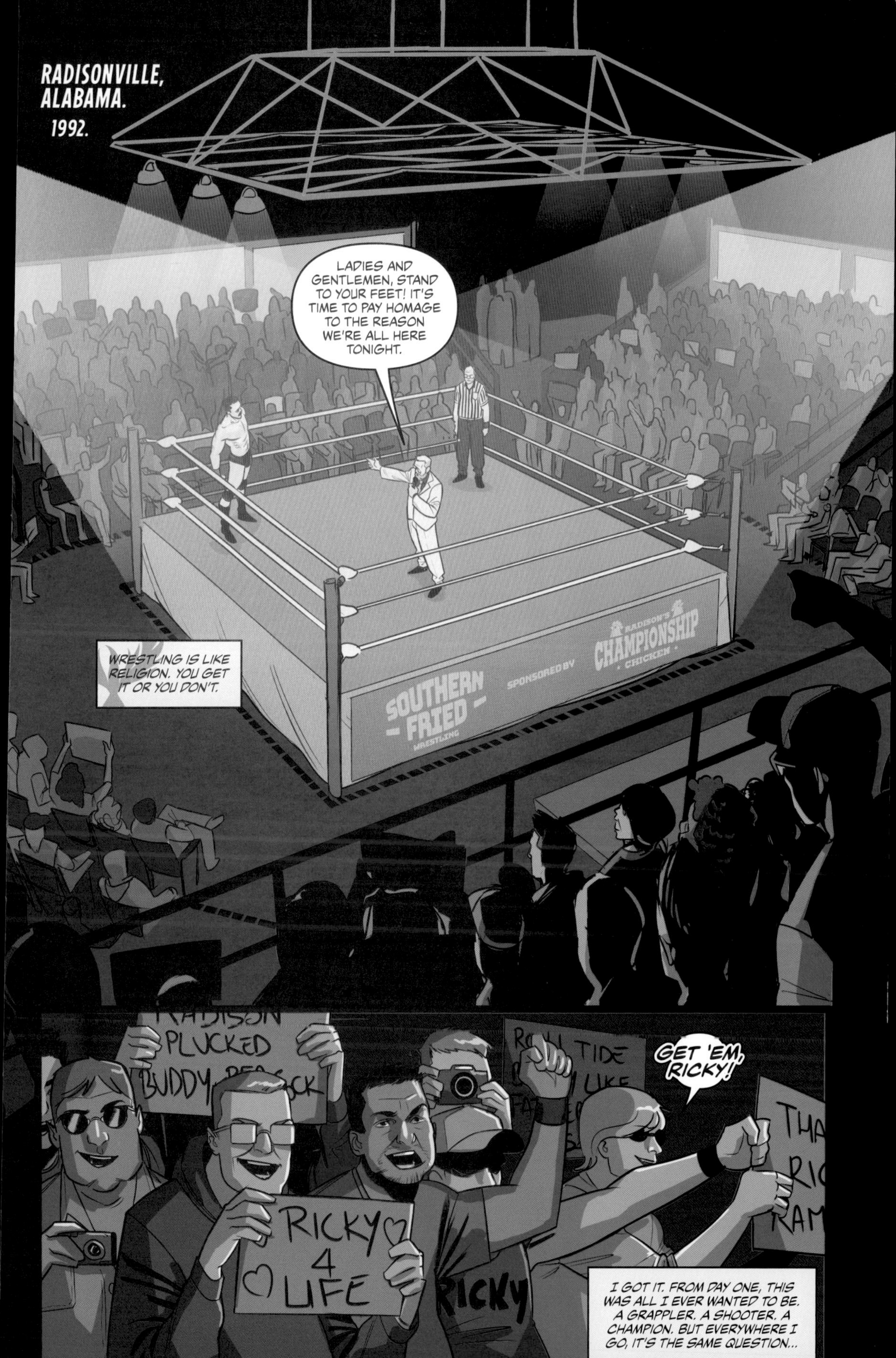
RADISONVILLE, ALABAMA.
1992.
LADIES AND GENTLEMEN, STAND TO YOUR FEET! IT'S TIME TO PAY HOMAGE TO THE REASON WE'RE ALL HERE TONIGHT.
WRESTLING IS LIKE RELIGION. YOU GET IT OR YOU DON'T.
SOUTHERN FRIED WRESTLING
SPONSORED BY
RADISON'S CHAMPIONSHIP CHICKEN
PLUCKED
GET 'EM, RICKY!
RICKY 4 LIFE
RICKY
I GOT IT. FROM DAY ONE, THIS WAS ALL I EVER WANTED TO BE. A GRAPPLER. A SHOOTER. A CHAMPION. BUT EVERYWHERE I GO, IT'S THE SAME QUESTION...

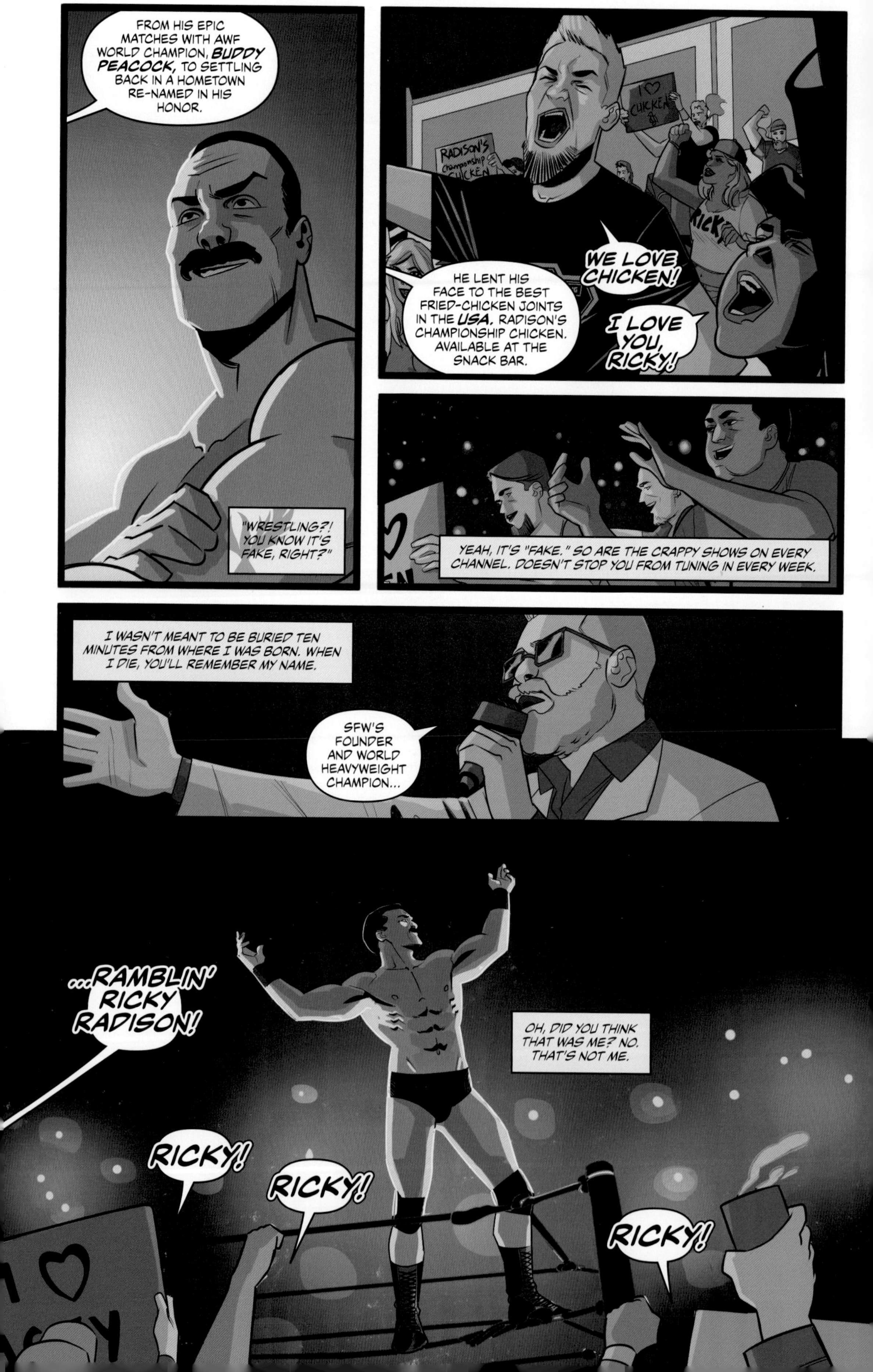
FROM HIS EPIC MATCHES WITH AWF WORLD CHAMPION, BUDDY PEACOCK, TO SETTLING BACK IN A HOMETOWN RE-NAMED IN HIS HONOR.
"WRESTLING?! YOU KNOW IT'S FAKE, RIGHT?"
I ♡ CHICKEN
RADISON'S Championship CHICKEN
WE LOVE CHICKEN!
HE LENT HIS FACE TO THE BEST FRIED-CHICKEN JOINTS IN THE USA. RADISON'S CHAMPIONSHIP CHICKEN. AVAILABLE AT THE SNACK BAR.
I LOVE YOU, RICKY!
YEAH, IT'S "FAKE." SO ARE THE CRAPPY SHOWS ON EVERY CHANNEL. DOESN'T STOP YOU FROM TUNING IN EVERY WEEK.
I WASN'T MEANT TO BE BURIED TEN MINUTES FROM WHERE I WAS BORN. WHEN I DIE, YOU'LL REMEMBER MY NAME.
SFW'S FOUNDER AND WORLD HEAVYWEIGHT CHAMPION...
...RAMBLIN' RICKY RADISON!
OH, DID YOU THINK THAT WAS ME? NO. THAT'S NOT ME.
RICKY!
RICKY!
RICKY!

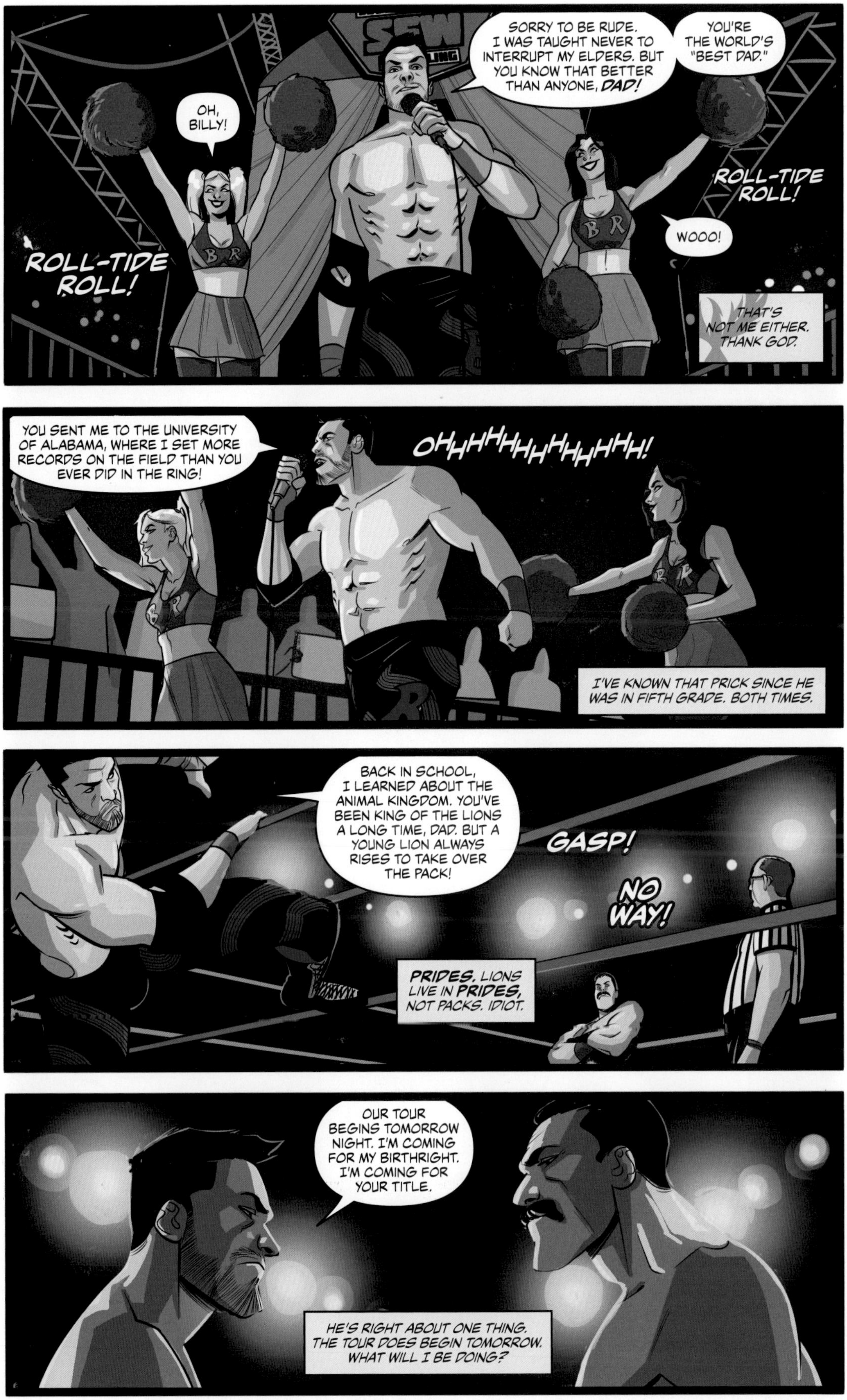

SORRY TO BE RUDE. I WAS TAUGHT NEVER TO INTERRUPT MY ELDERS. BUT YOU KNOW THAT BETTER THAN ANYONE, DAD!
YOU'RE THE WORLD'S "BEST DAD."
OH, BILLY!
ROLL-TIDE ROLL!
WOOO!
ROLL-TIDE ROLL!
THAT'S NOT ME EITHER. THANK GOD.
YOU SENT ME TO THE UNIVERSITY OF ALABAMA, WHERE I SET MORE RECORDS ON THE FIELD THAN YOU EVER DID IN THE RING!
OHHHHHHHHHHHHH!
I'VE KNOWN THAT PRICK SINCE HE WAS IN FIFTH GRADE. BOTH TIMES.
BACK IN SCHOOL, I LEARNED ABOUT THE ANIMAL KINGDOM. YOU'VE BEEN KING OF THE LIONS A LONG TIME, DAD. BUT A YOUNG LION ALWAYS RISES TO TAKE OVER THE PACK!
GASP!
NO WAY!
PRIDES. LIONS LIVE IN PRIDES, NOT PACKS. IDIOT.
OUR TOUR BEGINS TOMORROW NIGHT. I'M COMING FOR MY BIRTHRIGHT. I'M COMING FOR YOUR TITLE.
HE'S RIGHT ABOUT ONE THING. THE TOUR DOES BEGIN TOMORROW. WHAT WILL I BE DOING?

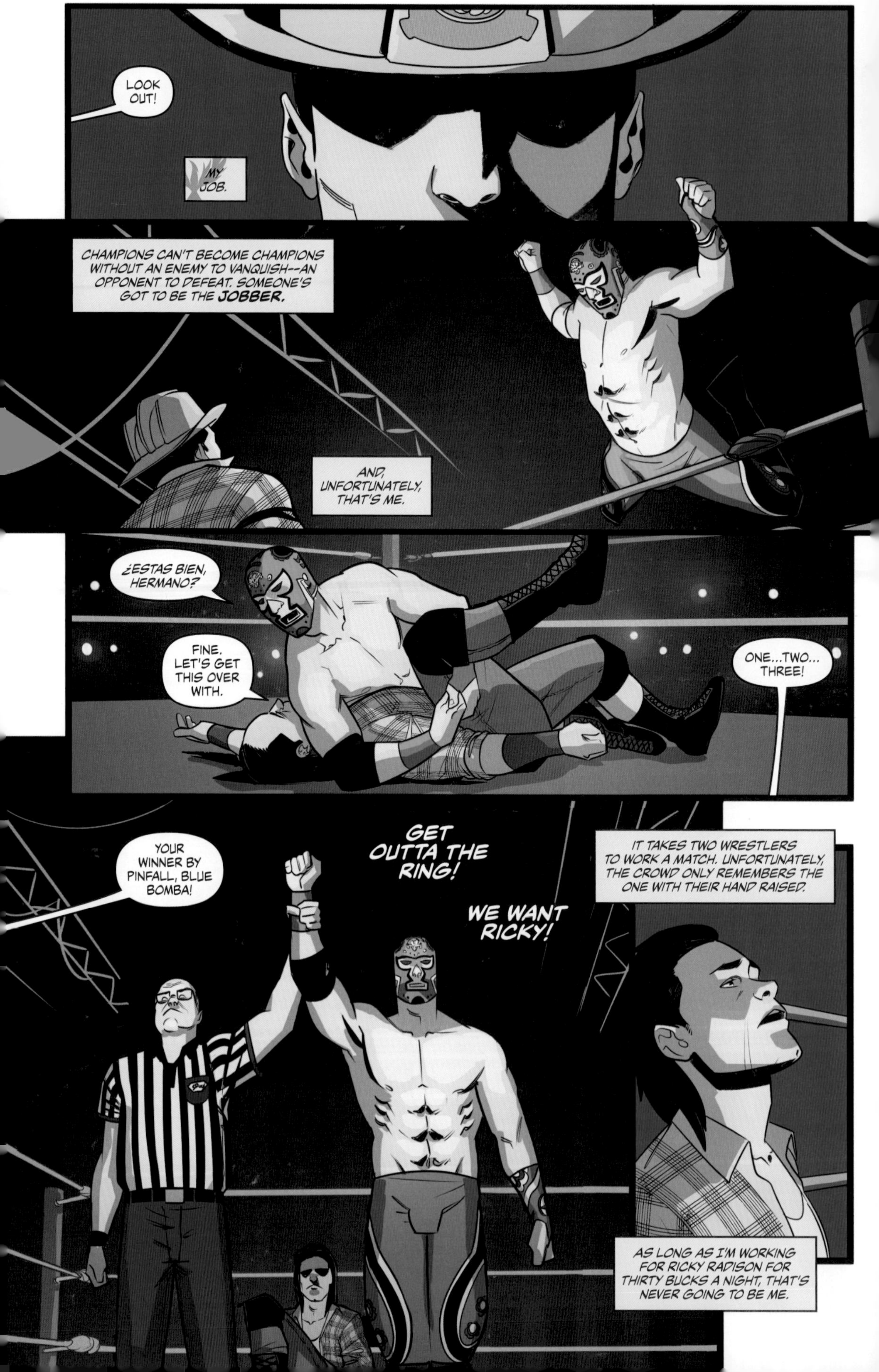
LOOK OUT!
MY JOB.
CHAMPIONS CAN'T BECOME CHAMPIONS WITHOUT AN ENEMY TO VANQUISH--AN OPPONENT TO DEFEAT. SOMEONE'S GOT TO BE THE JOBBER.
AND, UNFORTUNATELY, THAT'S ME.
¿ESTAS BIEN, HERMANO?
FINE. LET'S GET THIS OVER WITH.
ONE...TWO... THREE!
YOUR WINNER BY PINFALL, BLUE BOMBA!
GET OUTTA THE RING!
WE WANT RICKY!
IT TAKES TWO WRESTLERS TO WORK A MATCH. UNFORTUNATELY, THE CROWD ONLY REMEMBERS THE ONE WITH THEIR HAND RAISED.
AS LONG AS I'M WORKING FOR RICKY RADISON FOR THIRTY BUCKS A NIGHT, THAT'S NEVER GOING TO BE ME.

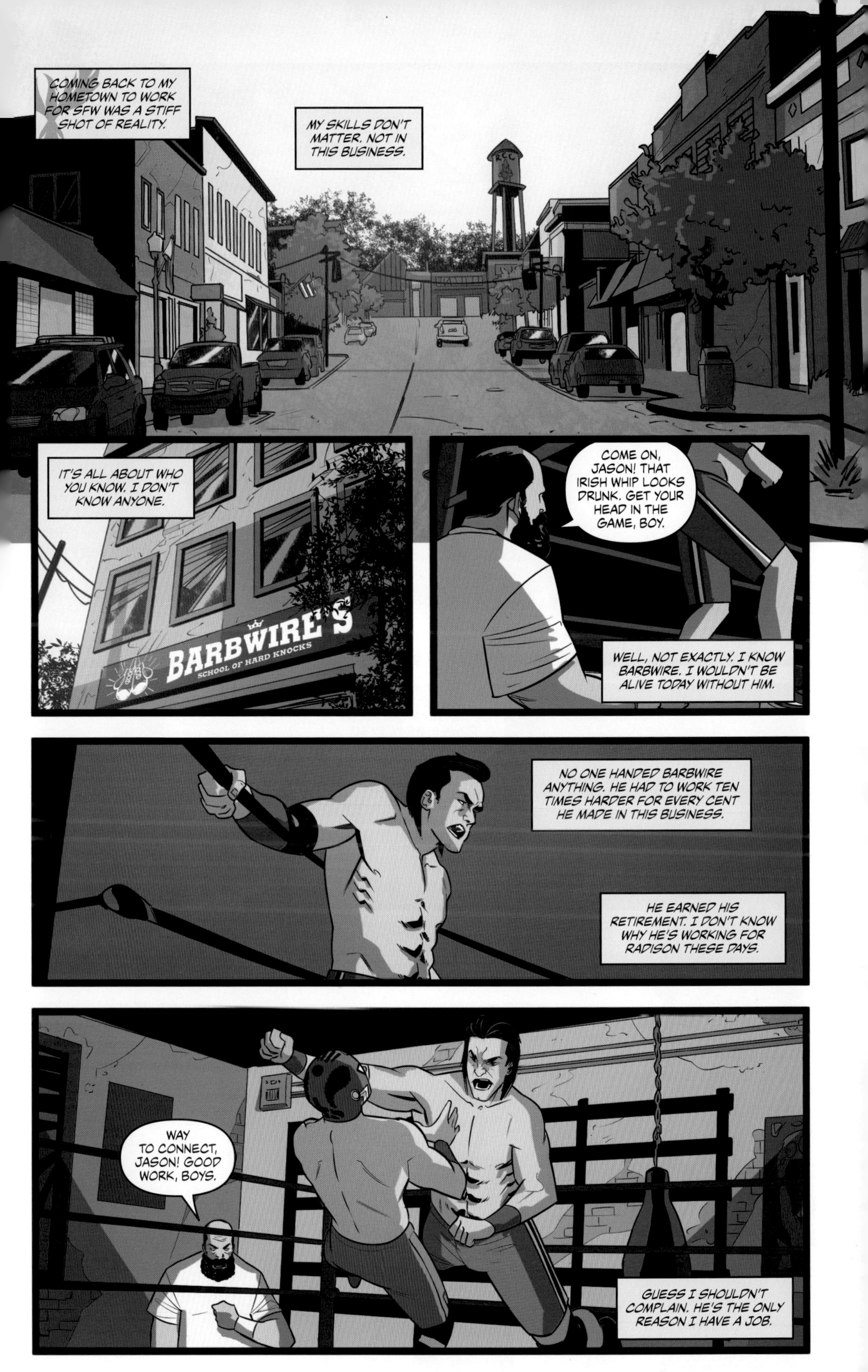
COMING BACK TO MY HOMETOWN TO WORK FOR SFW WAS A STIFF SHOT OF REALITY.
MY SKILLS DON'T MATTER. NOT IN THIS BUSINESS.
IT'S ALL ABOUT WHO YOU KNOW. I DON'T KNOW ANYONE.
BARBWIRE'S
SCHOOL OF HARD KNOCKS
COME ON, JASON! THAT IRISH WHIP LOOKS DRUNK. GET YOUR HEAD IN THE GAME, BOY.
WELL, NOT EXACTLY. I KNOW BARBWIRE. I WOULDN'T BE ALIVE TODAY WITHOUT HIM.
NO ONE HANDED BARBWIRE ANYTHING. HE HAD TO WORK TEN TIMES HARDER FOR EVERY CENT HE MADE IN THIS BUSINESS.
HE EARNED HIS RETIREMENT. I DON'T KNOW WHY HE'S WORKING FOR RADISON THESE DAYS.
WAY TO CONNECT, JASON! GOOD WORK, BOYS.
GUESS I SHOULDN'T COMPLAIN. HE'S THE ONLY REASON I HAVE A JOB.

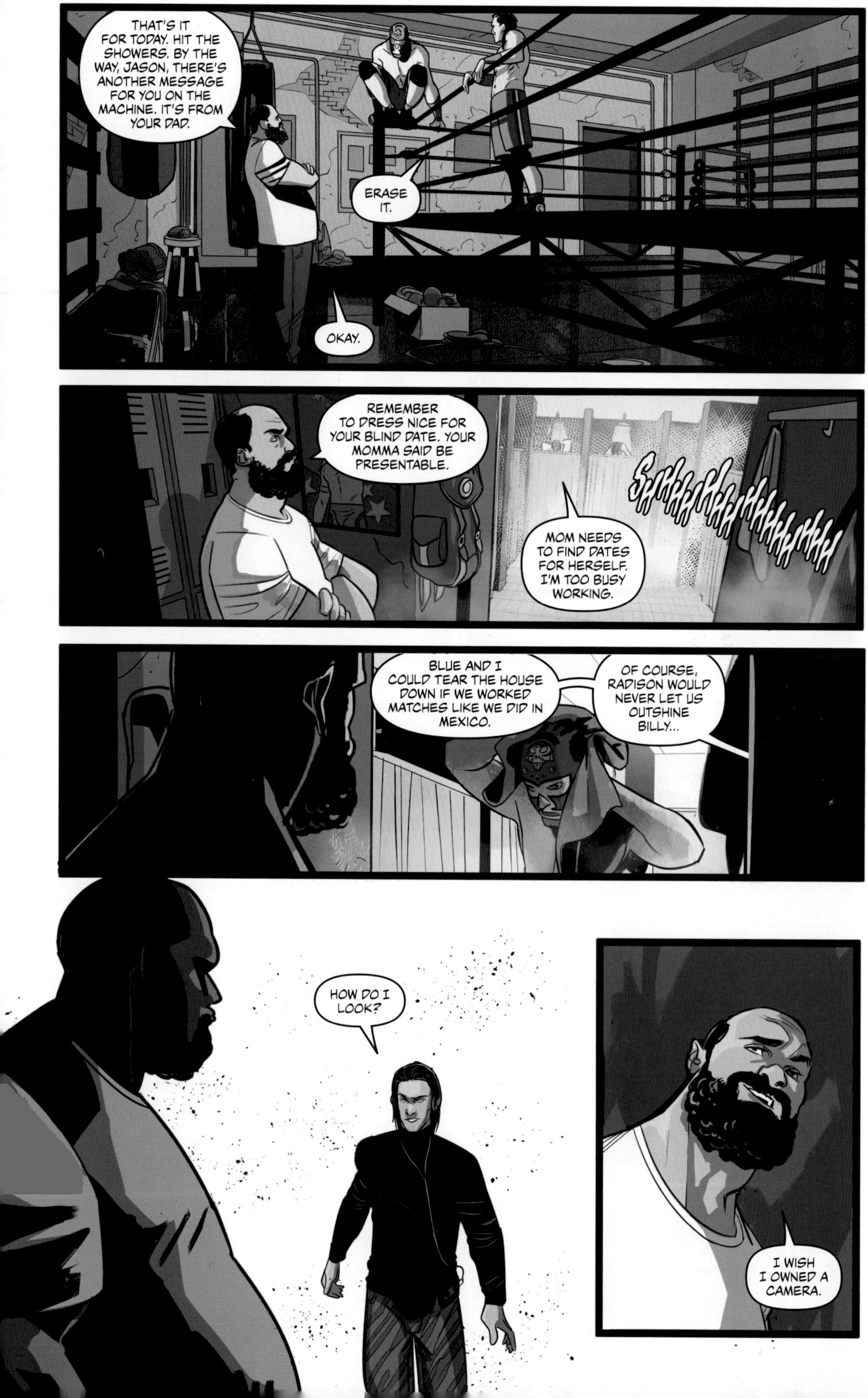
THAT'S IT FOR TODAY. HIT THE SHOWERS. BY THE WAY, JASON, THERE'S ANOTHER MESSAGE FOR YOU ON THE MACHINE. IT'S FROM YOUR DAD.
ERASE IT.
OKAY.
REMEMBER TO DRESS NICE FOR YOUR BLIND DATE. YOUR MOMMA SAID BE PRESENTABLE.
SHHHHHHHHHHHHHHHHH
MOM NEEDS TO FIND DATES FOR HERSELF. I'M TOO BUSY WORKING.
BLUE AND I COULD TEAR THE HOUSE DOWN IF WE WORKED MATCHES LIKE WE DID IN MEXICO.
OF COURSE, RADISON WOULD NEVER LET US OUTSHINE BILLY...
HOW DO I LOOK?
I WISH I OWNED A CAMERA.

WRESTLING?! YOU KNOW IT'S FAKE, RIGHT?

I MEAN, IT'S COOL. EVERYONE HAS DREAMS. I KNEW LOTS OF GUYS THAT GREW UP WANTING TO BE WRESTLERS--THEY WANTED TO BE *RICKY RADISON* OR *BUDDY PEACOCK.*

I'M NOTHING LIKE THEM.

OKAY...NEW SUBJECT. DO YOU LIKE TO READ? I DO. FROST, EMERSON, DICKINSON, ÷PSHH÷ I FEEL LIKE I'VE KNOWN THE BRONTË SISTERS FOR YEARS.

SHELLEY.

UM, MY NAME IS COURTNEY. COURTNEY HART.

I DO LIKE TO READ. MARY SHELLEY. WROTE *FRANKENSTEIN.*

PIONEERED SCIENCE FICTION WHEN SHE WAS ABOUT SEVENTEEN.

HAVE UNIVERSITY STANDARDS FALLEN THAT MUCH?

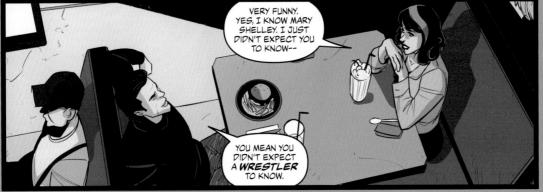

VERY FUNNY. YES, I KNOW MARY SHELLEY. I JUST DIDN'T EXPECT YOU TO KNOW--

YOU MEAN YOU DIDN'T EXPECT A *WRESTLER* TO KNOW.

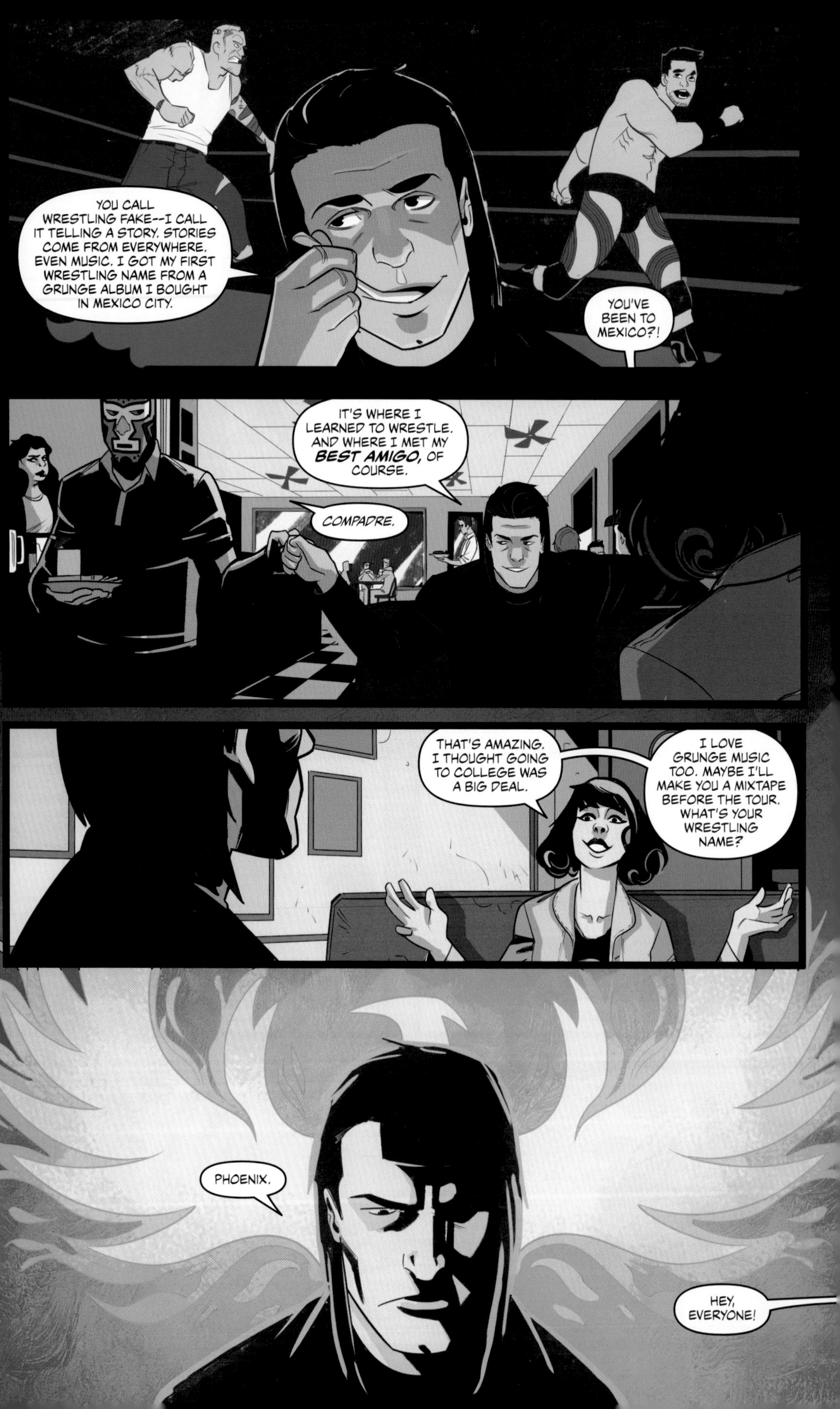
YOU CALL WRESTLING FAKE--I CALL IT TELLING A STORY. STORIES COME FROM EVERYWHERE. EVEN MUSIC. I GOT MY FIRST WRESTLING NAME FROM A GRUNGE ALBUM I BOUGHT IN MEXICO CITY.
YOU'VE BEEN TO MEXICO?!
IT'S WHERE I LEARNED TO WRESTLE. AND WHERE I MET MY BEST AMIGO, OF COURSE.
COMPADRE.
THAT'S AMAZING. I THOUGHT GOING TO COLLEGE WAS A BIG DEAL.
I LOVE GRUNGE MUSIC TOO. MAYBE I'LL MAKE YOU A MIXTAPE BEFORE THE TOUR. WHAT'S YOUR WRESTLING NAME?
PHOENIX.
HEY, EVERYONE!

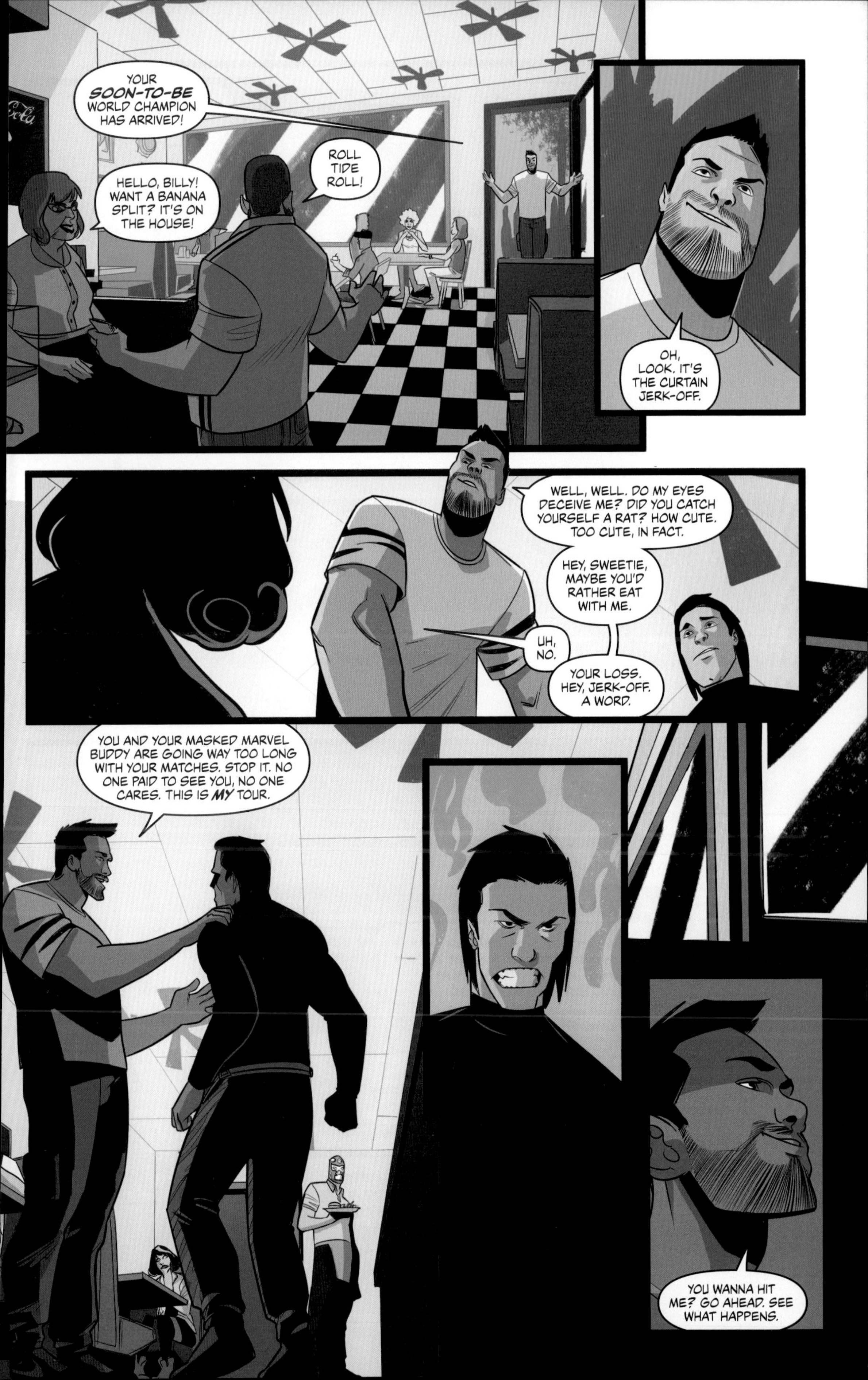
YOUR SOON-TO-BE WORLD CHAMPION HAS ARRIVED!
HELLO, BILLY! WANT A BANANA SPLIT? IT'S ON THE HOUSE!
ROLL TIDE ROLL!
OH, LOOK. IT'S THE CURTAIN JERK-OFF.
WELL, WELL. DO MY EYES DECEIVE ME? DID YOU CATCH YOURSELF A RAT? HOW CUTE. TOO CUTE, IN FACT.
HEY, SWEETIE, MAYBE YOU'D RATHER EAT WITH ME.
UH, NO.
YOUR LOSS. HEY, JERK-OFF. A WORD.
YOU AND YOUR MASKED MARVEL BUDDY ARE GOING WAY TOO LONG WITH YOUR MATCHES. STOP IT. NO ONE PAID TO SEE YOU, NO ONE CARES. THIS IS MY TOUR.
YOU WANNA HIT ME? GO AHEAD. SEE WHAT HAPPENS.

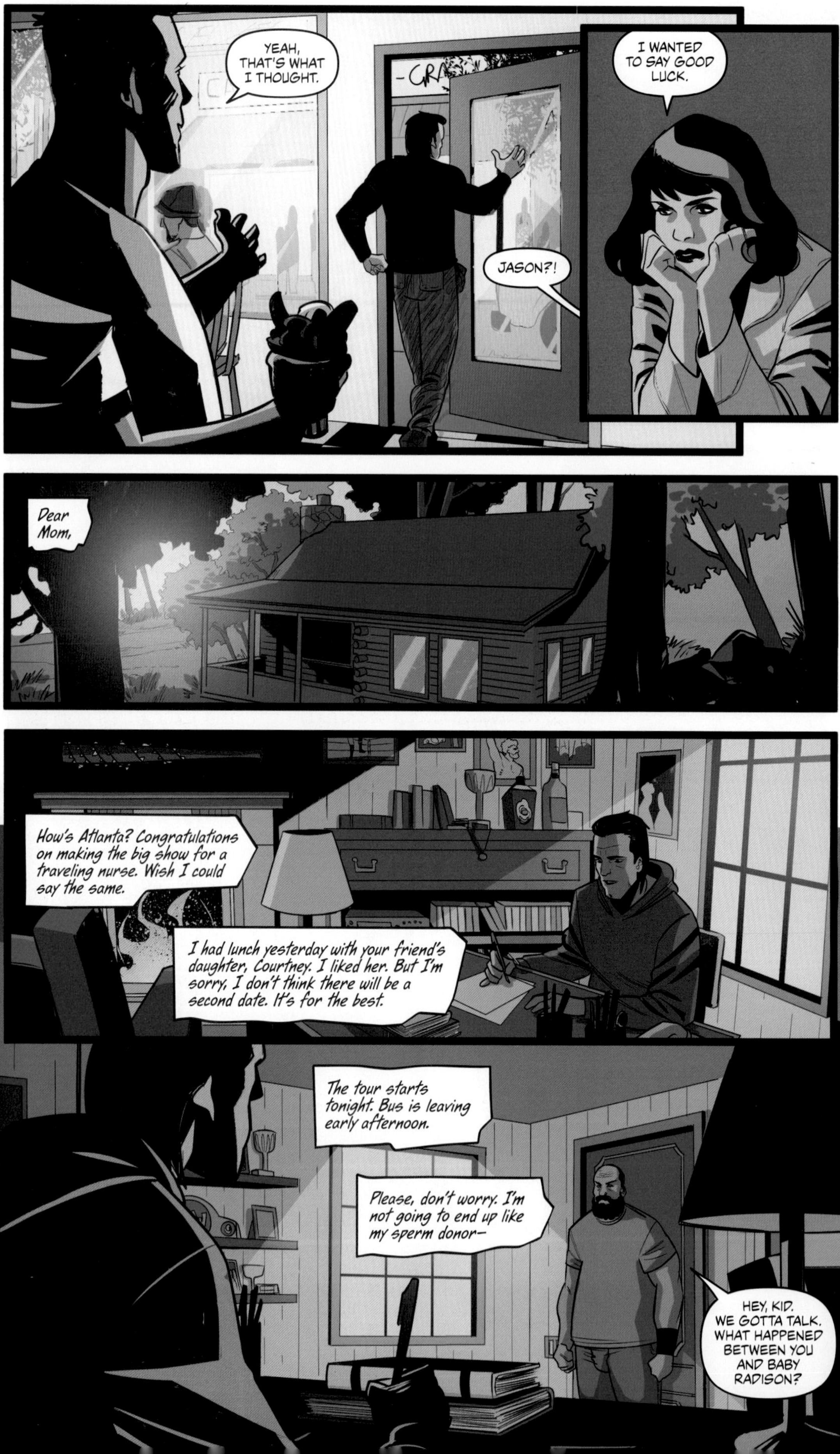
YEAH, THAT'S WHAT I THOUGHT.
I WANTED TO SAY GOOD LUCK.
JASON?!
Dear Mom,
How's Atlanta? Congratulations on making the big show for a traveling nurse. Wish I could say the same.
I had lunch yesterday with your friend's daughter, Courtney. I liked her. But I'm sorry, I don't think there will be a second date. It's for the best.
The tour starts tonight. Bus is leaving early afternoon.
Please, don't worry. I'm not going to end up like my sperm donor—
HEY, KID. WE GOTTA TALK. WHAT HAPPENED BETWEEN YOU AND BABY RADISON?

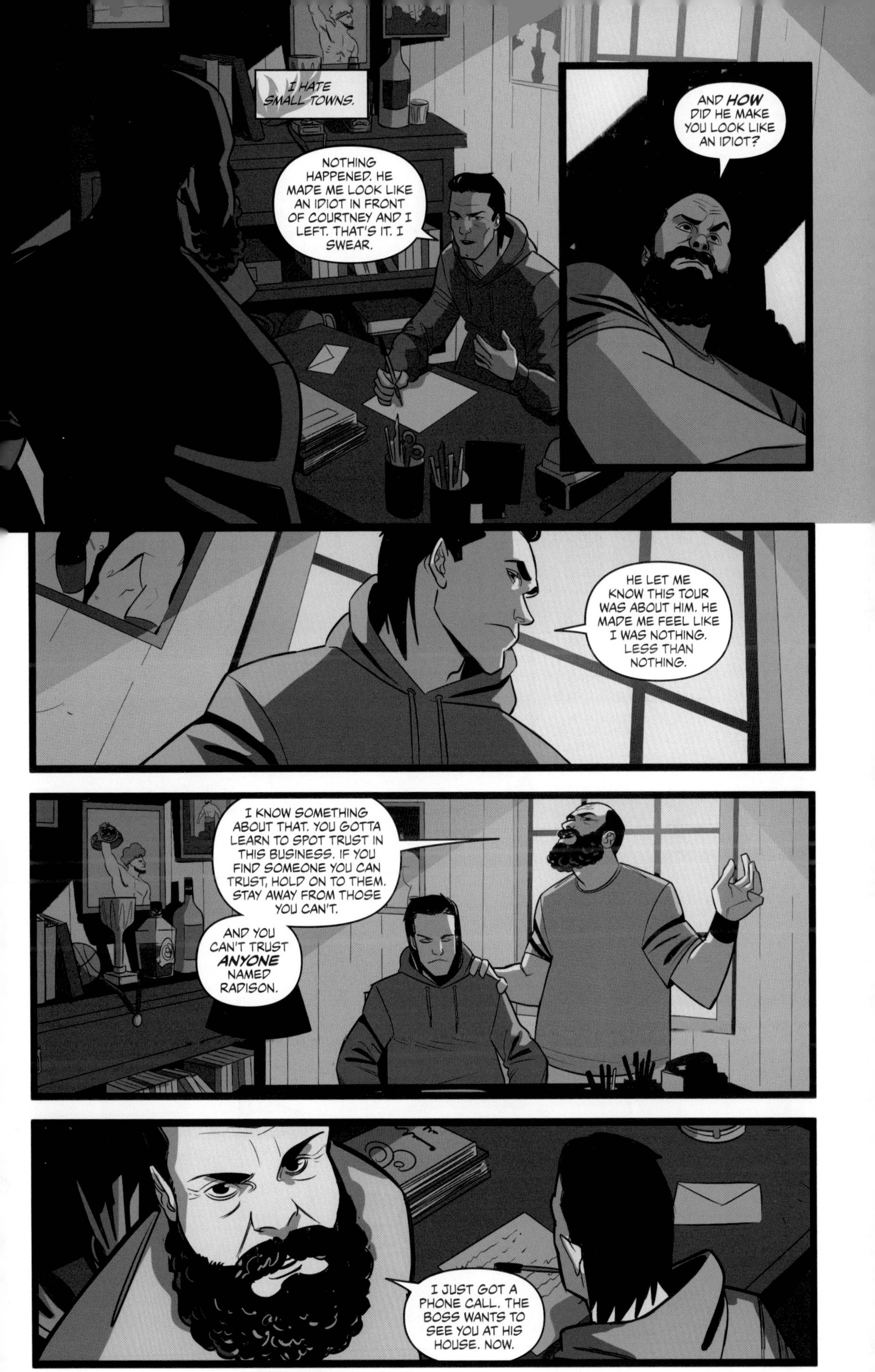
I HATE SMALL TOWNS.
NOTHING HAPPENED. HE MADE ME LOOK LIKE AN IDIOT IN FRONT OF COURTNEY AND I LEFT. THAT'S IT. I SWEAR.
AND **HOW** DID HE MAKE YOU LOOK LIKE AN IDIOT?
HE LET ME KNOW THIS TOUR WAS ABOUT HIM. HE MADE ME FEEL LIKE I WAS NOTHING. LESS THAN NOTHING.
I KNOW SOMETHING ABOUT THAT. YOU GOTTA LEARN TO SPOT TRUST IN THIS BUSINESS. IF YOU FIND SOMEONE YOU CAN TRUST, HOLD ON TO THEM. STAY AWAY FROM THOSE YOU CAN'T.
AND YOU CAN'T TRUST ***ANYONE*** NAMED RADISON.
I JUST GOT A PHONE CALL. THE BOSS WANTS TO SEE YOU AT HIS HOUSE. NOW.

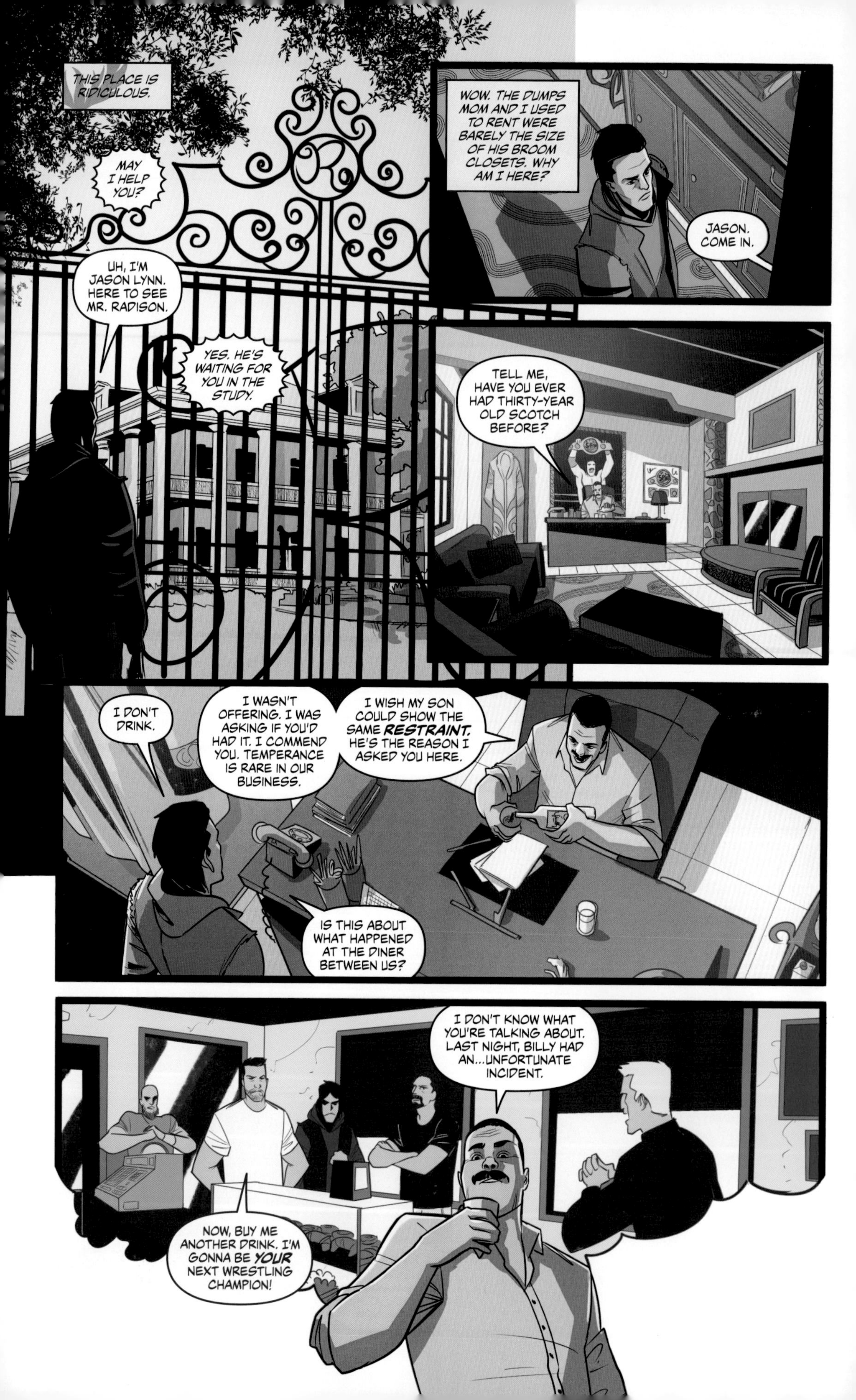
THIS PLACE IS RIDICULOUS.
MAY I HELP YOU?
UH, I'M JASON LYNN. HERE TO SEE MR. RADISON.
YES. HE'S WAITING FOR YOU IN THE STUDY.
WOW. THE DUMPS MOM AND I USED TO RENT WERE BARELY THE SIZE OF HIS BROOM CLOSETS. WHY AM I HERE?
JASON. COME IN.
TELL ME, HAVE YOU EVER HAD THIRTY-YEAR OLD SCOTCH BEFORE?
I DON'T DRINK.
I WASN'T OFFERING. I WAS ASKING IF YOU'D HAD IT. I COMMEND YOU. TEMPERANCE IS RARE IN OUR BUSINESS.
I WISH MY SON COULD SHOW THE SAME **RESTRAINT.** HE'S THE REASON I ASKED YOU HERE.
IS THIS ABOUT WHAT HAPPENED AT THE DINER BETWEEN US?
I DON'T KNOW WHAT YOU'RE TALKING ABOUT. LAST NIGHT, BILLY HAD AN...UNFORTUNATE INCIDENT.
NOW, BUY ME ANOTHER DRINK. I'M GONNA BE ***YOUR*** NEXT WRESTLING CHAMPION!

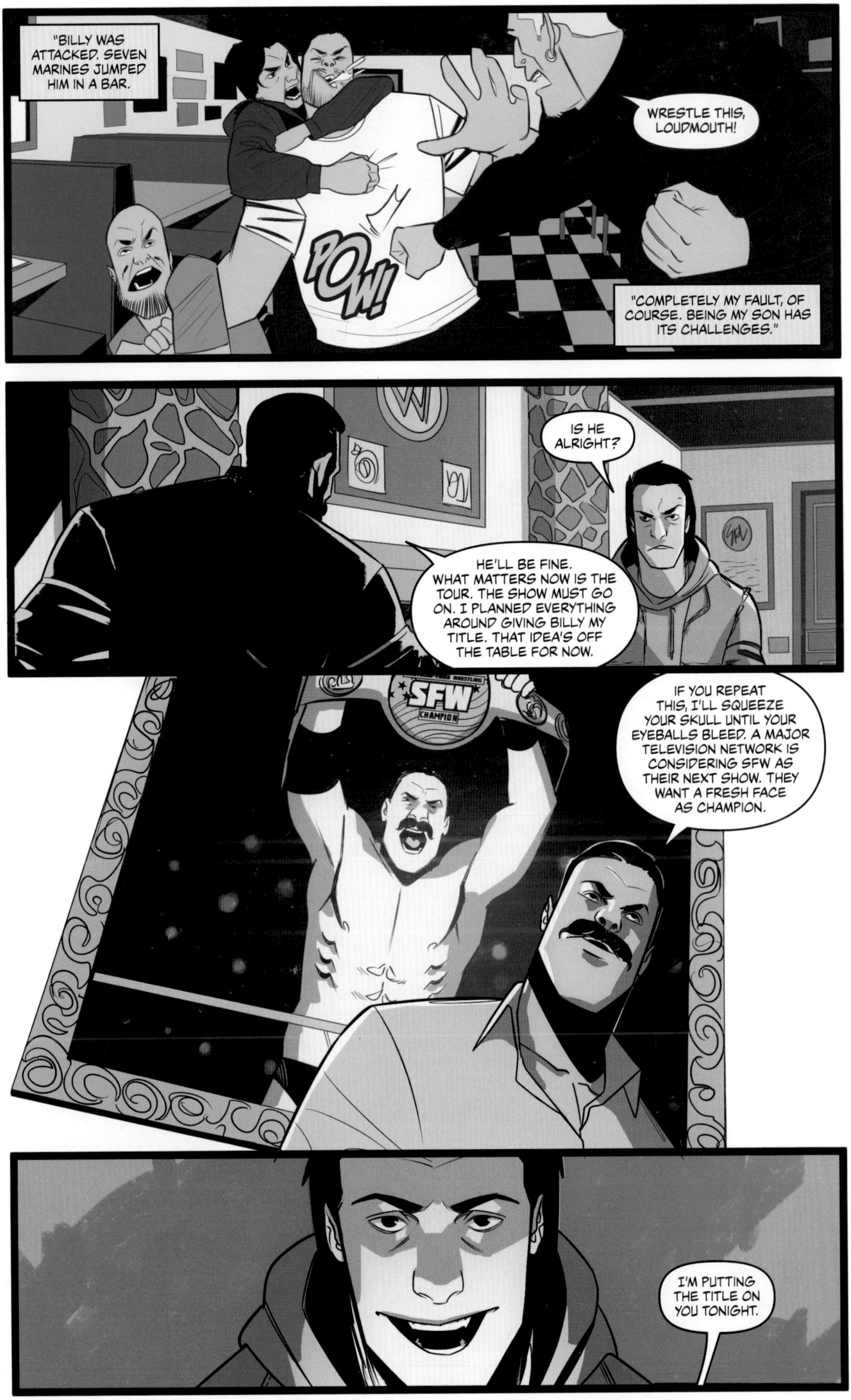
"BILLY WAS ATTACKED. SEVEN MARINES JUMPED HIM IN A BAR.
WRESTLE THIS, LOUDMOUTH!
POW!
"COMPLETELY MY FAULT, OF COURSE. BEING MY SON HAS ITS CHALLENGES."
IS HE ALRIGHT?
HE'LL BE FINE. WHAT MATTERS NOW IS THE TOUR. THE SHOW MUST GO ON. I PLANNED EVERYTHING AROUND GIVING BILLY MY TITLE. THAT IDEA'S OFF THE TABLE FOR NOW.
SFW
CHAMPION
IF YOU REPEAT THIS, I'LL SQUEEZE YOUR SKULL UNTIL YOUR EYEBALLS BLEED. A MAJOR TELEVISION NETWORK IS CONSIDERING SFW AS THEIR NEXT SHOW. THEY WANT A FRESH FACE AS CHAMPION.
I'M PUTTING THE TITLE ON YOU TONIGHT.

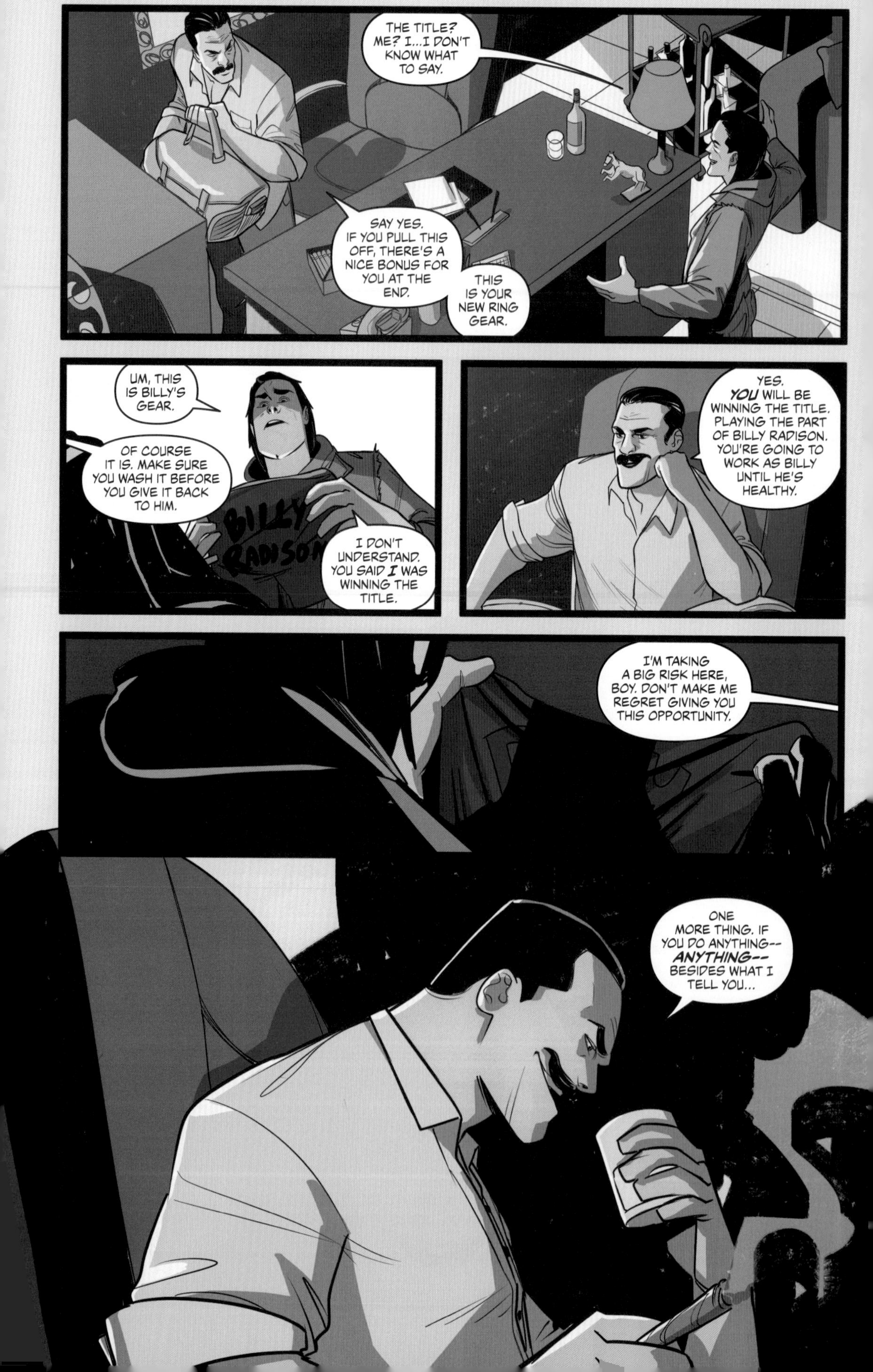
THE TITLE? ME? I...I DON'T KNOW WHAT TO SAY.
SAY YES. IF YOU PULL THIS OFF, THERE'S A NICE BONUS FOR YOU AT THE END.
THIS IS YOUR NEW RING GEAR.
UM, THIS IS BILLY'S GEAR.
OF COURSE IT IS. MAKE SURE YOU WASH IT BEFORE YOU GIVE IT BACK TO HIM.
BILLY RADISON
I DON'T UNDERSTAND. YOU SAID *I* WAS WINNING THE TITLE.
YES. ***YOU*** WILL BE WINNING THE TITLE. PLAYING THE PART OF BILLY RADISON. YOU'RE GOING TO WORK AS BILLY UNTIL HE'S HEALTHY.
I'M TAKING A BIG RISK HERE, BOY. DON'T MAKE ME REGRET GIVING YOU THIS OPPORTUNITY.
ONE MORE THING. IF YOU DO ANYTHING-- ***ANYTHING--*** BESIDES WHAT I TELL YOU...

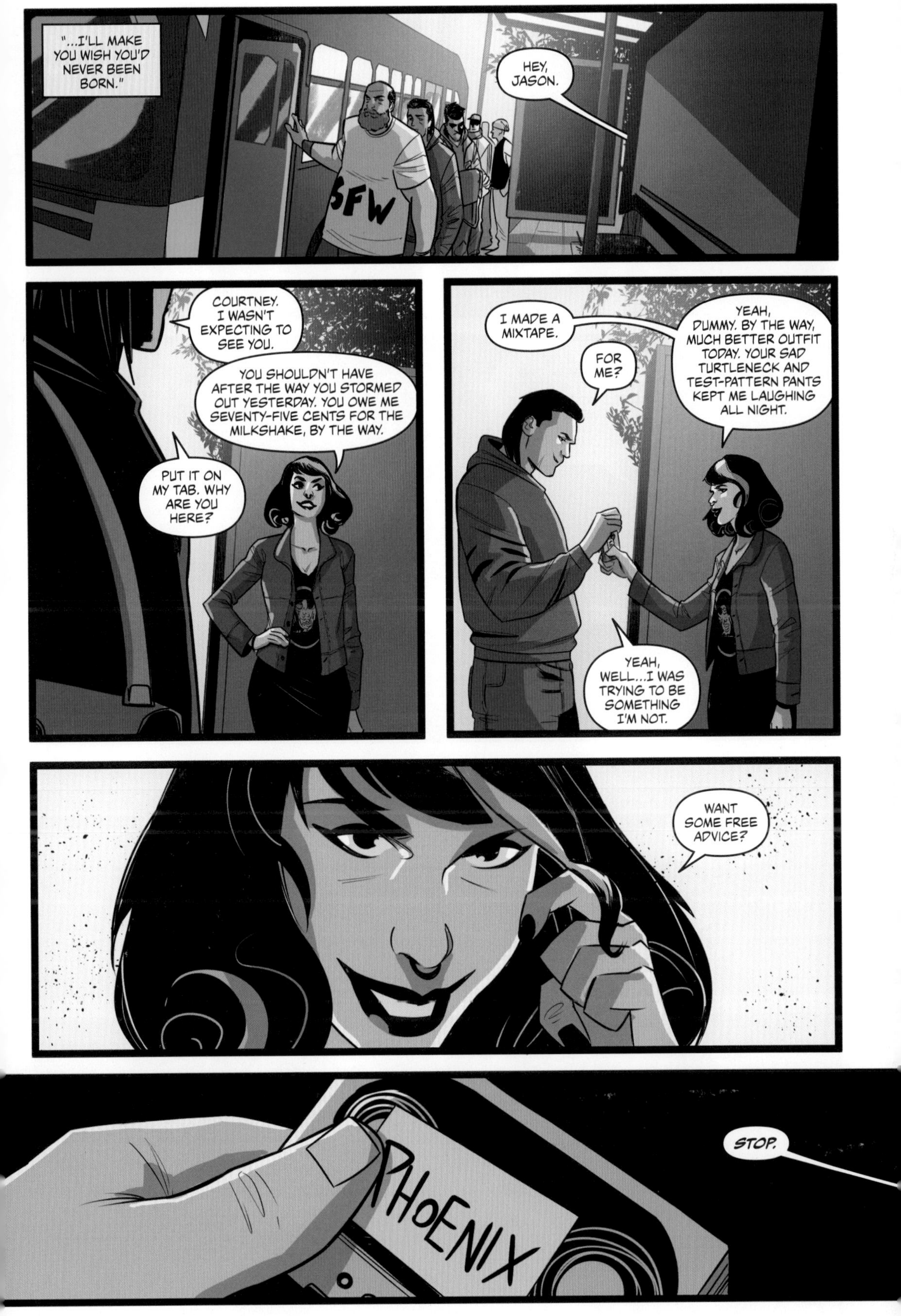
"...I'LL MAKE YOU WISH YOU'D NEVER BEEN BORN."
HEY, JASON.
SFW
COURTNEY. I WASN'T EXPECTING TO SEE YOU.
YOU SHOULDN'T HAVE AFTER THE WAY YOU STORMED OUT YESTERDAY. YOU OWE ME SEVENTY-FIVE CENTS FOR THE MILKSHAKE, BY THE WAY.
PUT IT ON MY TAB. WHY ARE YOU HERE?
I MADE A MIXTAPE.
FOR ME?
YEAH, DUMMY. BY THE WAY, MUCH BETTER OUTFIT TODAY. YOUR SAD TURTLENECK AND TEST-PATTERN PANTS KEPT ME LAUGHING ALL NIGHT.
YEAH, WELL...I WAS TRYING TO BE SOMETHING I'M NOT.
WANT SOME FREE ADVICE?
PHOENIX
STOP.

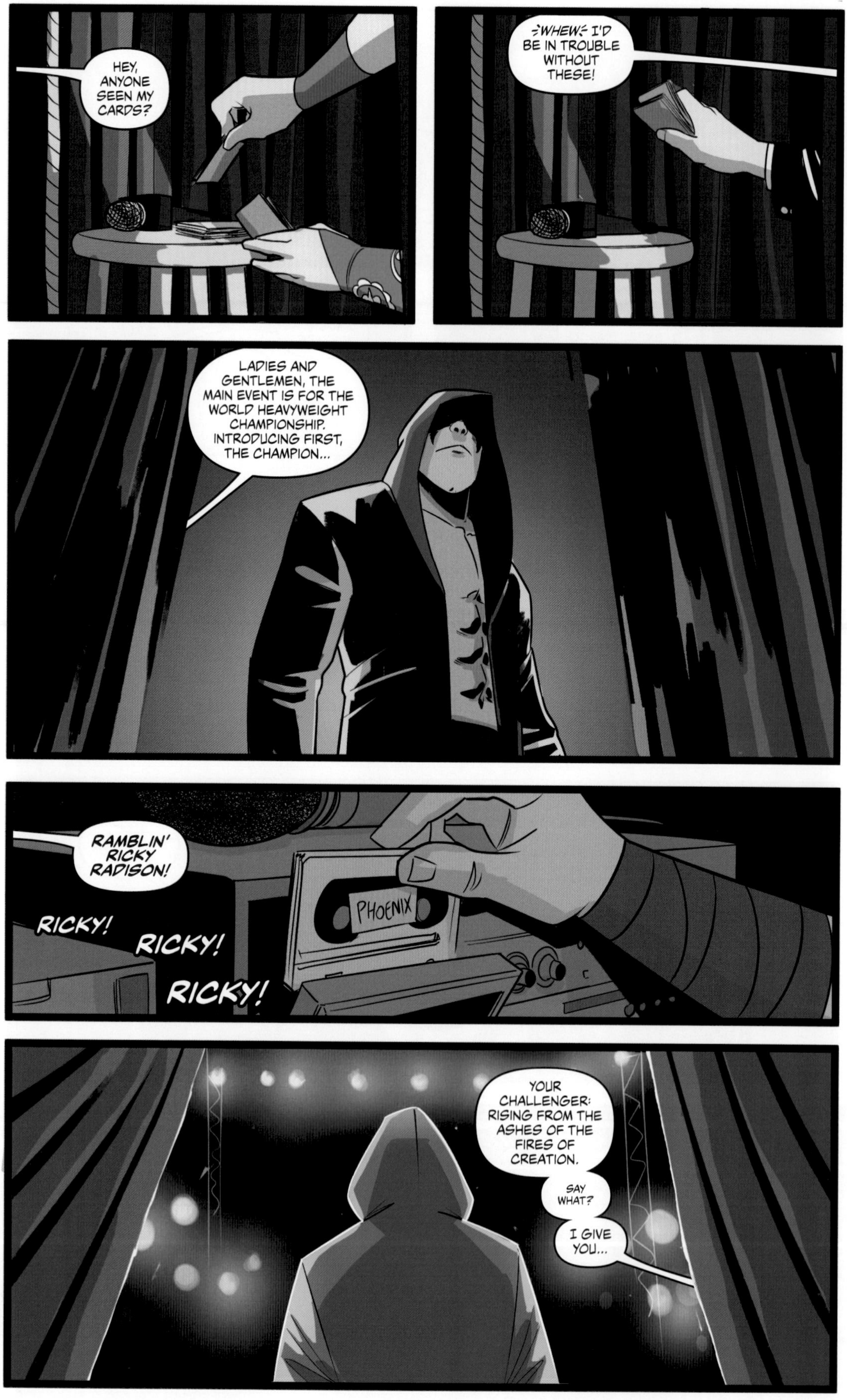
HEY, ANYONE SEEN MY CARDS?
-WHEW- I'D BE IN TROUBLE WITHOUT THESE!
LADIES AND GENTLEMEN, THE MAIN EVENT IS FOR THE WORLD HEAVYWEIGHT CHAMPIONSHIP. INTRODUCING FIRST, THE CHAMPION...
RAMBLIN' RICKY RADISON!
PHOENIX
RICKY!
RICKY!
RICKY!
YOUR CHALLENGER: RISING FROM THE ASHES OF THE FIRES OF CREATION.
SAY WHAT?
I GIVE YOU...

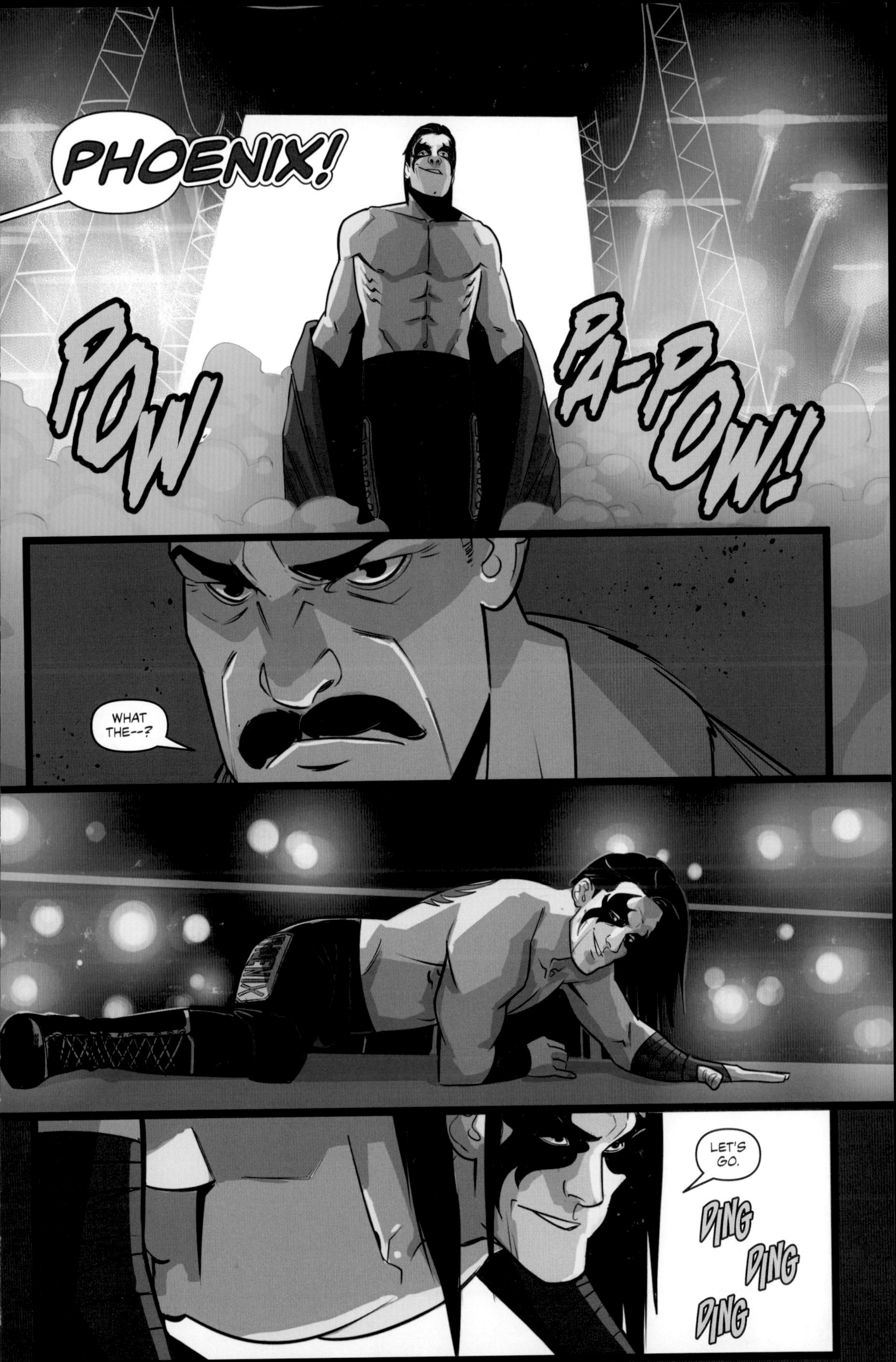
PHOENIX!
POW
PA-POW!
WHAT THE--?
PHOENIX
LET'S GO.
DING
DING
DING

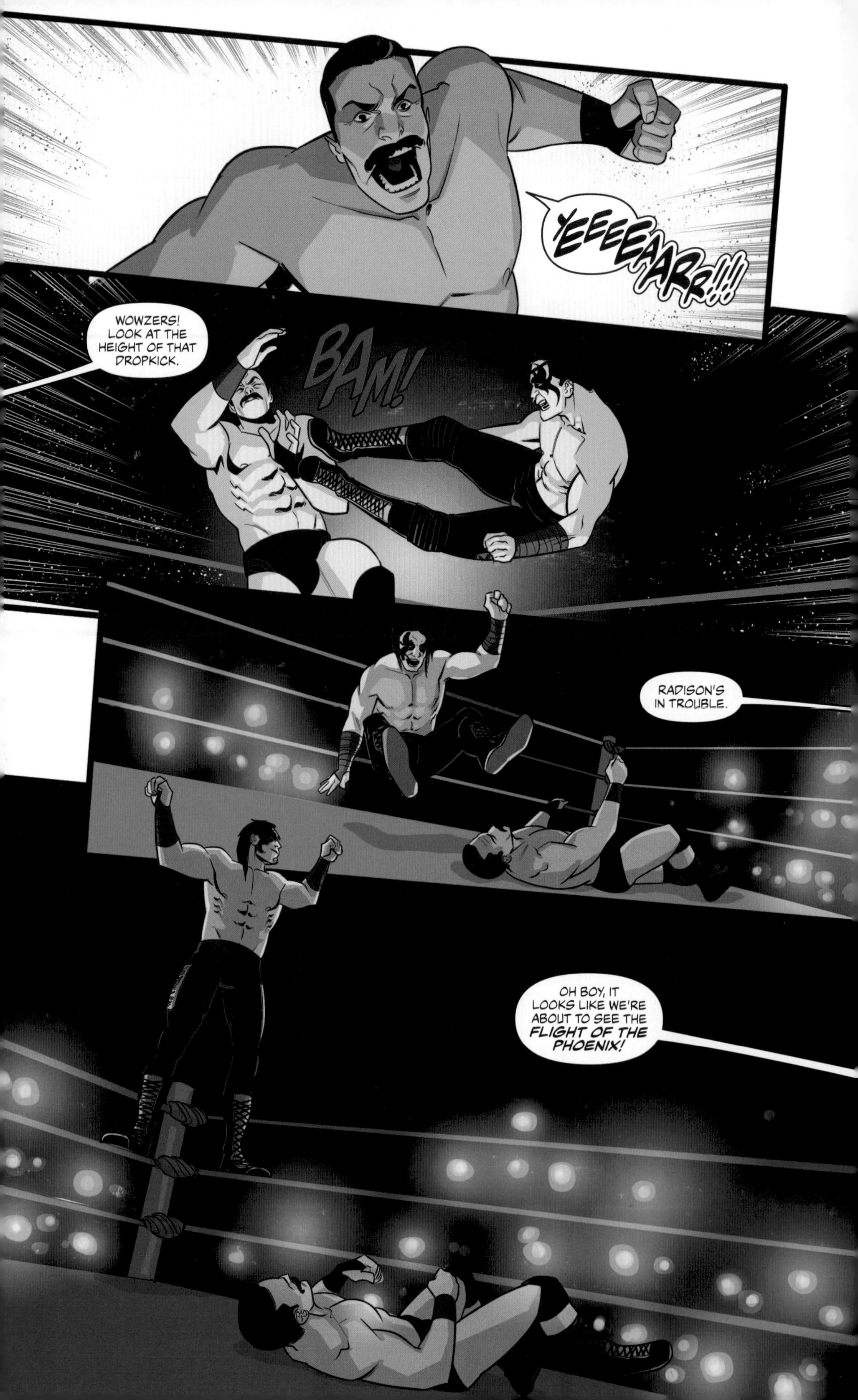
YEEEEAARR!!!
WOWZERS! LOOK AT THE HEIGHT OF THAT DROPKICK.
BAM!
RADISON'S IN TROUBLE.
OH BOY, IT LOOKS LIKE WE'RE ABOUT TO SEE THE *FLIGHT OF THE PHOENIX!*

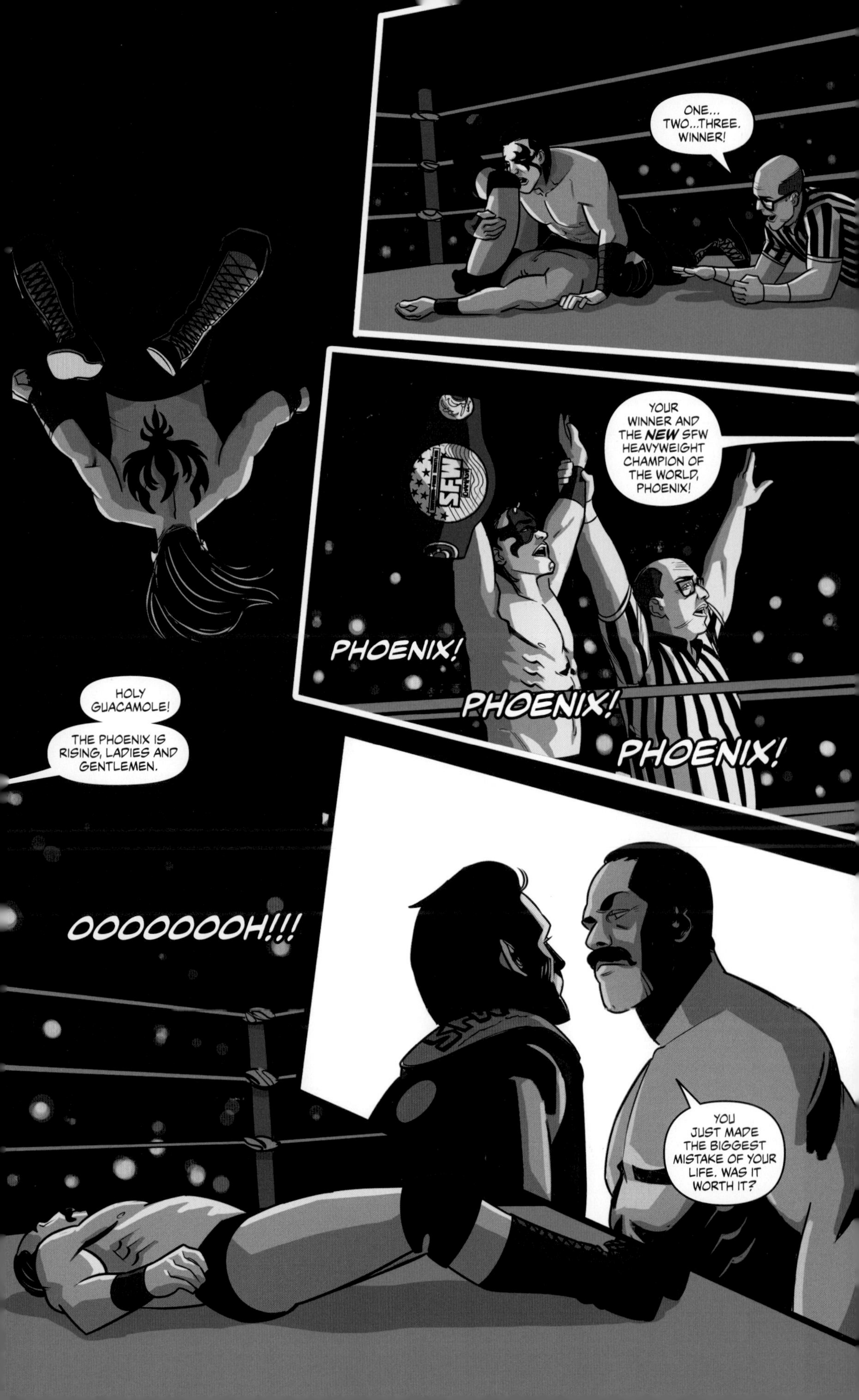
ONE... TWO...THREE. WINNER!
YOUR WINNER AND THE NEW SFW HEAVYWEIGHT CHAMPION OF THE WORLD, PHOENIX!
SFW
PHOENIX!
PHOENIX!
PHOENIX!
HOLY GUACAMOLE!
THE PHOENIX IS RISING, LADIES AND GENTLEMEN.
OOOOOOOH!!!
YOU JUST MADE THE BIGGEST MISTAKE OF YOUR LIFE. WAS IT WORTH IT?

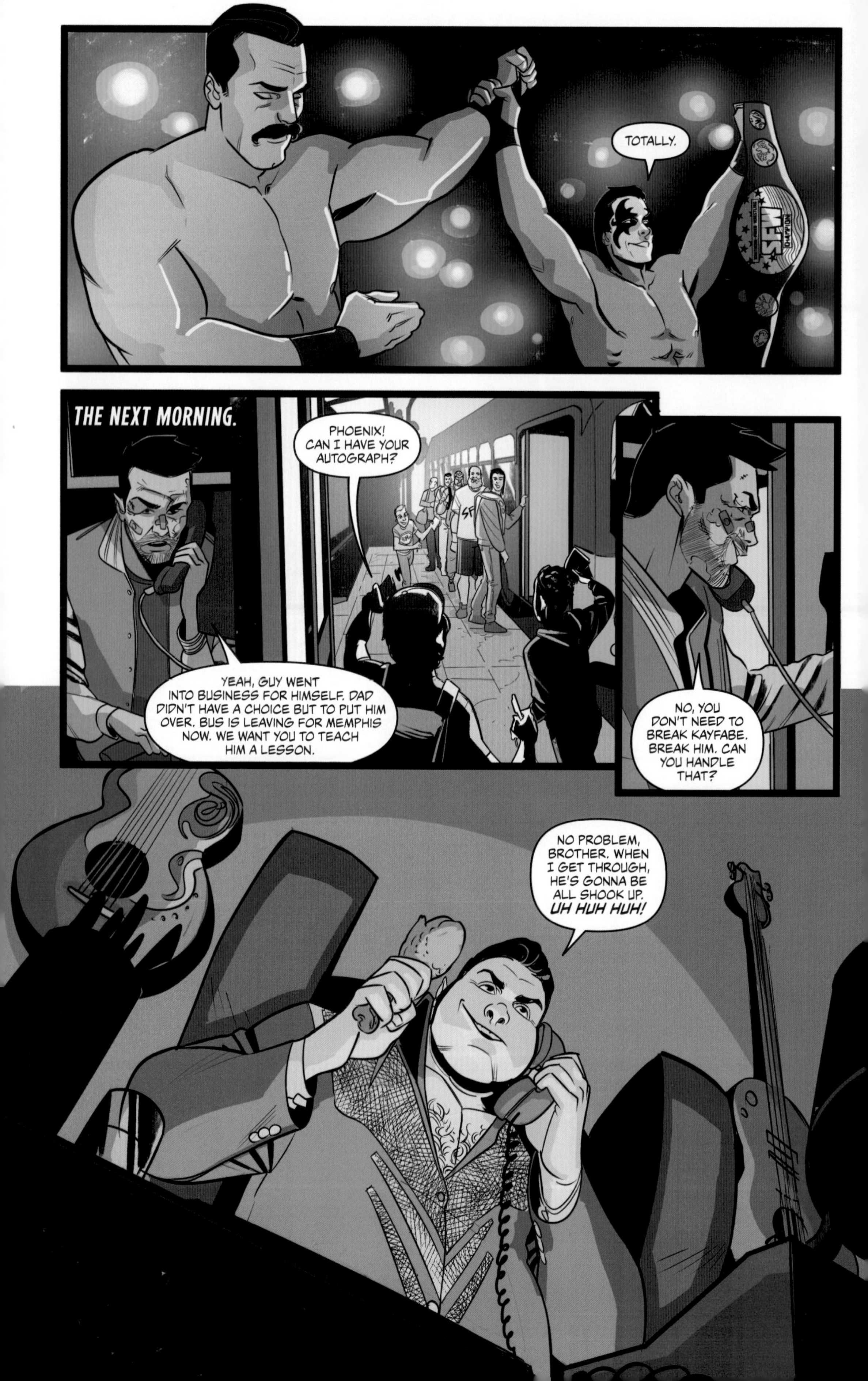

TOTALLY.
THE NEXT MORNING.
PHOENIX! CAN I HAVE YOUR AUTOGRAPH?
YEAH, GUY WENT INTO BUSINESS FOR HIMSELF. DAD DIDN'T HAVE A CHOICE BUT TO PUT HIM OVER. BUS IS LEAVING FOR MEMPHIS NOW. WE WANT YOU TO TEACH HIM A LESSON.
NO, YOU DON'T NEED TO BREAK KAYFABE. BREAK HIM. CAN YOU HANDLE THAT?
NO PROBLEM, BROTHER. WHEN I GET THROUGH, HE'S GONNA BE ALL SHOOK UP. *UH HUH HUH!*

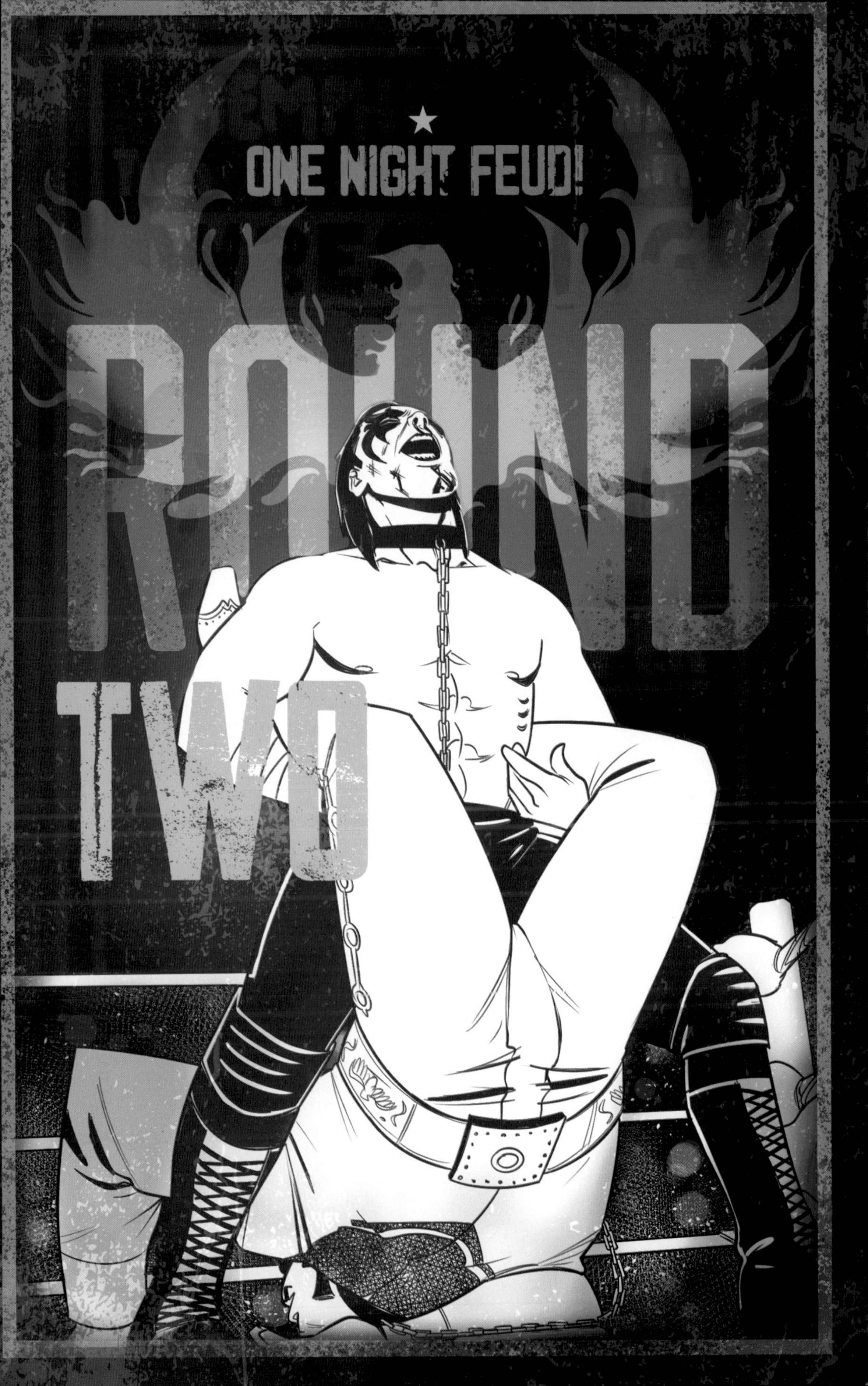
ONE NIGHT FEUD!
ROUND
TWO

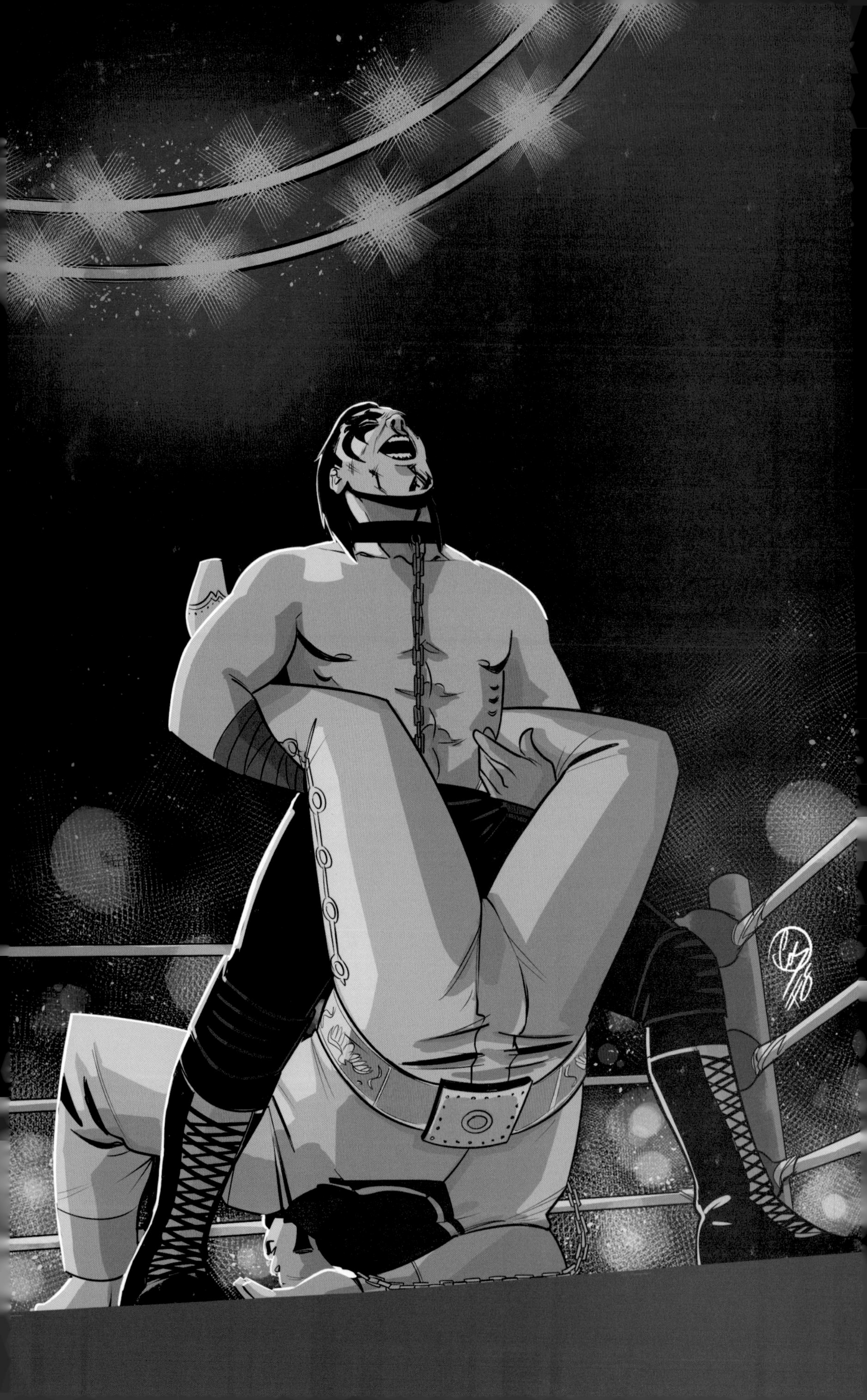

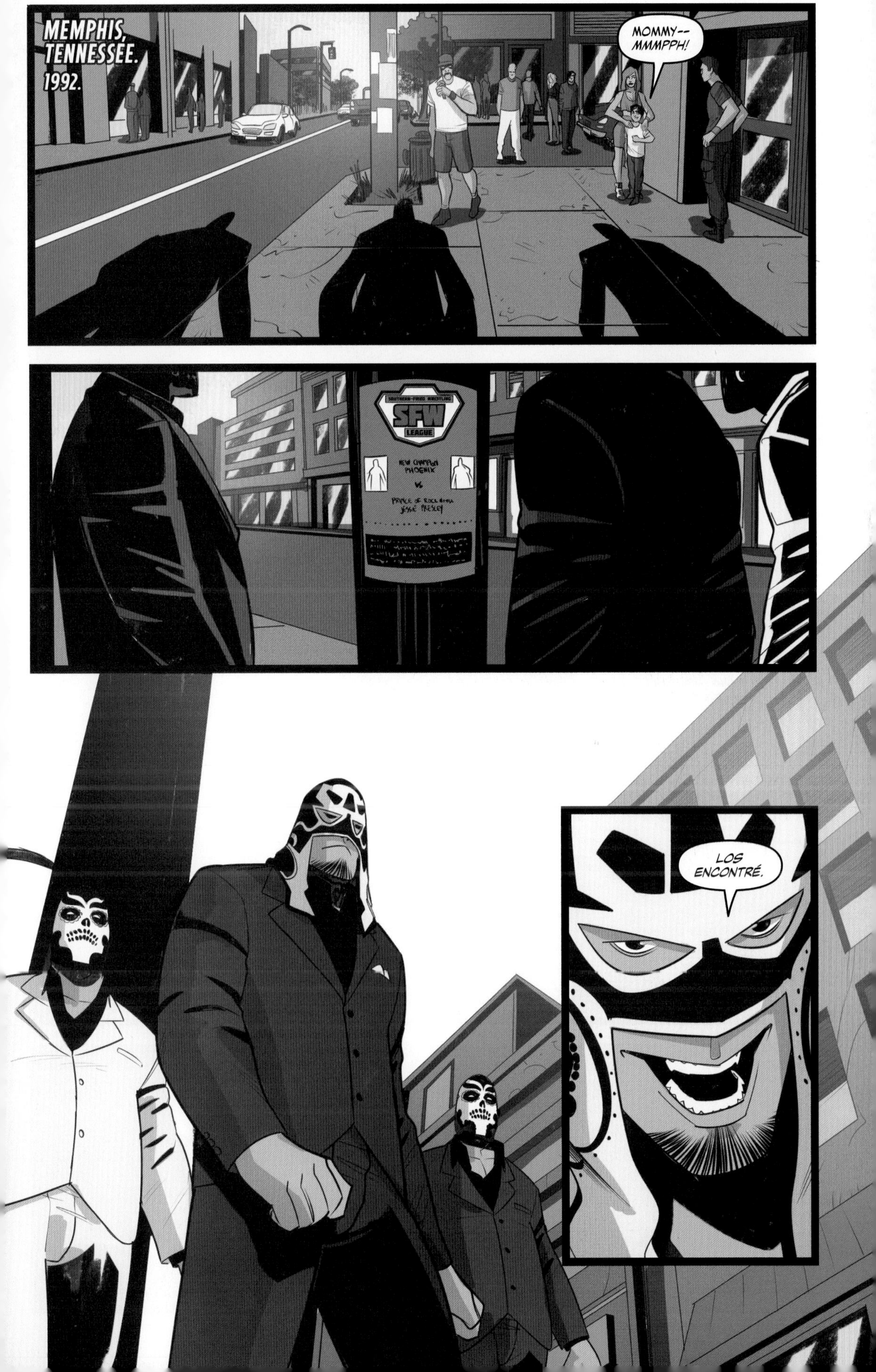
MEMPHIS, TENNESSEE. 1992.
MOMMY-- MMMPPH!
SOUTHERN-FRIED WRESTLING
SFW
LEAGUE
NEW CHAMPION PHOENIX
VS
PRINCE OF ROCK N ROLL JESSIE PRESLEY
LOS ENCONTRÉ.

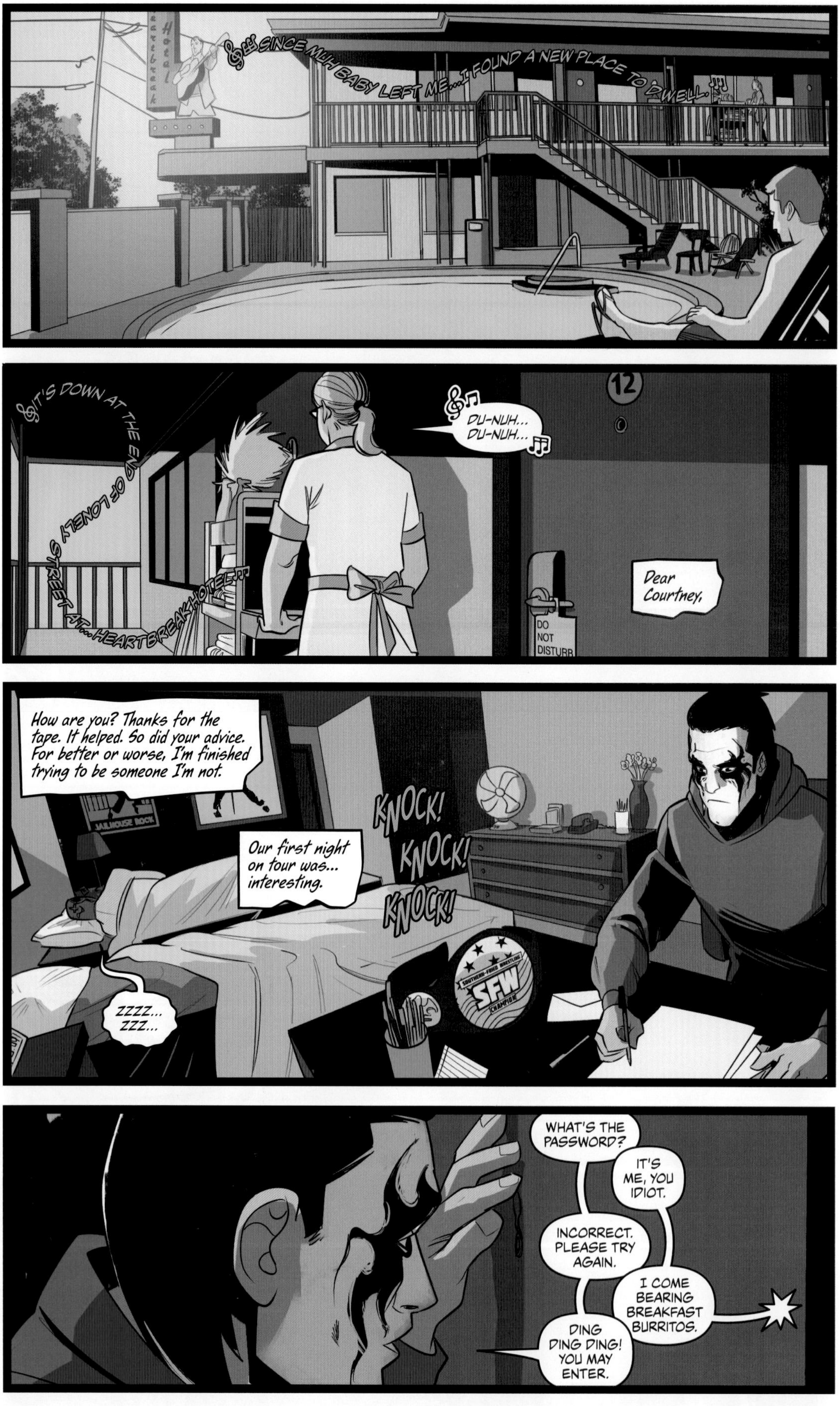
Heartbreak Hotel
SINCE MUH BABY LEFT ME... I FOUND A NEW PLACE TO DWELL.
IT'S DOWN AT THE END OF LONELY STREET AT... HEARTBREAK HOTEL.
DU-NUH... DU-NUH...
12
DO NOT DISTURB
Dear Courtney,
How are you? Thanks for the tape. It helped. So did your advice. For better or worse, I'm finished trying to be someone I'm not.
JAILHOUSE ROCK
Our first night on tour was... interesting.
KNOCK! KNOCK! KNOCK!
SFW
SOUTHERN-FRIED WRESTLING
CHAMPION
ZZZZ... ZZZ...
WHAT'S THE PASSWORD?
IT'S ME, YOU IDIOT.
INCORRECT. PLEASE TRY AGAIN.
I COME BEARING BREAKFAST BURRITOS.
DING DING DING! YOU MAY ENTER.

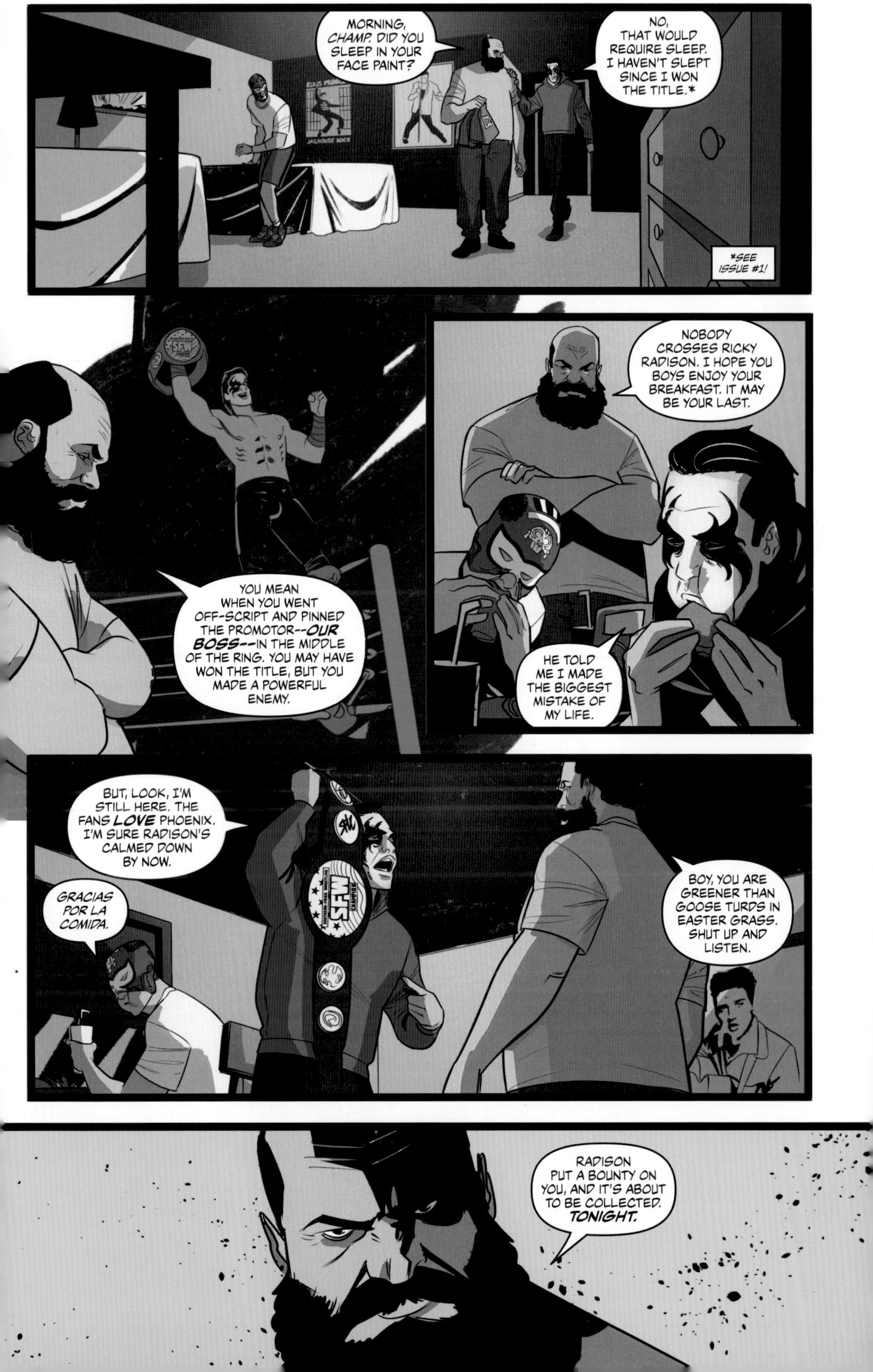
MORNING, CHAMP. DID YOU SLEEP IN YOUR FACE PAINT?
NO, THAT WOULD REQUIRE SLEEP. I HAVEN'T SLEPT SINCE I WON THE TITLE.*
*SEE ISSUE #1!
YOU MEAN WHEN YOU WENT OFF-SCRIPT AND PINNED THE PROMOTOR--OUR BOSS--IN THE MIDDLE OF THE RING. YOU MAY HAVE WON THE TITLE, BUT YOU MADE A POWERFUL ENEMY.
NOBODY CROSSES RICKY RADISON. I HOPE YOU BOYS ENJOY YOUR BREAKFAST. IT MAY BE YOUR LAST.
HE TOLD ME I MADE THE BIGGEST MISTAKE OF MY LIFE.
BUT, LOOK, I'M STILL HERE. THE FANS LOVE PHOENIX. I'M SURE RADISON'S CALMED DOWN BY NOW.
GRACIAS POR LA COMIDA.
BOY, YOU ARE GREENER THAN GOOSE TURDS IN EASTER GRASS. SHUT UP AND LISTEN.
RADISON PUT A BOUNTY ON YOU, AND IT'S ABOUT TO BE COLLECTED. TONIGHT.

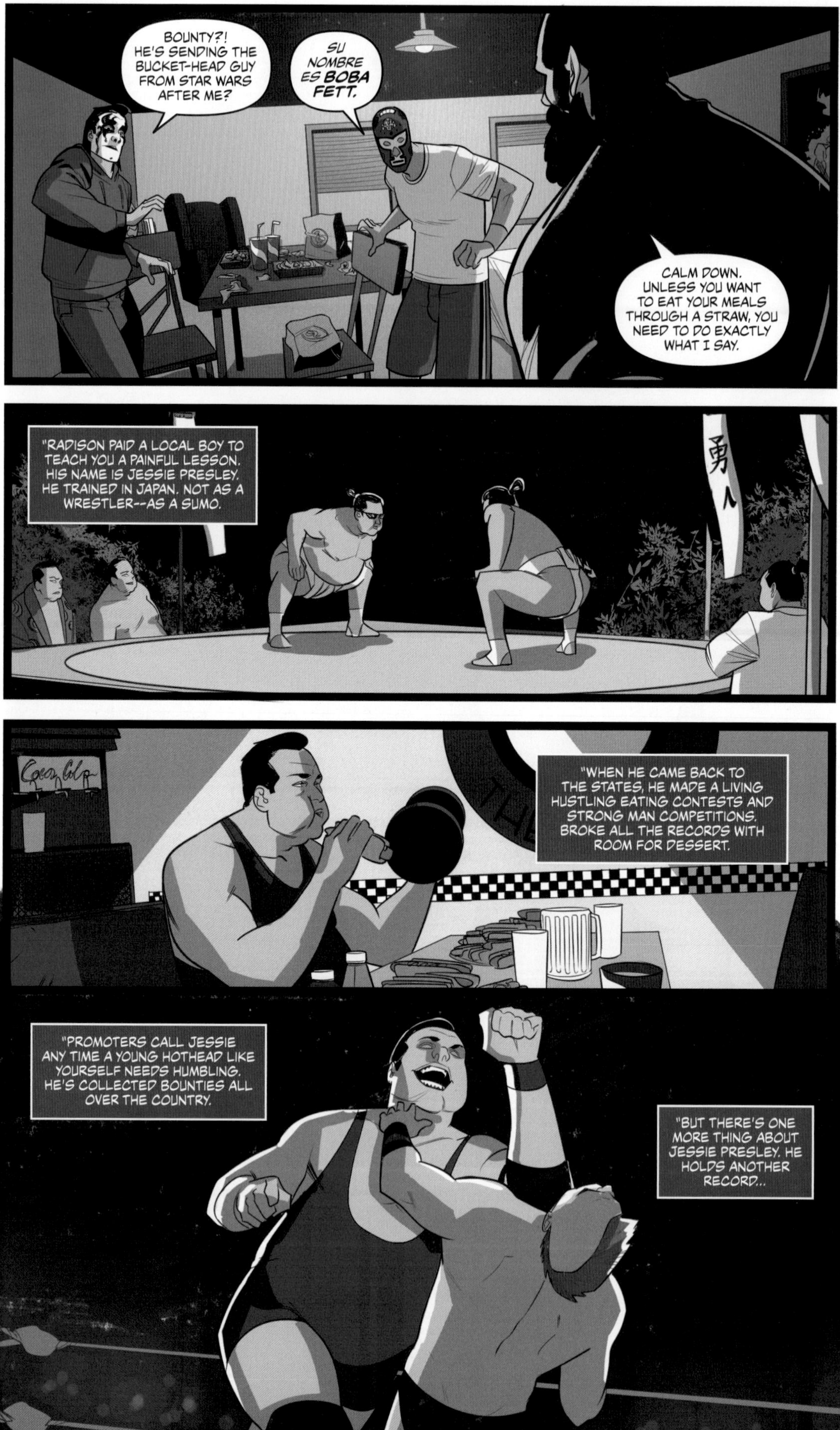
BOUNTY?! HE'S SENDING THE BUCKET-HEAD GUY FROM STAR WARS AFTER ME?
SU NOMBRE ES **BOBA FETT.**
CALM DOWN. UNLESS YOU WANT TO EAT YOUR MEALS THROUGH A STRAW, YOU NEED TO DO EXACTLY WHAT I SAY.
"RADISON PAID A LOCAL BOY TO TEACH YOU A PAINFUL LESSON. HIS NAME IS JESSIE PRESLEY. HE TRAINED IN JAPAN. NOT AS A WRESTLER--AS A SUMO.
"WHEN HE CAME BACK TO THE STATES, HE MADE A LIVING HUSTLING EATING CONTESTS AND STRONG MAN COMPETITIONS. BROKE ALL THE RECORDS WITH ROOM FOR DESSERT.
"PROMOTERS CALL JESSIE ANY TIME A YOUNG HOTHEAD LIKE YOURSELF NEEDS HUMBLING. HE'S COLLECTED BOUNTIES ALL OVER THE COUNTRY.
"BUT THERE'S ONE MORE THING ABOUT JESSIE PRESLEY. HE HOLDS ANOTHER RECORD...

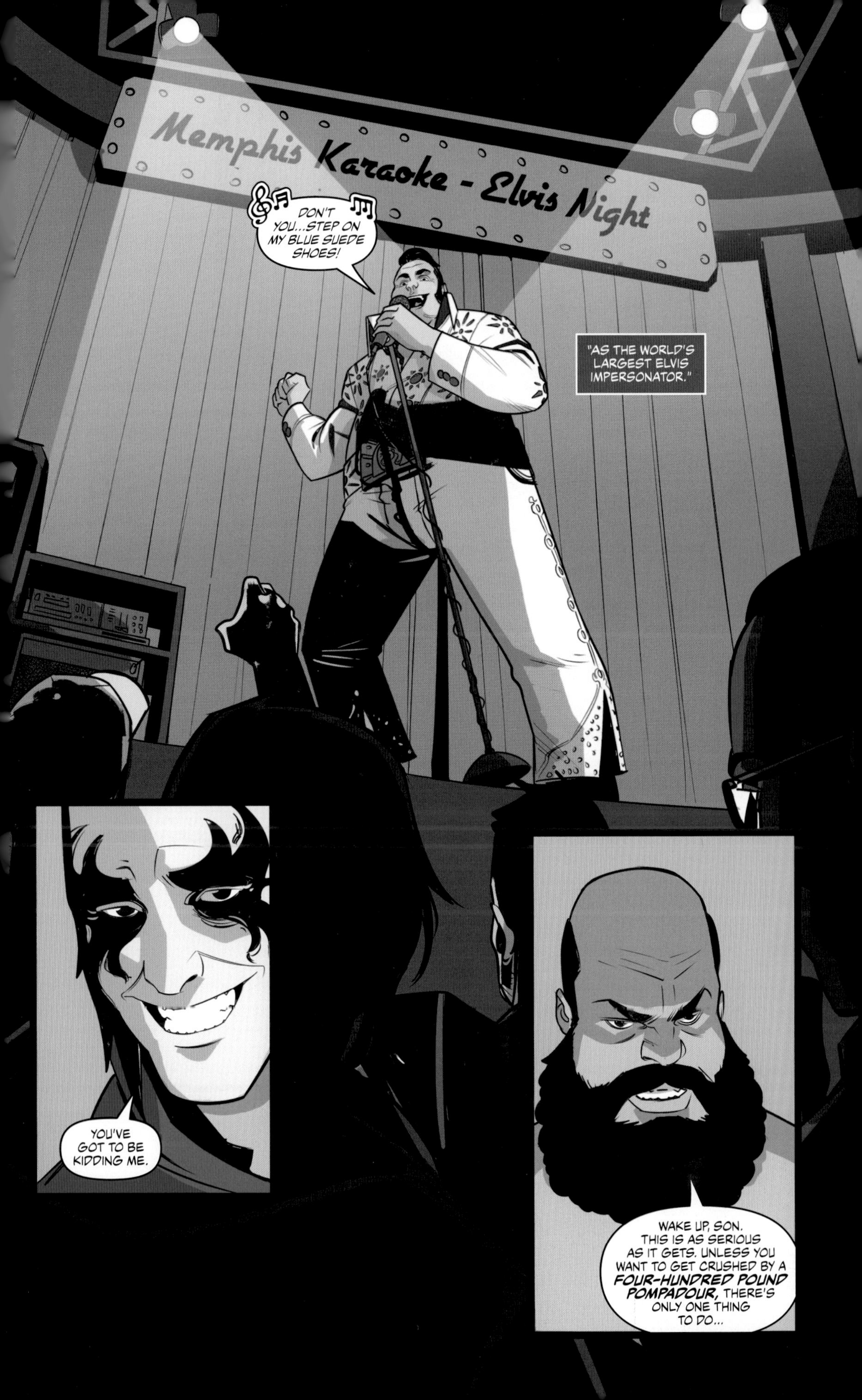
Memphis Karaoke - Elvis Night
DON'T YOU...STEP ON MY BLUE SUEDE SHOES!
"AS THE WORLD'S LARGEST ELVIS IMPERSONATOR."
YOU'VE GOT TO BE KIDDING ME.
WAKE UP, SON. THIS IS AS SERIOUS AS IT GETS. UNLESS YOU WANT TO GET CRUSHED BY A ***FOUR-HUNDRED POUND POMPADOUR,*** THERE'S ONLY ONE THING TO DO...

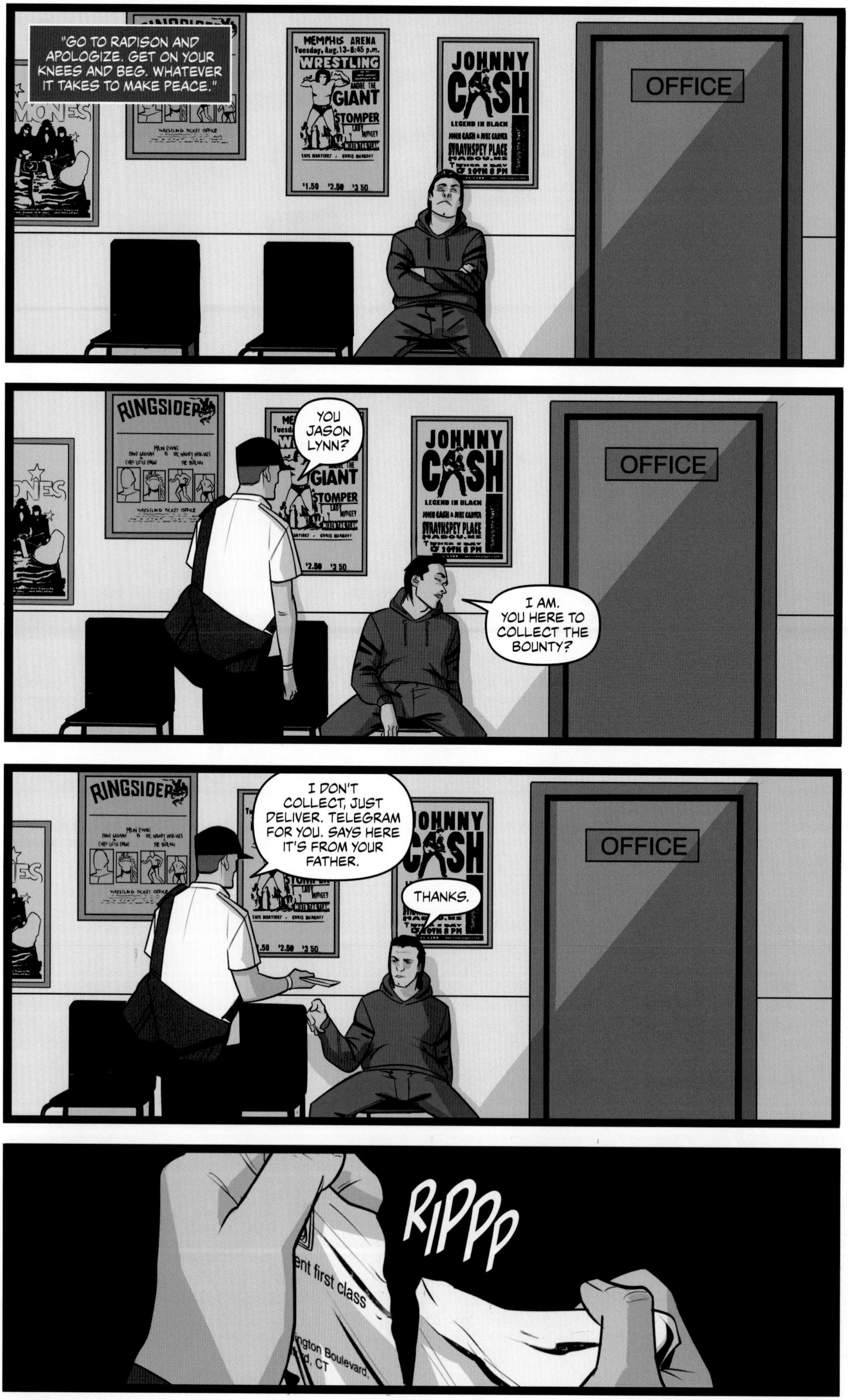
"GO TO RADISON AND APOLOGIZE. GET ON YOUR KNEES AND BEG. WHATEVER IT TAKES TO MAKE PEACE."
MEMPHIS ARENA
WRESTLING
GIANT
STOMPER
JOHNNY CASH
LEGEND IN BLACK
OFFICE
YOU JASON LYNN?
I AM. YOU HERE TO COLLECT THE BOUNTY?
RINGSIDER
I DON'T COLLECT, JUST DELIVER. TELEGRAM FOR YOU. SAYS HERE IT'S FROM YOUR FATHER.
THANKS.
RIPPP
ent first class
ington Boulevard,
d, CT

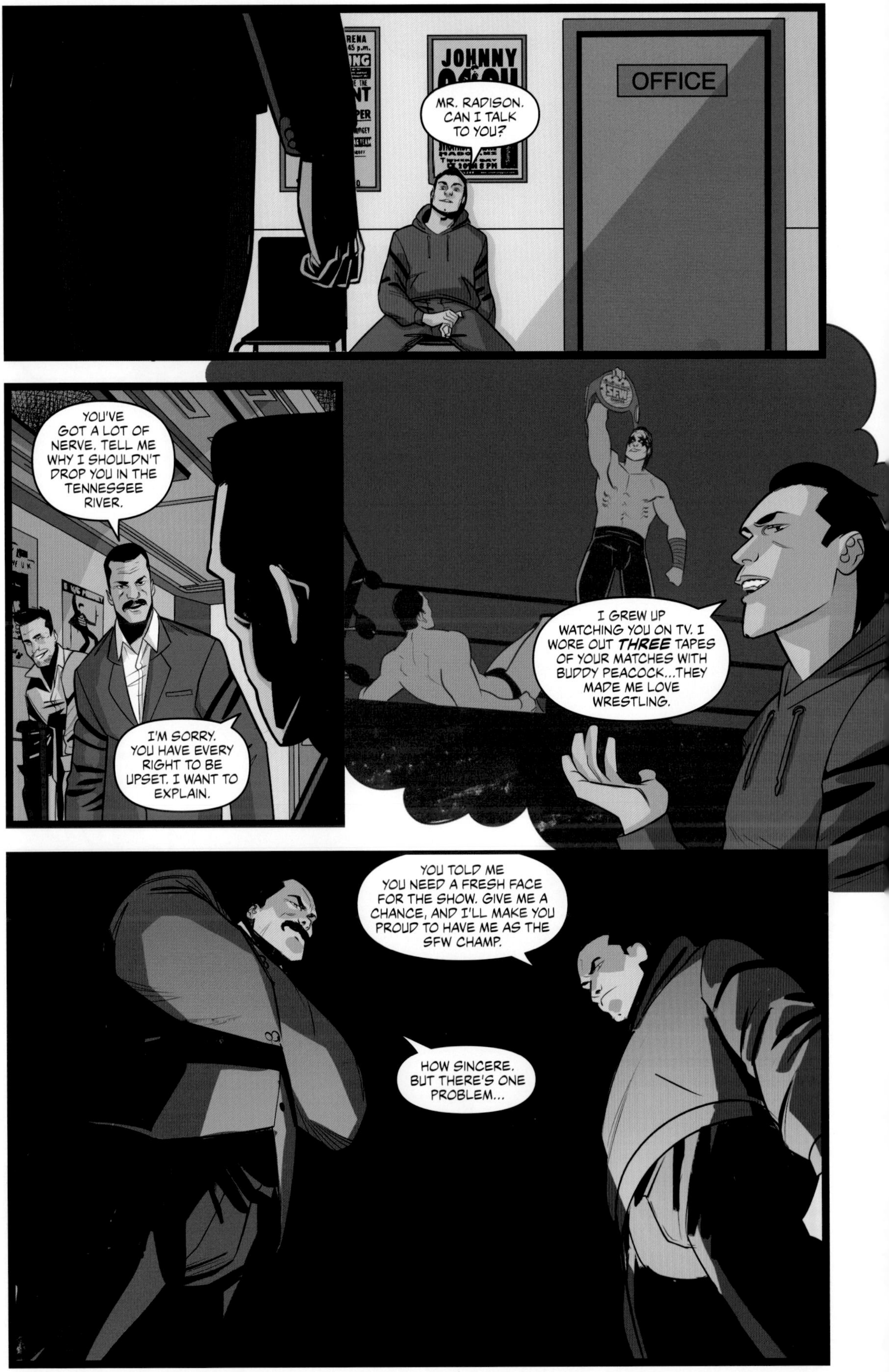
JOHNNY
OFFICE
MR. RADISON. CAN I TALK TO YOU?
YOU'VE GOT A LOT OF NERVE. TELL ME WHY I SHOULDN'T DROP YOU IN THE TENNESSEE RIVER.
I'M SORRY. YOU HAVE EVERY RIGHT TO BE UPSET. I WANT TO EXPLAIN.
SFW
I GREW UP WATCHING YOU ON TV. I WORE OUT ***THREE*** TAPES OF YOUR MATCHES WITH BUDDY PEACOCK...THEY MADE ME LOVE WRESTLING.
YOU TOLD ME YOU NEED A FRESH FACE FOR THE SHOW. GIVE ME A CHANCE, AND I'LL MAKE YOU PROUD TO HAVE ME AS THE SFW CHAMP.
HOW SINCERE. BUT THERE'S ONE PROBLEM...

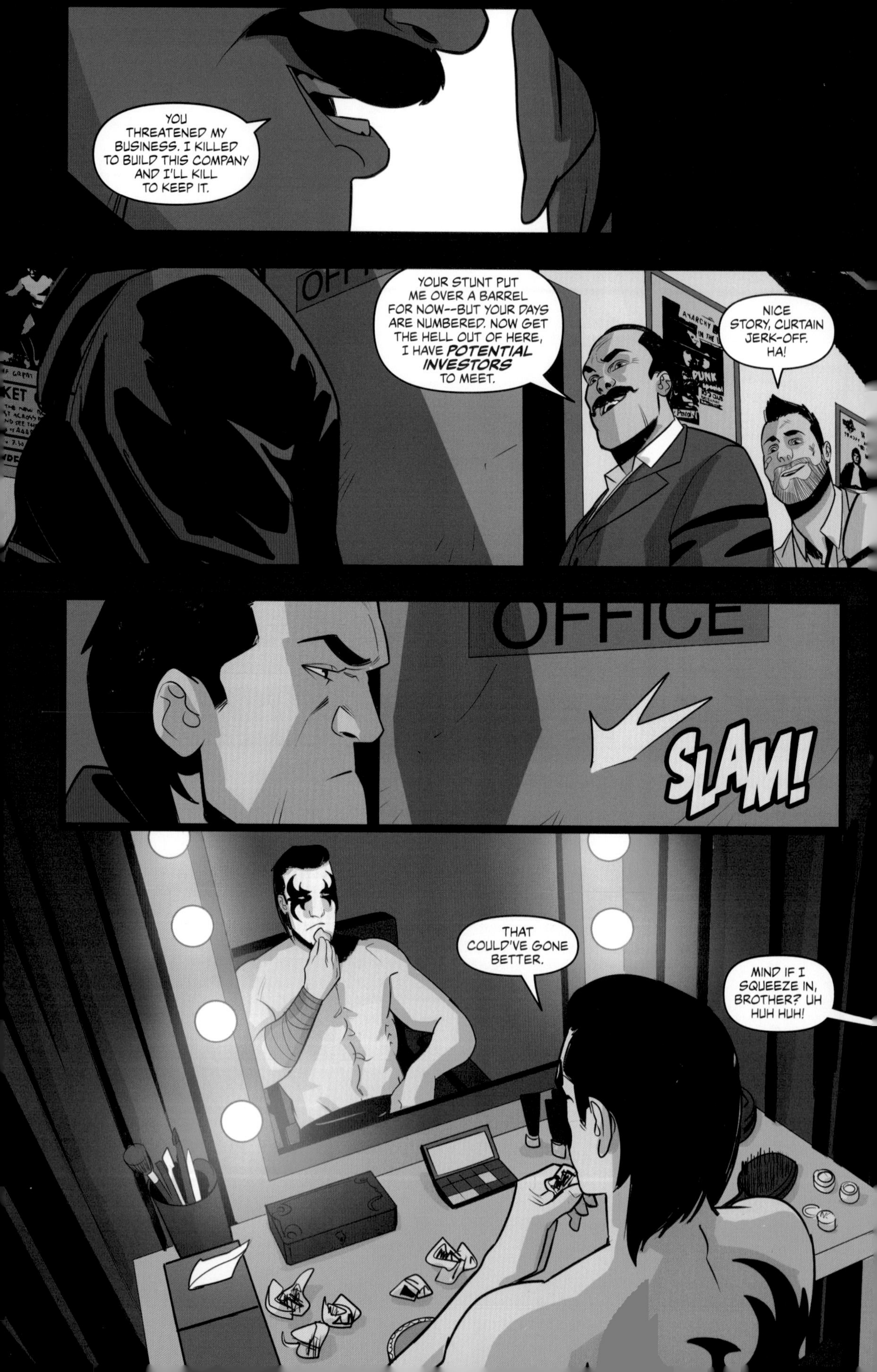
YOU THREATENED MY BUSINESS. I KILLED TO BUILD THIS COMPANY AND I'LL KILL TO KEEP IT.
YOUR STUNT PUT ME OVER A BARREL FOR NOW--BUT YOUR DAYS ARE NUMBERED. NOW GET THE HELL OUT OF HERE, I HAVE **POTENTIAL INVESTORS** TO MEET.
NICE STORY, CURTAIN JERK-OFF. HA!
OFFICE
SLAM!
THAT COULD'VE GONE BETTER.
MIND IF I SQUEEZE IN, BROTHER? UH HUH HUH!

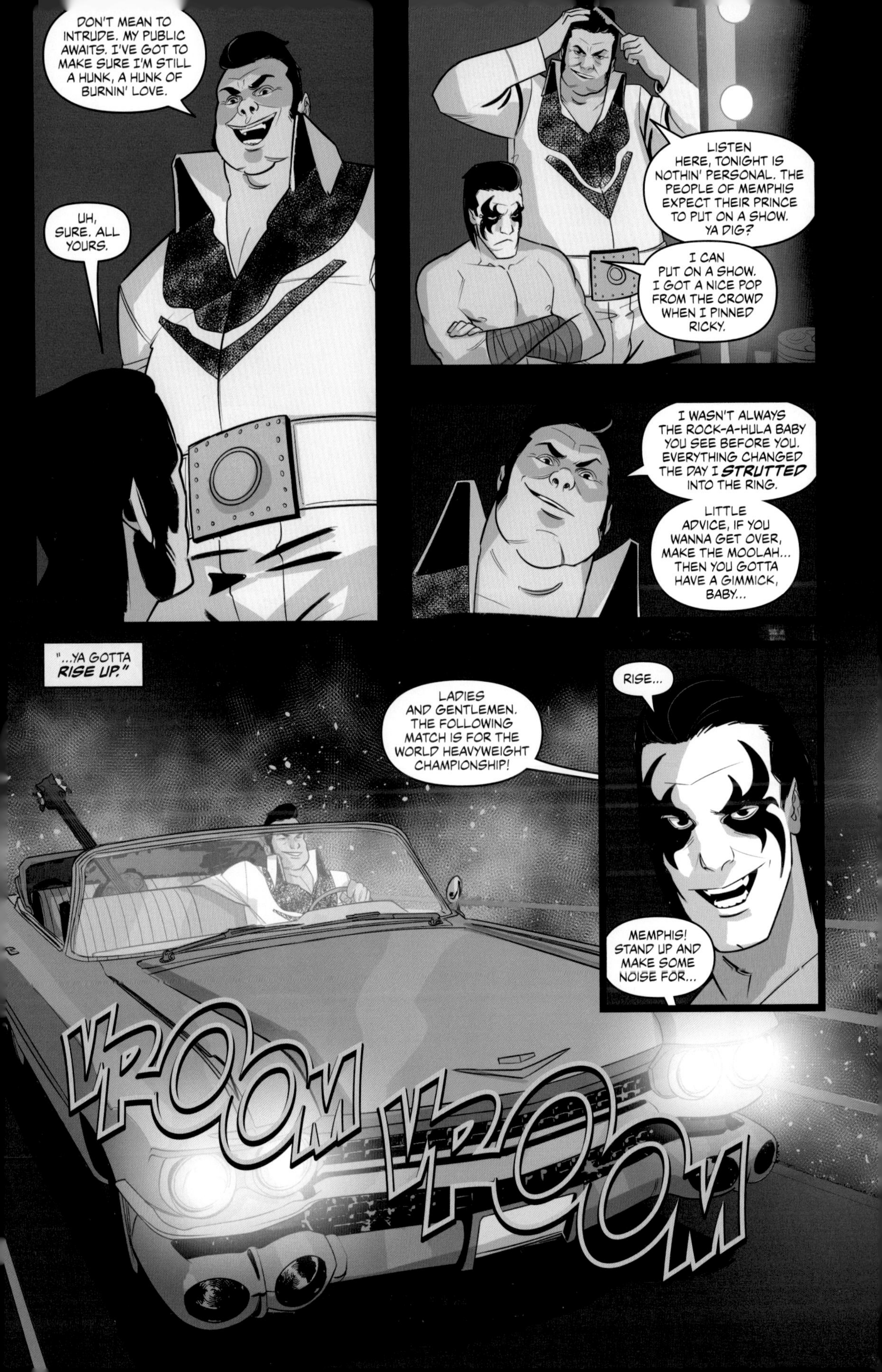
DON'T MEAN TO INTRUDE. MY PUBLIC AWAITS. I'VE GOT TO MAKE SURE I'M STILL A HUNK, A HUNK OF BURNIN' LOVE.
UH, SURE. ALL YOURS.
LISTEN HERE, TONIGHT IS NOTHIN' PERSONAL. THE PEOPLE OF MEMPHIS EXPECT THEIR PRINCE TO PUT ON A SHOW. YA DIG?
I CAN PUT ON A SHOW. I GOT A NICE POP FROM THE CROWD WHEN I PINNED RICKY.
I WASN'T ALWAYS THE ROCK-A-HULA BABY YOU SEE BEFORE YOU. EVERYTHING CHANGED THE DAY I STRUTTED INTO THE RING.
LITTLE ADVICE, IF YOU WANNA GET OVER, MAKE THE MOOLAH... THEN YOU GOTTA HAVE A GIMMICK, BABY...
"...YA GOTTA RISE UP."
LADIES AND GENTLEMEN. THE FOLLOWING MATCH IS FOR THE WORLD HEAVYWEIGHT CHAMPIONSHIP!
RISE...
MEMPHIS! STAND UP AND MAKE SOME NOISE FOR...
VROOM
VROOM

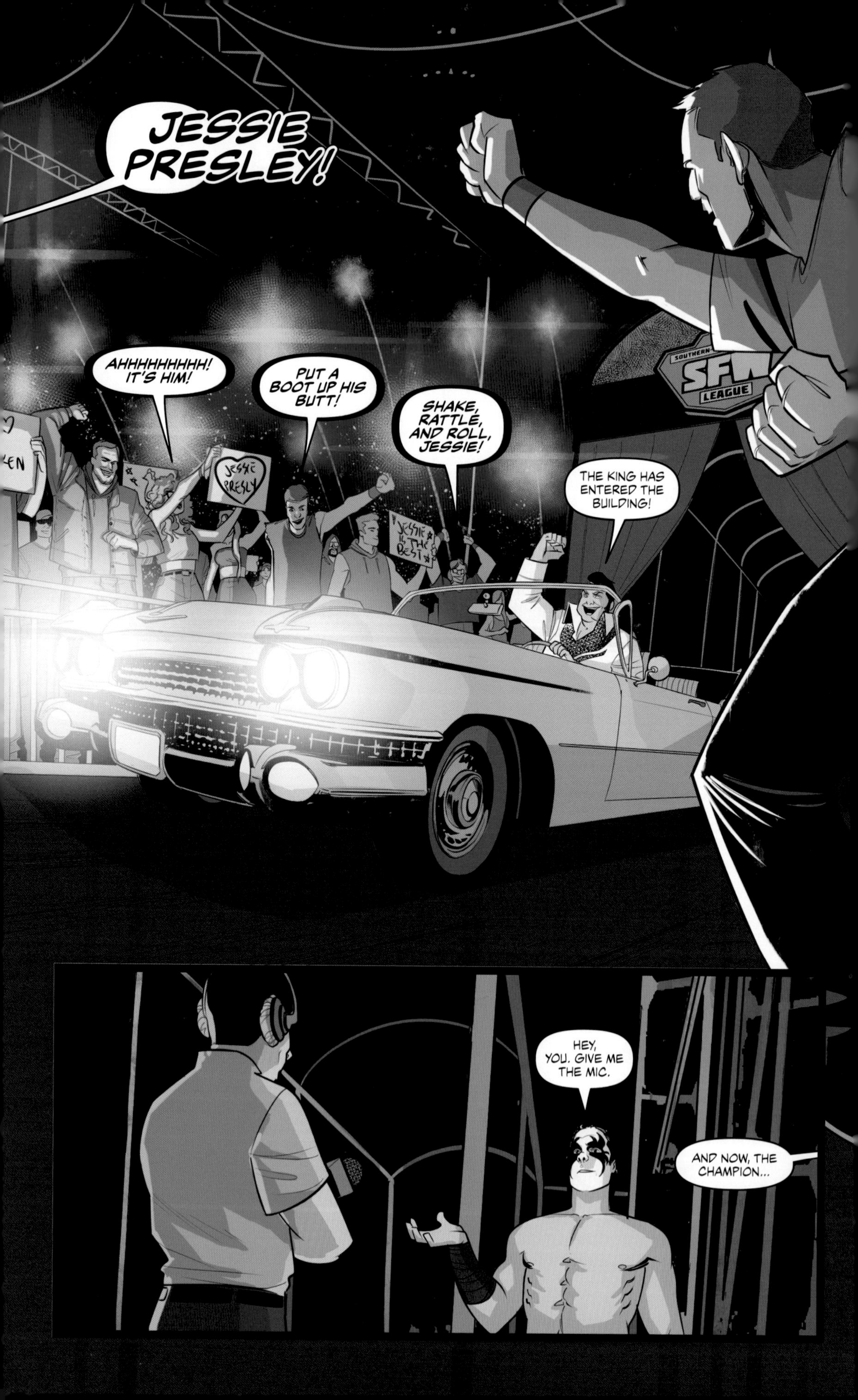
JESSIE PRESLEY!
AHHHHHHHHH! IT'S HIM!
PUT A BOOT UP HIS BUTT!
SHAKE, RATTLE, AND ROLL, JESSIE!
JESSIE PRESLEY
JESSIE IS THE BEST
SOUTHERN SFW LEAGUE
THE KING HAS ENTERED THE BUILDING!
HEY, YOU. GIVE ME THE MIC.
AND NOW, THE CHAMPION...

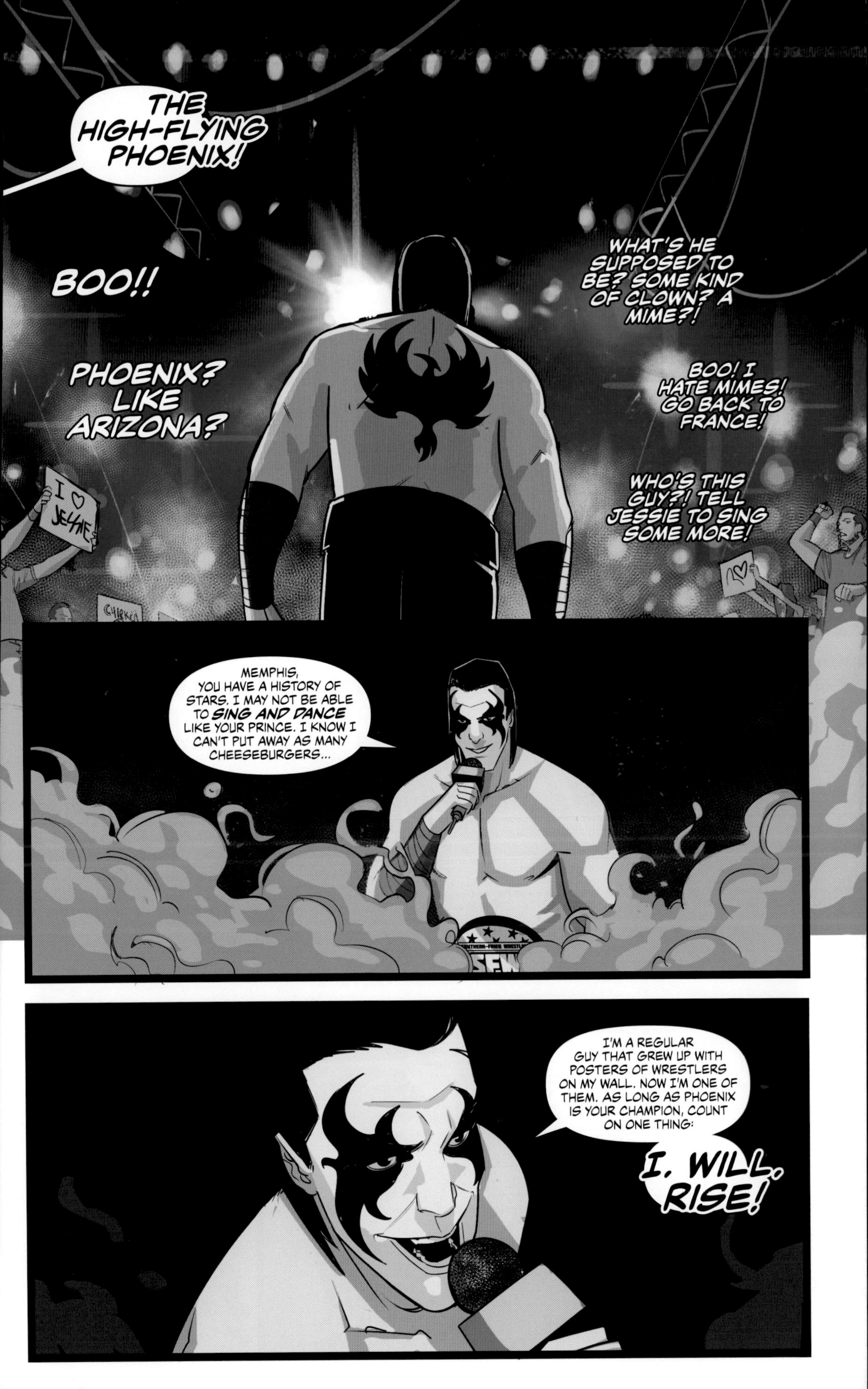
THE HIGH-FLYING PHOENIX!
BOO!!
WHAT'S HE SUPPOSED TO BE? SOME KIND OF CLOWN? A MIME?!
PHOENIX? LIKE ARIZONA?
BOO! I HATE MIMES! GO BACK TO FRANCE!
WHO'S THIS GUY?! TELL JESSIE TO SING SOME MORE!
I ♡ JESSIE
MEMPHIS, YOU HAVE A HISTORY OF STARS. I MAY NOT BE ABLE TO SING AND DANCE LIKE YOUR PRINCE. I KNOW I CAN'T PUT AWAY AS MANY CHEESEBURGERS...
I'M A REGULAR GUY THAT GREW UP WITH POSTERS OF WRESTLERS ON MY WALL. NOW I'M ONE OF THEM. AS LONG AS PHOENIX IS YOUR CHAMPION, COUNT ON ONE THING:
I. WILL. RISE!

NICE SPEECH. I CAN'T PROMISE TO LOVE YOU TENDER, BUT IF YOU COOPERATE, I'LL MAKE THIS QUICK.

NEVER WAS ANY GOOD AT COOPERATING. LET'S DANCE.

ARE YOU SURE? THAT'S NOT IN MY FORMAT. OKAY, YES, SIR. OF COURSE.

FOLKS, AS AN ADDED TREAT, THIS CONTEST HAS AN *UNADVERTISED* STIPULATION.

LET'S HOPE OUR COMBATANTS HAVE HAD ALL THEIR SHOTS. BECAUSE TONIGHT'S MAIN EVENT IS A *DOG COLLAR MATCH!*

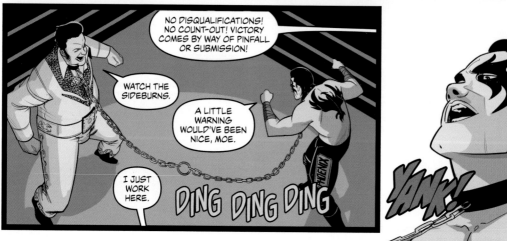

NO DISQUALIFICATIONS! NO COUNT-OUT! VICTORY COMES BY WAY OF PINFALL OR SUBMISSION!

WATCH THE SIDEBURNS.

A LITTLE WARNING WOULD'VE BEEN NICE, MOE.

I JUST WORK HERE.

DING DING DING

YANK!

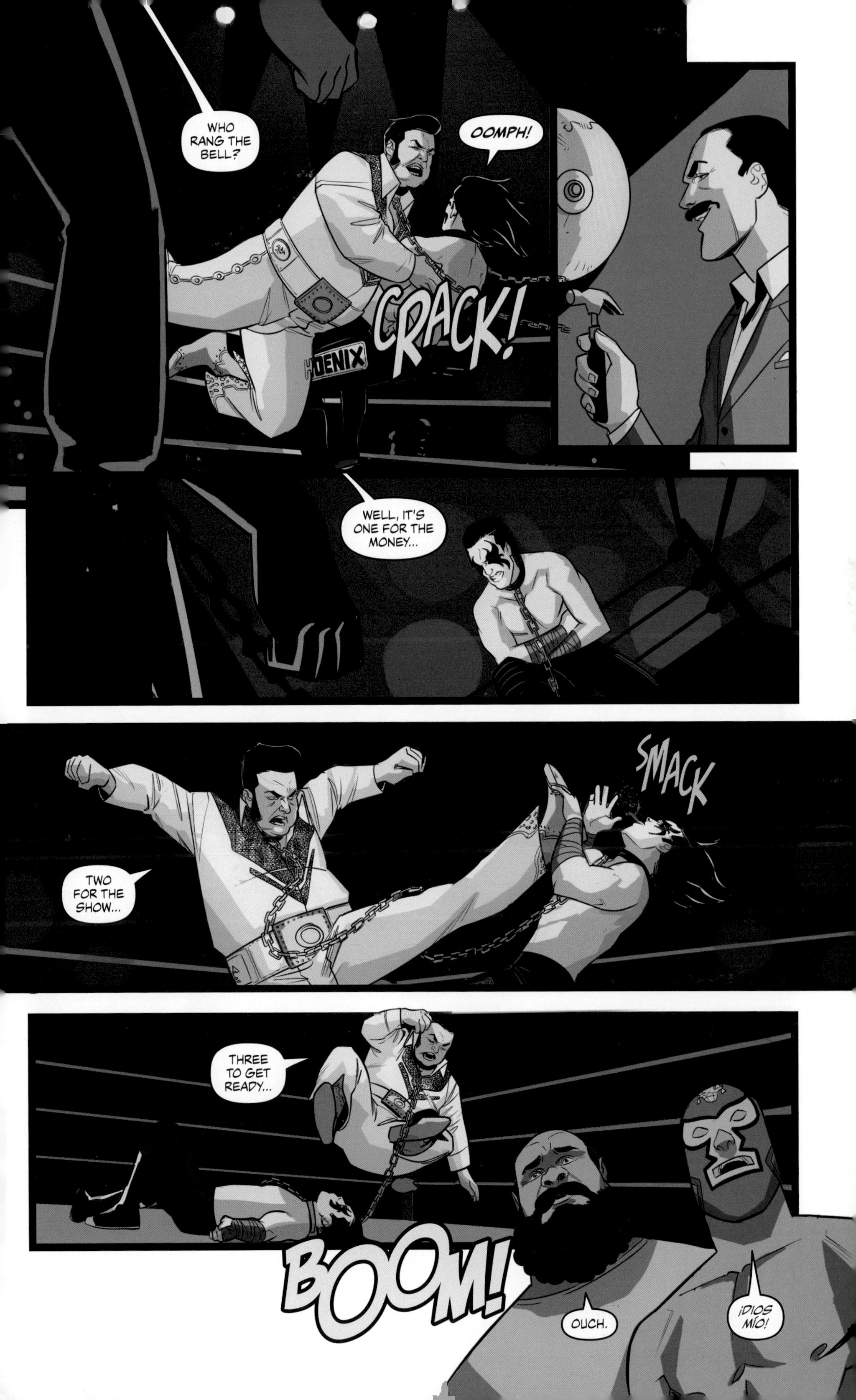
WHO RANG THE BELL?
OOMPH!
CRACK!
WELL, IT'S ONE FOR THE MONEY...
SMACK
TWO FOR THE SHOW...
THREE TO GET READY...
BOOM!
OUCH.
¡DIOS MÍO!

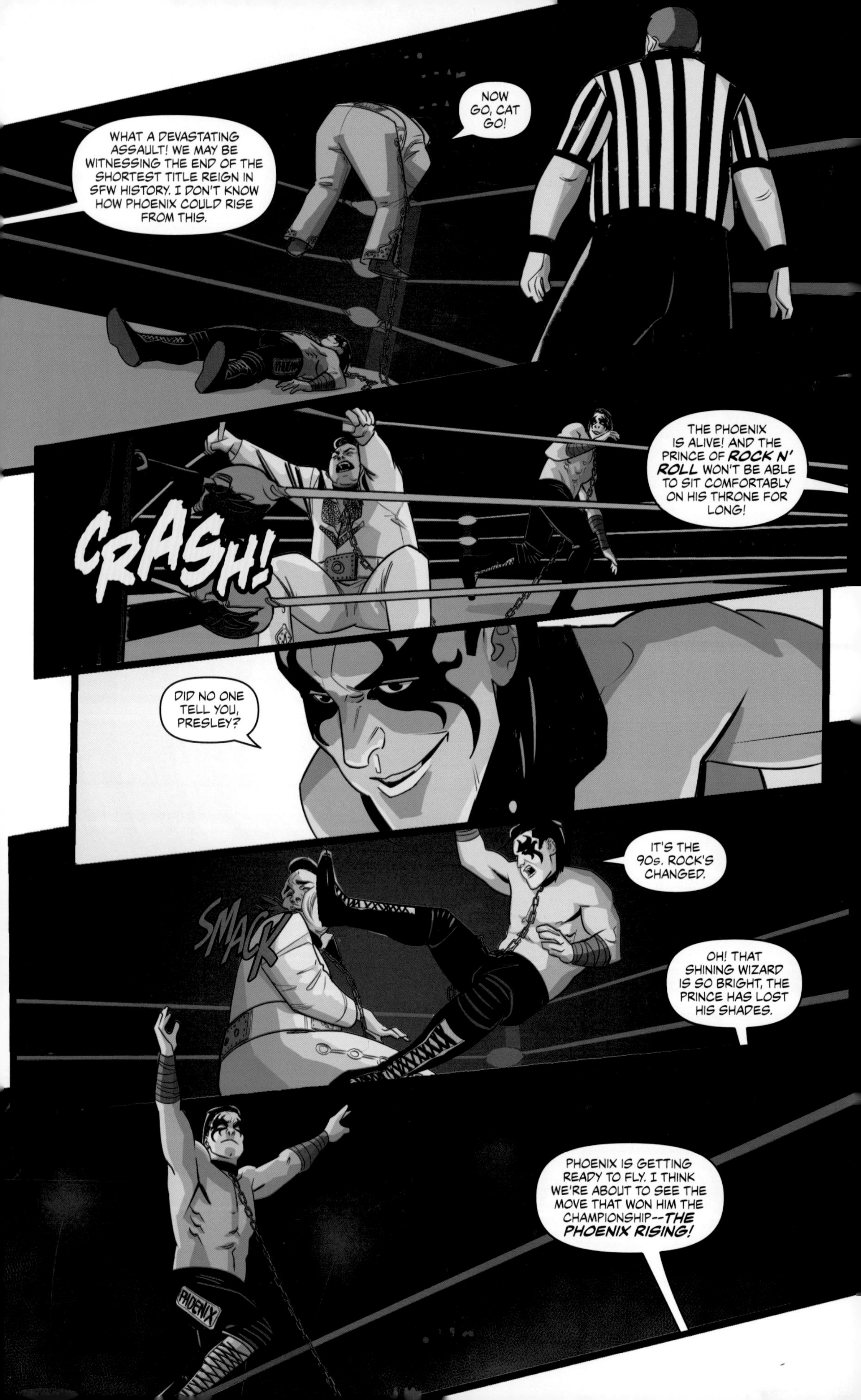
WHAT A DEVASTATING ASSAULT! WE MAY BE WITNESSING THE END OF THE SHORTEST TITLE REIGN IN SFW HISTORY. I DON'T KNOW HOW PHOENIX COULD RISE FROM THIS.
NOW GO, CAT GO!
THE PHOENIX IS ALIVE! AND THE PRINCE OF ROCK N' ROLL WON'T BE ABLE TO SIT COMFORTABLY ON HIS THRONE FOR LONG!
CRASH!
DID NO ONE TELL YOU, PRESLEY?
IT'S THE 90s. ROCK'S CHANGED.
SMACK
OH! THAT SHINING WIZARD IS SO BRIGHT, THE PRINCE HAS LOST HIS SHADES.
PHOENIX IS GETTING READY TO FLY. I THINK WE'RE ABOUT TO SEE THE MOVE THAT WON HIM THE CHAMPIONSHIP--THE PHOENIX RISING!

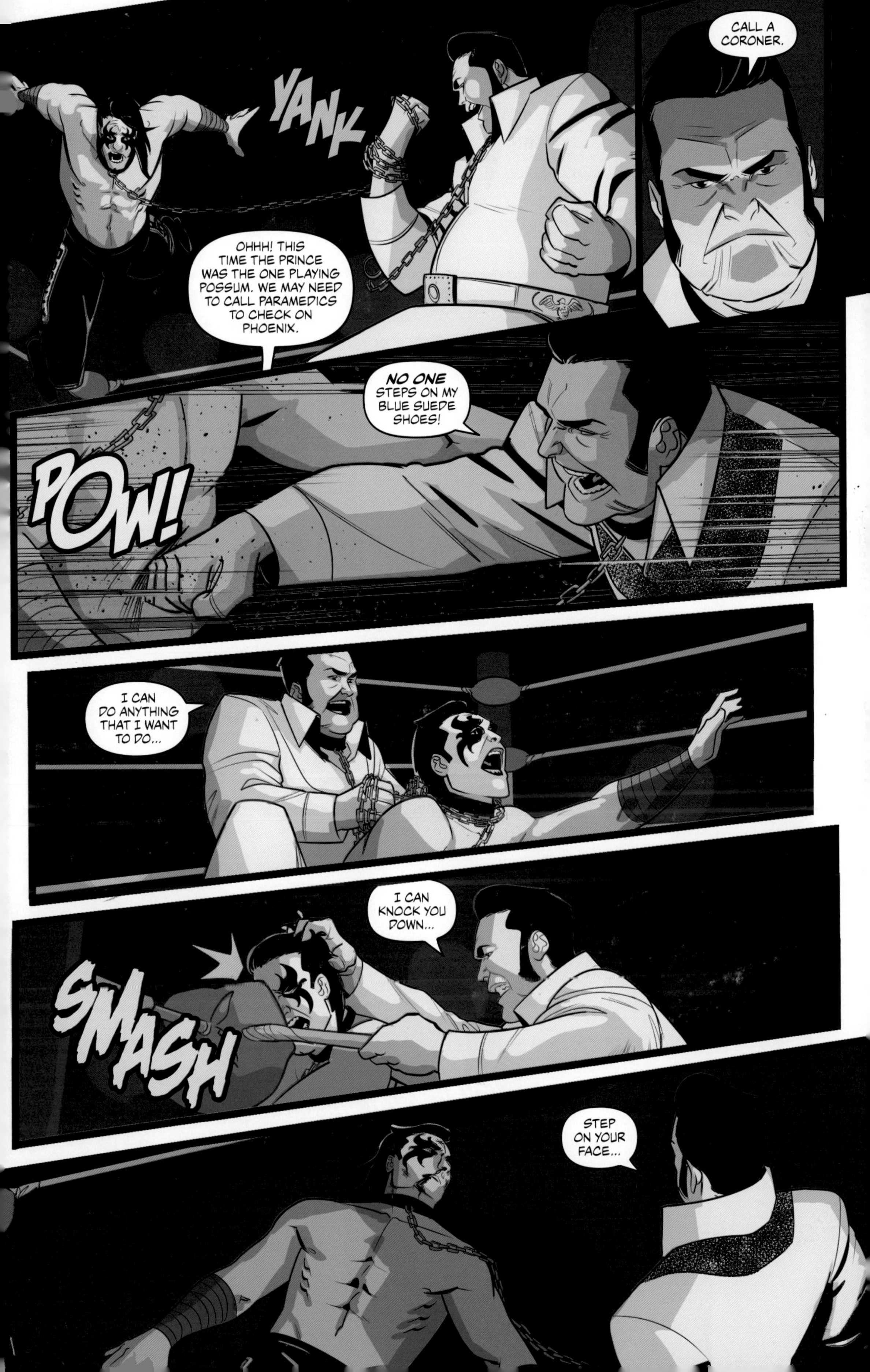
YANK
CALL A CORONER.
OHHH! THIS TIME THE PRINCE WAS THE ONE PLAYING POSSUM. WE MAY NEED TO CALL PARAMEDICS TO CHECK ON PHOENIX.
NO ONE STEPS ON MY BLUE SUEDE SHOES!
POW!
I CAN DO ANYTHING THAT I WANT TO DO...
I CAN KNOCK YOU DOWN...
SMASH
STEP ON YOUR FACE...

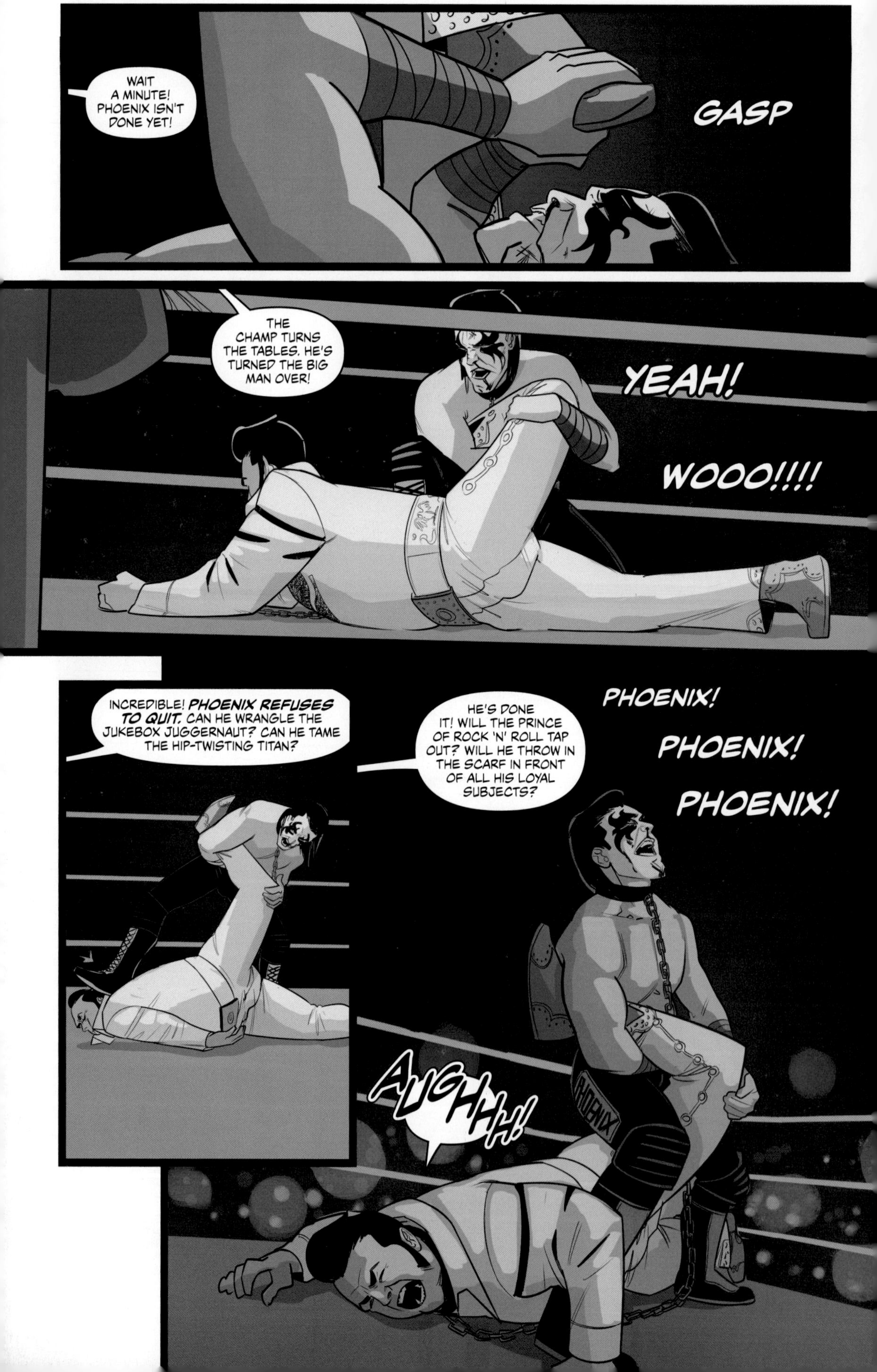
WAIT A MINUTE! PHOENIX ISN'T DONE YET!
GASP
THE CHAMP TURNS THE TABLES. HE'S TURNED THE BIG MAN OVER!
YEAH!
WOOO!!!!
INCREDIBLE! **PHOENIX REFUSES TO QUIT.** CAN HE WRANGLE THE JUKEBOX JUGGERNAUT? CAN HE TAME THE HIP-TWISTING TITAN?
HE'S DONE IT! WILL THE PRINCE OF ROCK 'N' ROLL TAP OUT? WILL HE THROW IN THE SCARF IN FRONT OF ALL HIS LOYAL SUBJECTS?
PHOENIX!
PHOENIX!
PHOENIX!
AUGHHH!
PHOENIX

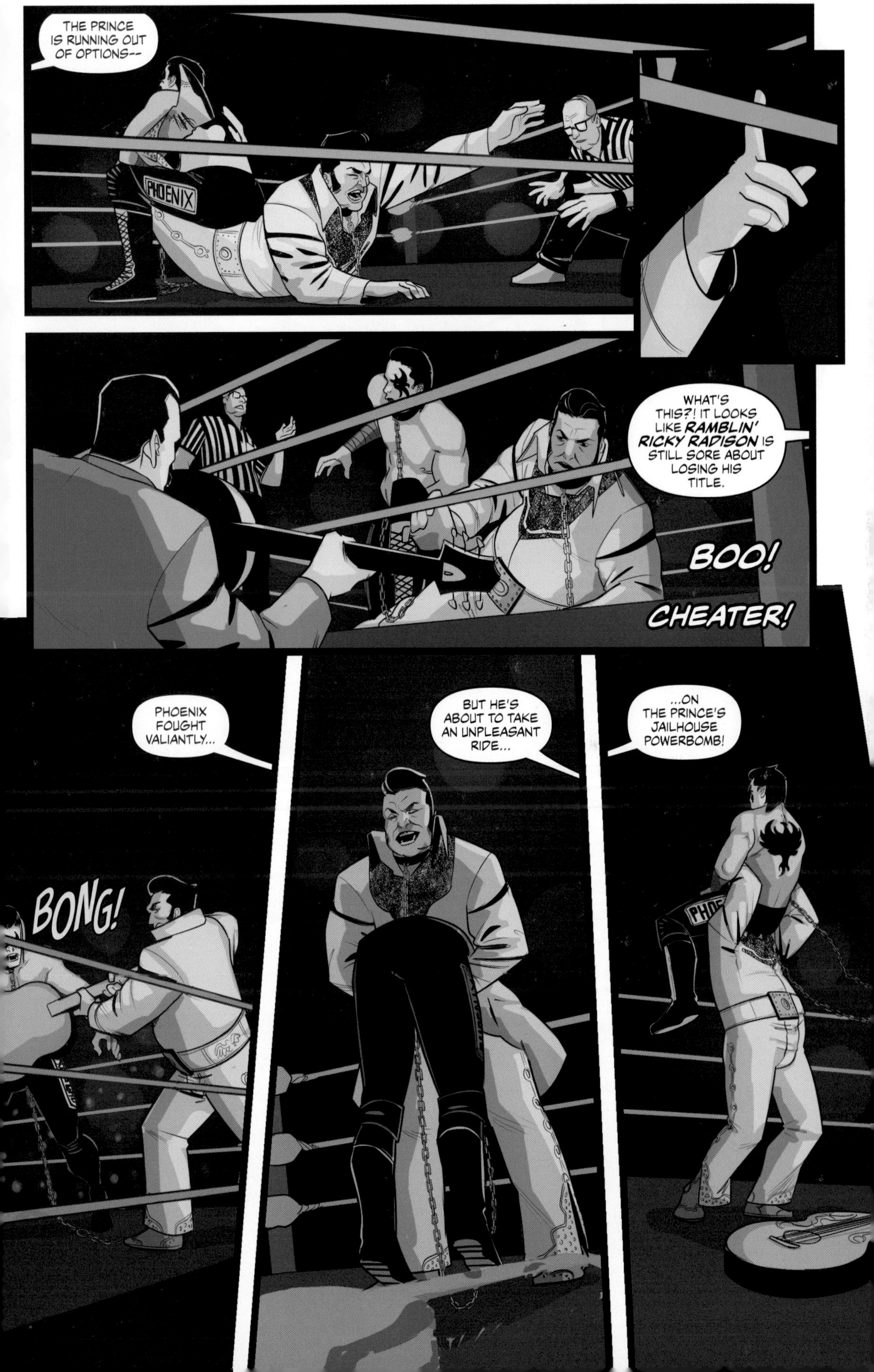
THE PRINCE IS RUNNING OUT OF OPTIONS--
PHOENIX
WHAT'S THIS?! IT LOOKS LIKE **RAMBLIN' RICKY RADISON** IS STILL SORE ABOUT LOSING HIS TITLE.
BOO!
CHEATER!
PHOENIX FOUGHT VALIANTLY...
BONG!
BUT HE'S ABOUT TO TAKE AN UNPLEASANT RIDE...
...ON THE PRINCE'S JAILHOUSE POWERBOMB!

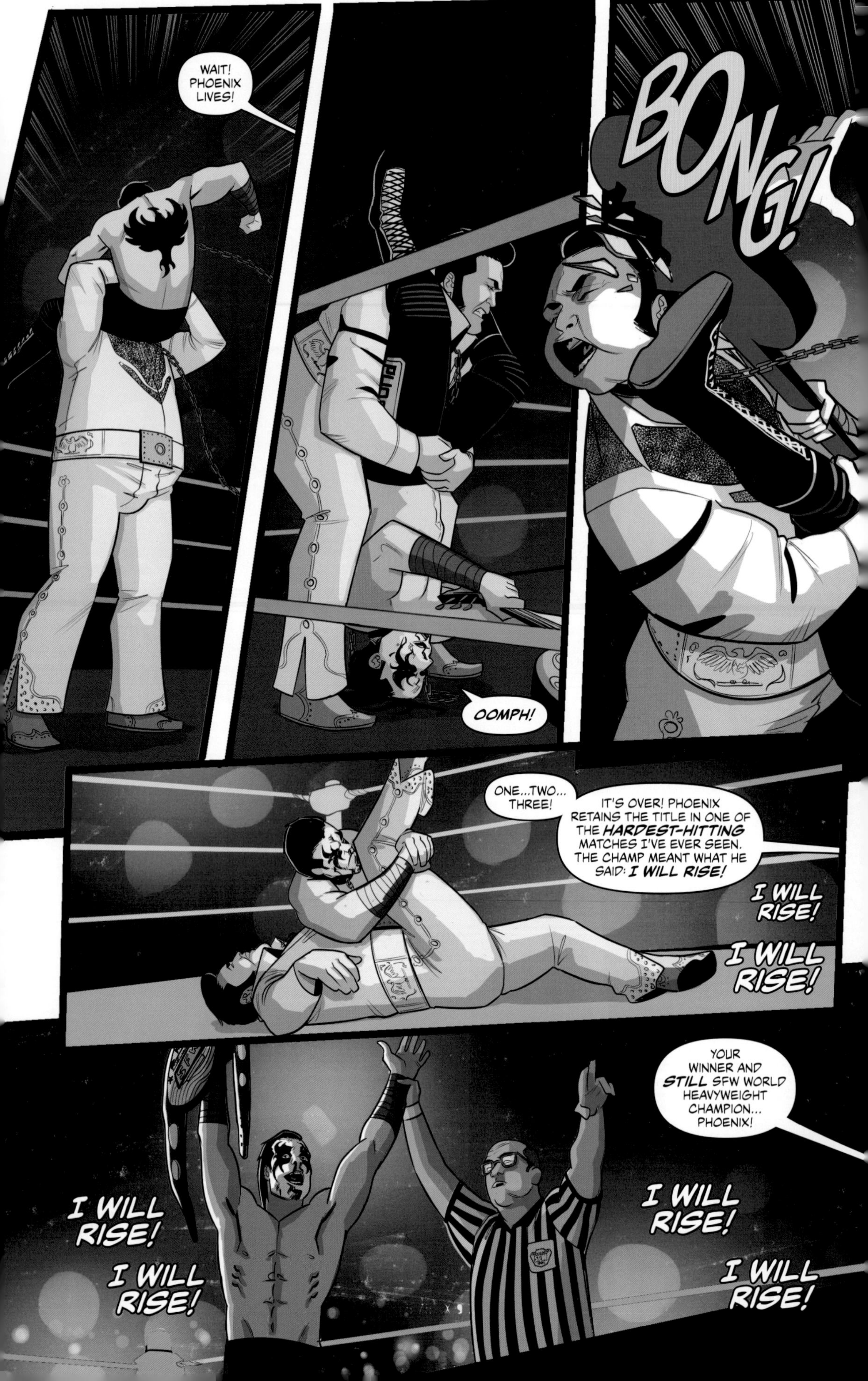
WAIT! PHOENIX LIVES!
BONG!
OOMPH!
ONE...TWO... THREE!
IT'S OVER! PHOENIX RETAINS THE TITLE IN ONE OF THE **HARDEST-HITTING** MATCHES I'VE EVER SEEN. THE CHAMP MEANT WHAT HE SAID: **I WILL RISE!**
I WILL RISE!
I WILL RISE!
YOUR WINNER AND **STILL** SFW WORLD HEAVYWEIGHT CHAMPION... PHOENIX!
I WILL RISE!
I WILL RISE!
I WILL RISE!
I WILL RISE!

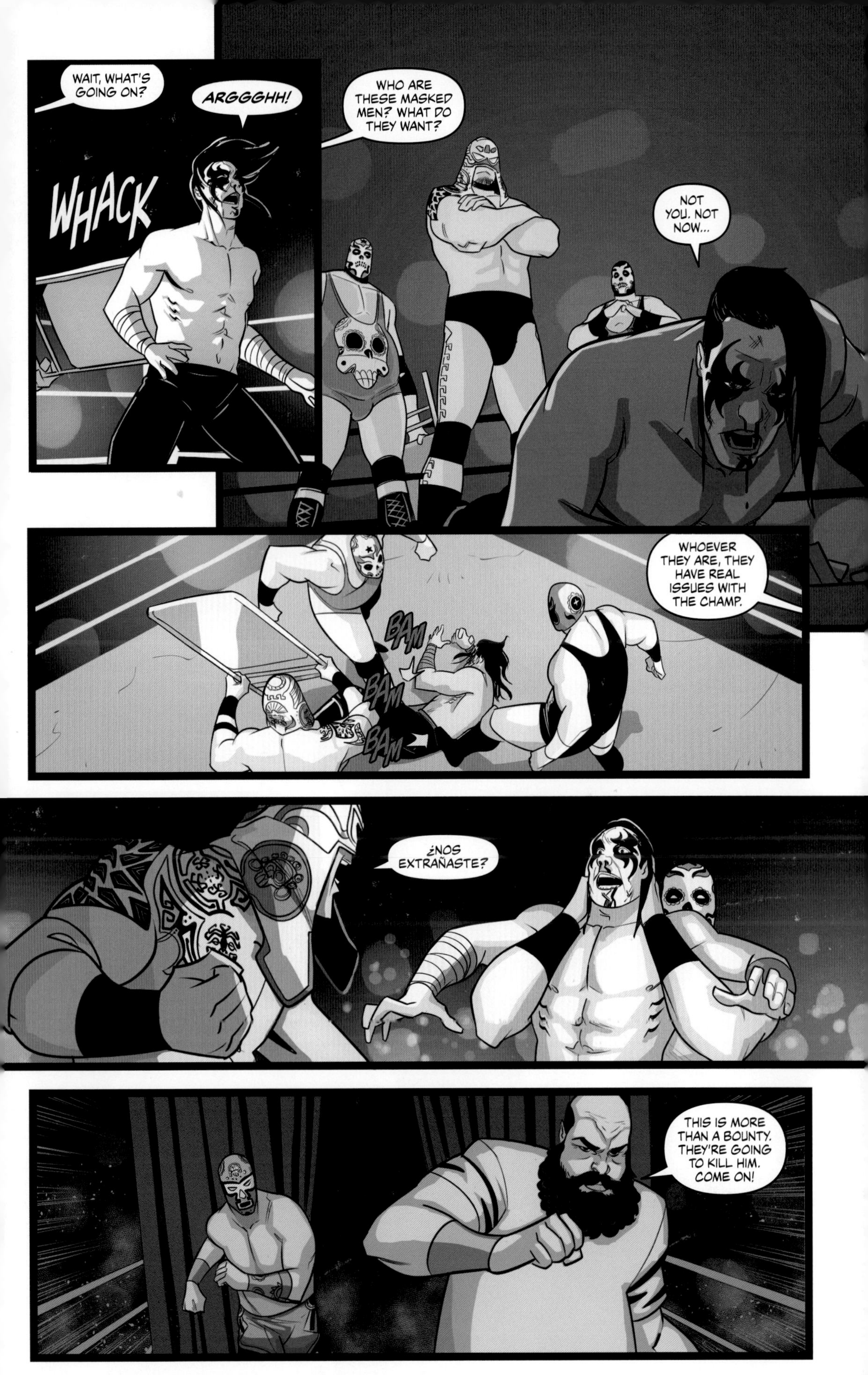
WAIT, WHAT'S GOING ON?
ARGGGHH!
WHACK
WHO ARE THESE MASKED MEN? WHAT DO THEY WANT?
NOT YOU. NOT NOW...
WHOEVER THEY ARE, THEY HAVE REAL ISSUES WITH THE CHAMP.
BAM
BAM
BAM
¿NOS EXTRAÑASTE?
THIS IS MORE THAN A BOUNTY. THEY'RE GOING TO KILL HIM. COME ON!

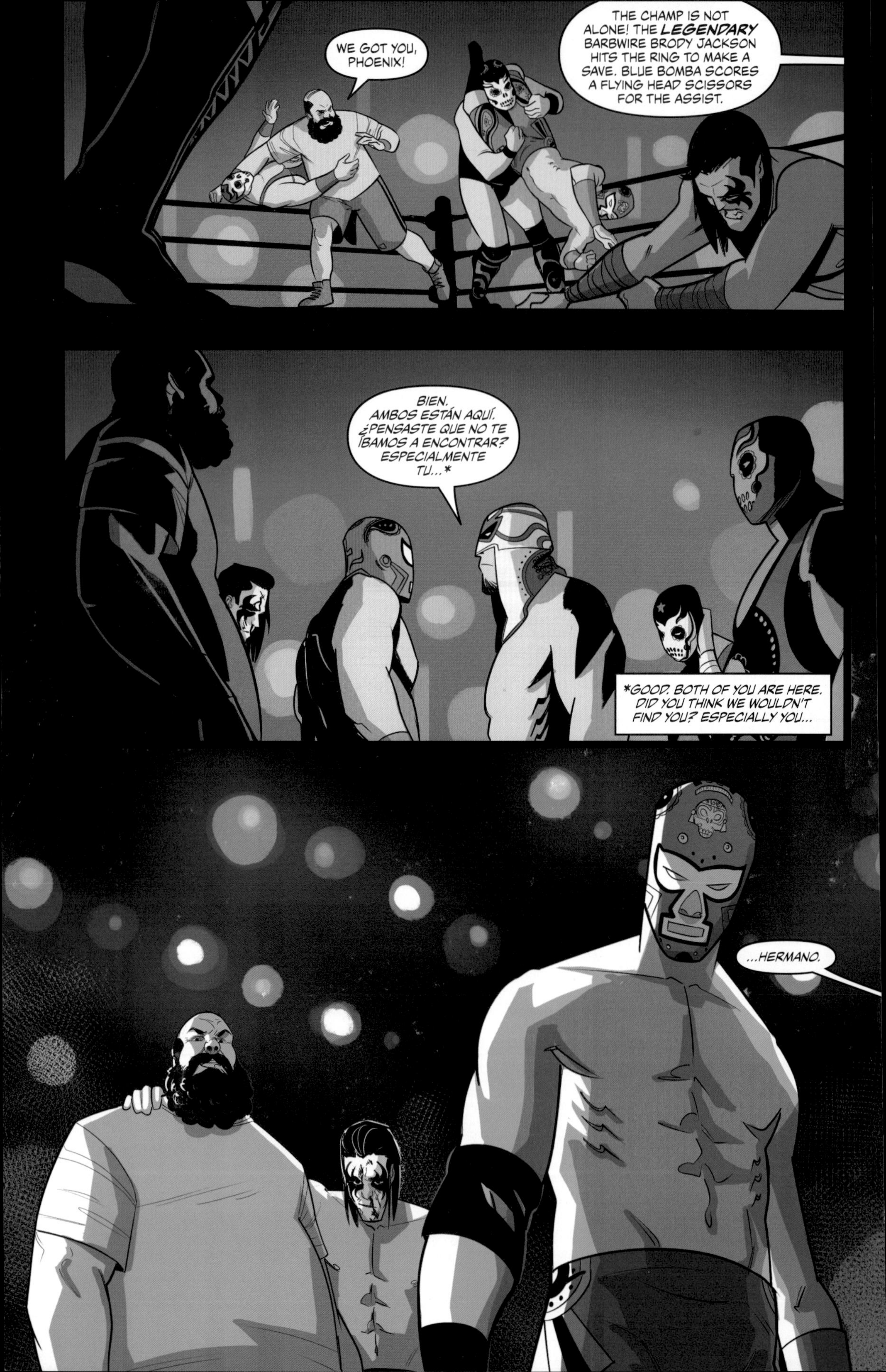
WE GOT YOU, PHOENIX!
THE CHAMP IS NOT ALONE! THE LEGENDARY BARBWIRE BRODY JACKSON HITS THE RING TO MAKE A SAVE. BLUE BOMBA SCORES A FLYING HEAD SCISSORS FOR THE ASSIST.
BIEN. AMBOS ESTÁN AQUÍ. ¿PENSASTE QUE NO TE ÍBAMOS A ENCONTRAR? ESPECIALMENTE TU...*
*GOOD. BOTH OF YOU ARE HERE. DID YOU THINK WE WOULDN'T FIND YOU? ESPECIALLY YOU...
...HERMANO.

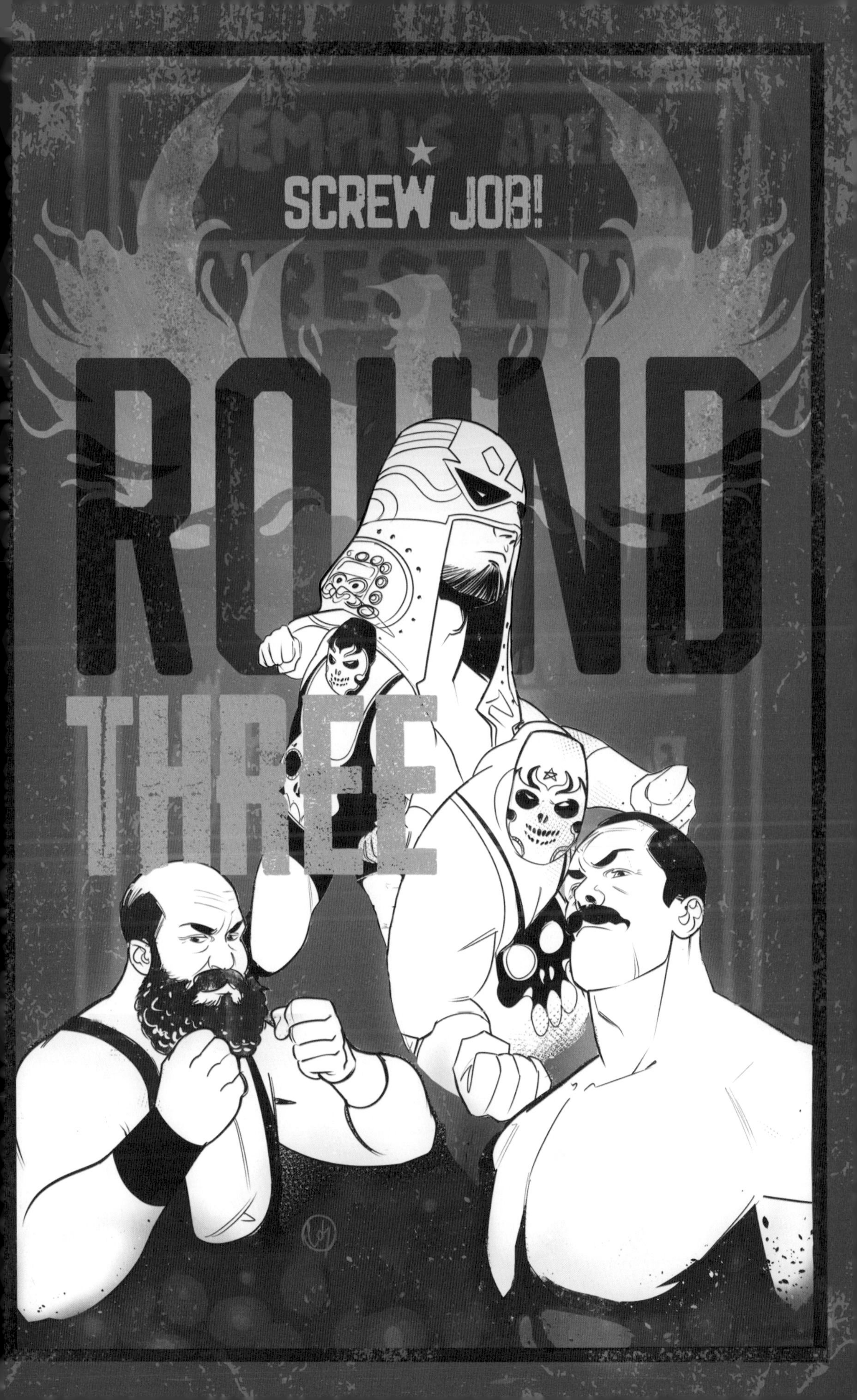
SCREW JOB!
ROUND
THREE

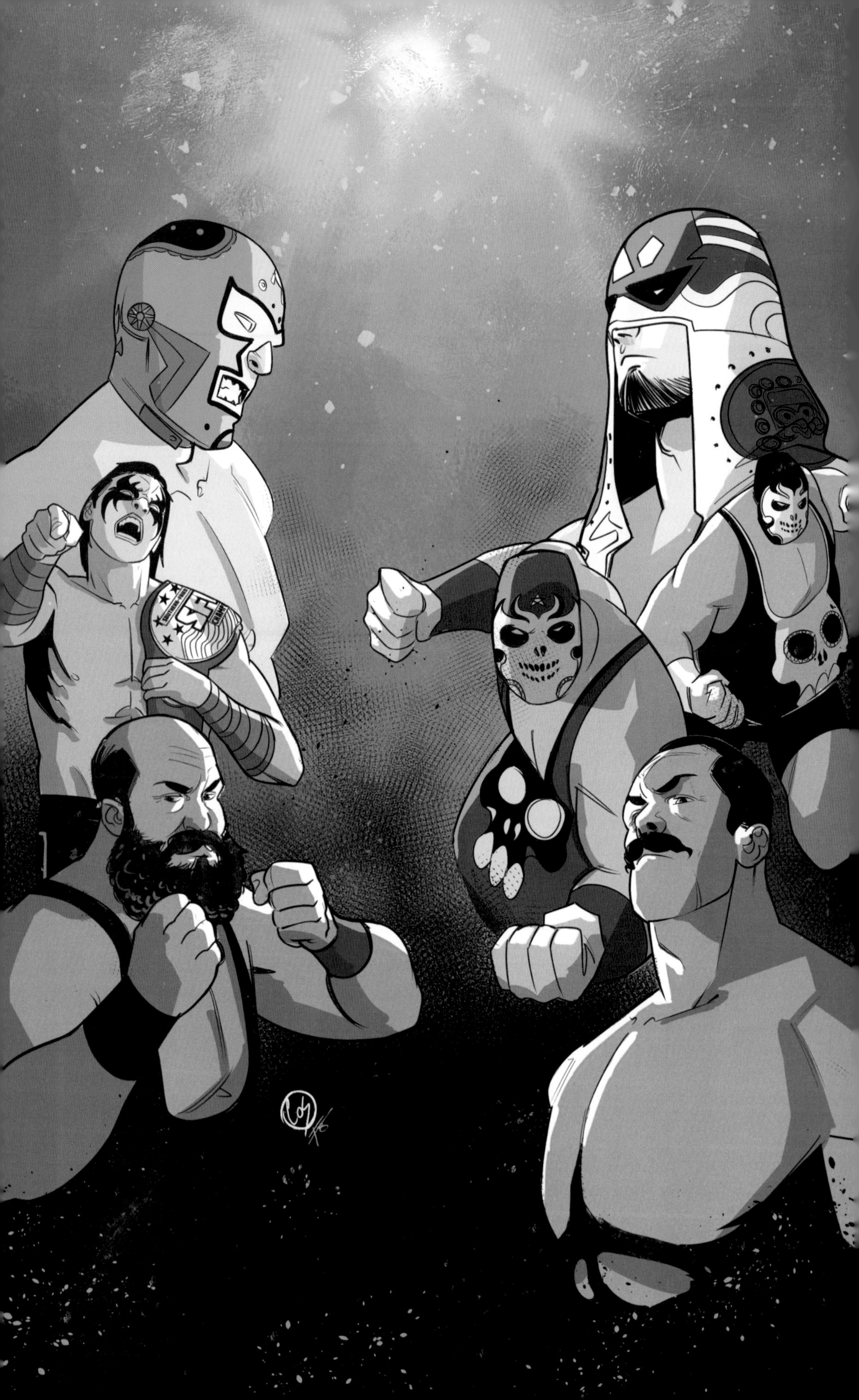

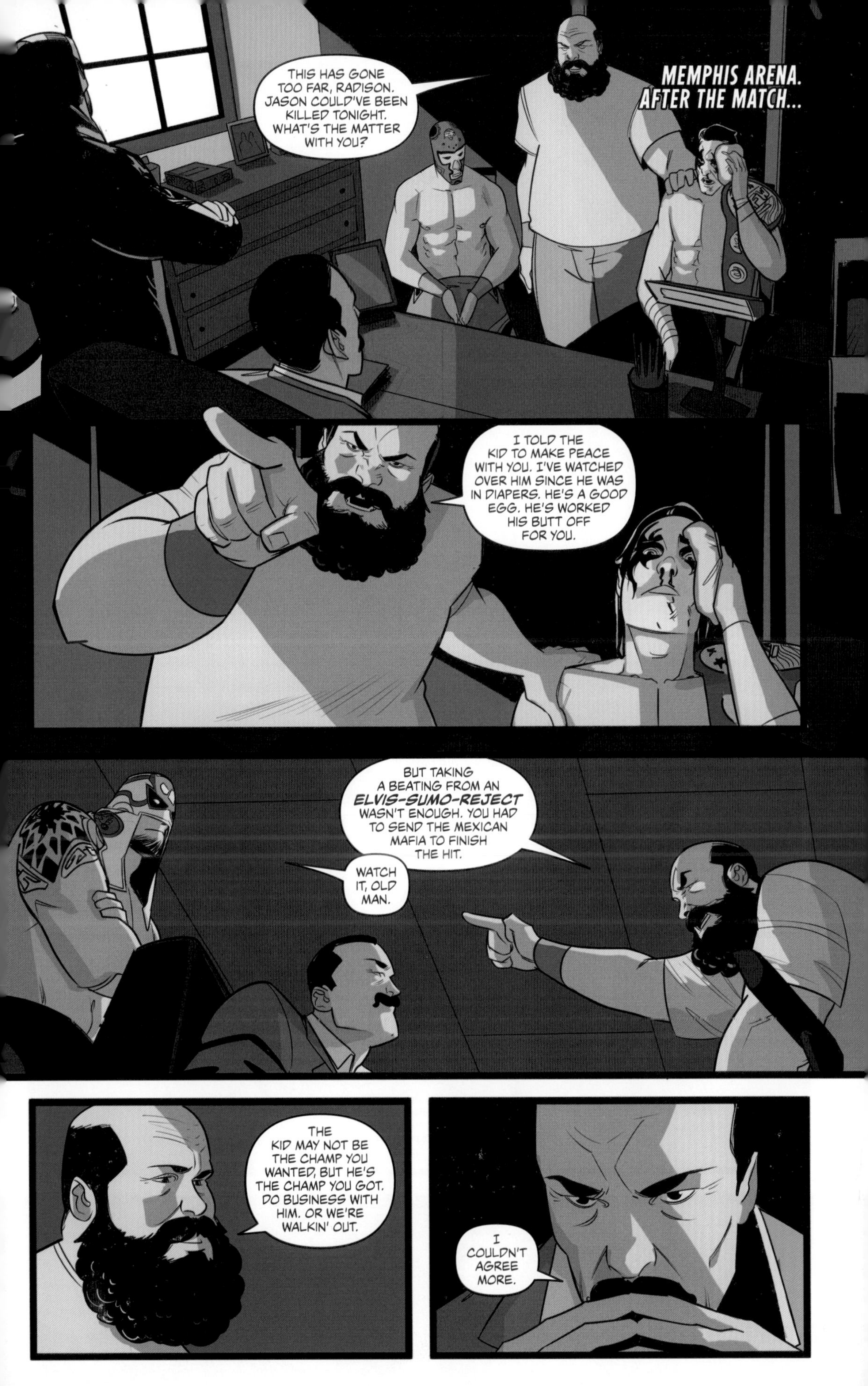
MEMPHIS ARENA. AFTER THE MATCH...
THIS HAS GONE TOO FAR, RADISON. JASON COULD'VE BEEN KILLED TONIGHT. WHAT'S THE MATTER WITH YOU?
I TOLD THE KID TO MAKE PEACE WITH YOU. I'VE WATCHED OVER HIM SINCE HE WAS IN DIAPERS. HE'S A GOOD EGG. HE'S WORKED HIS BUTT OFF FOR YOU.
BUT TAKING A BEATING FROM AN ELVIS-SUMO-REJECT WASN'T ENOUGH. YOU HAD TO SEND THE MEXICAN MAFIA TO FINISH THE HIT.
WATCH IT, OLD MAN.
THE KID MAY NOT BE THE CHAMP YOU WANTED, BUT HE'S THE CHAMP YOU GOT. DO BUSINESS WITH HIM. OR WE'RE WALKIN' OUT.
I COULDN'T AGREE MORE.

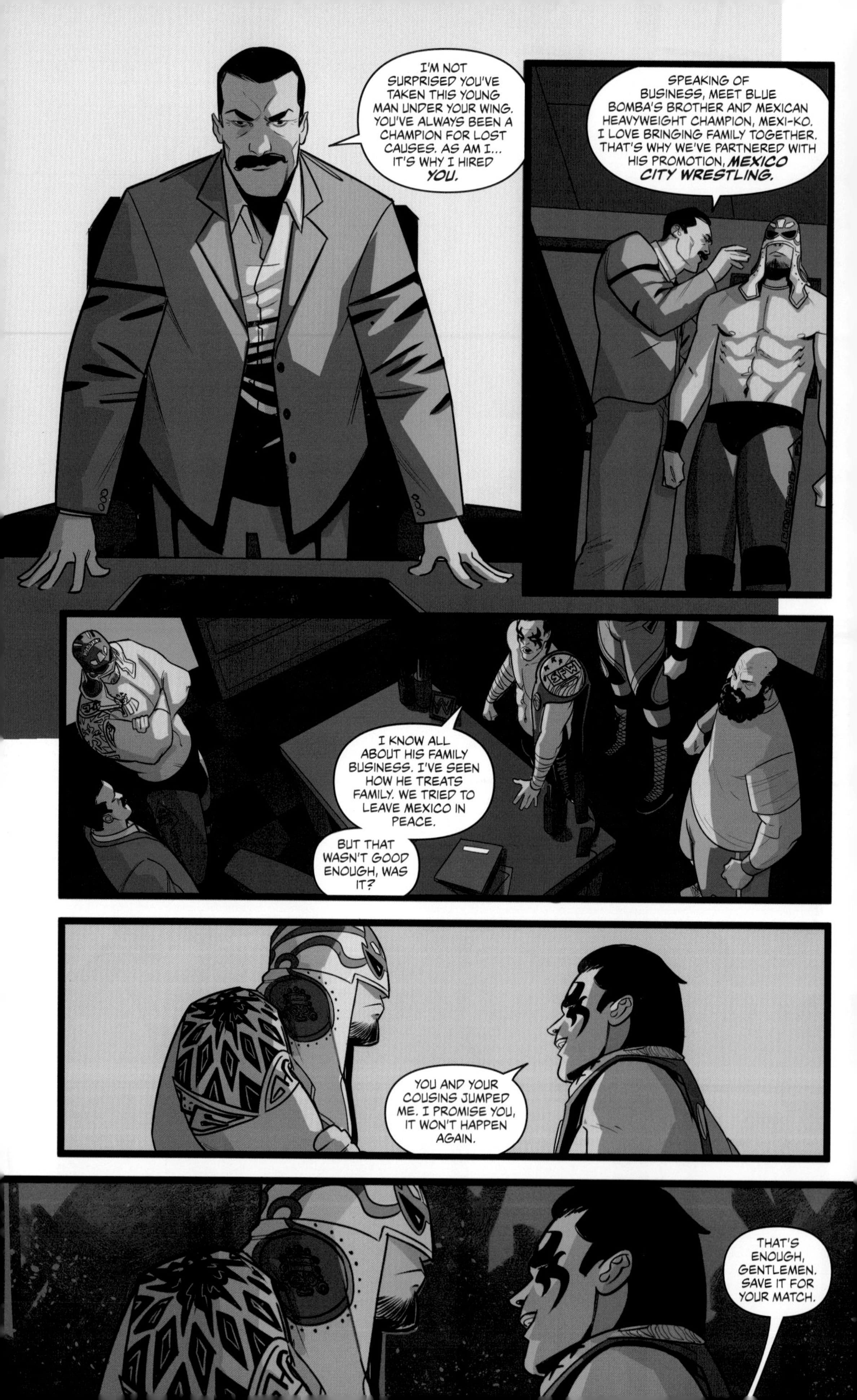
I'M NOT SURPRISED YOU'VE TAKEN THIS YOUNG MAN UNDER YOUR WING. YOU'VE ALWAYS BEEN A CHAMPION FOR LOST CAUSES. AS AM I... IT'S WHY I HIRED YOU.
SPEAKING OF BUSINESS, MEET BLUE BOMBA'S BROTHER AND MEXICAN HEAVYWEIGHT CHAMPION, MEXI-KO. I LOVE BRINGING FAMILY TOGETHER. THAT'S WHY WE'VE PARTNERED WITH HIS PROMOTION, MEXICO CITY WRESTLING.
I KNOW ALL ABOUT HIS FAMILY BUSINESS. I'VE SEEN HOW HE TREATS FAMILY. WE TRIED TO LEAVE MEXICO IN PEACE.
BUT THAT WASN'T GOOD ENOUGH, WAS IT?
YOU AND YOUR COUSINS JUMPED ME. I PROMISE YOU, IT WON'T HAPPEN AGAIN.
THAT'S ENOUGH, GENTLEMEN. SAVE IT FOR YOUR MATCH.

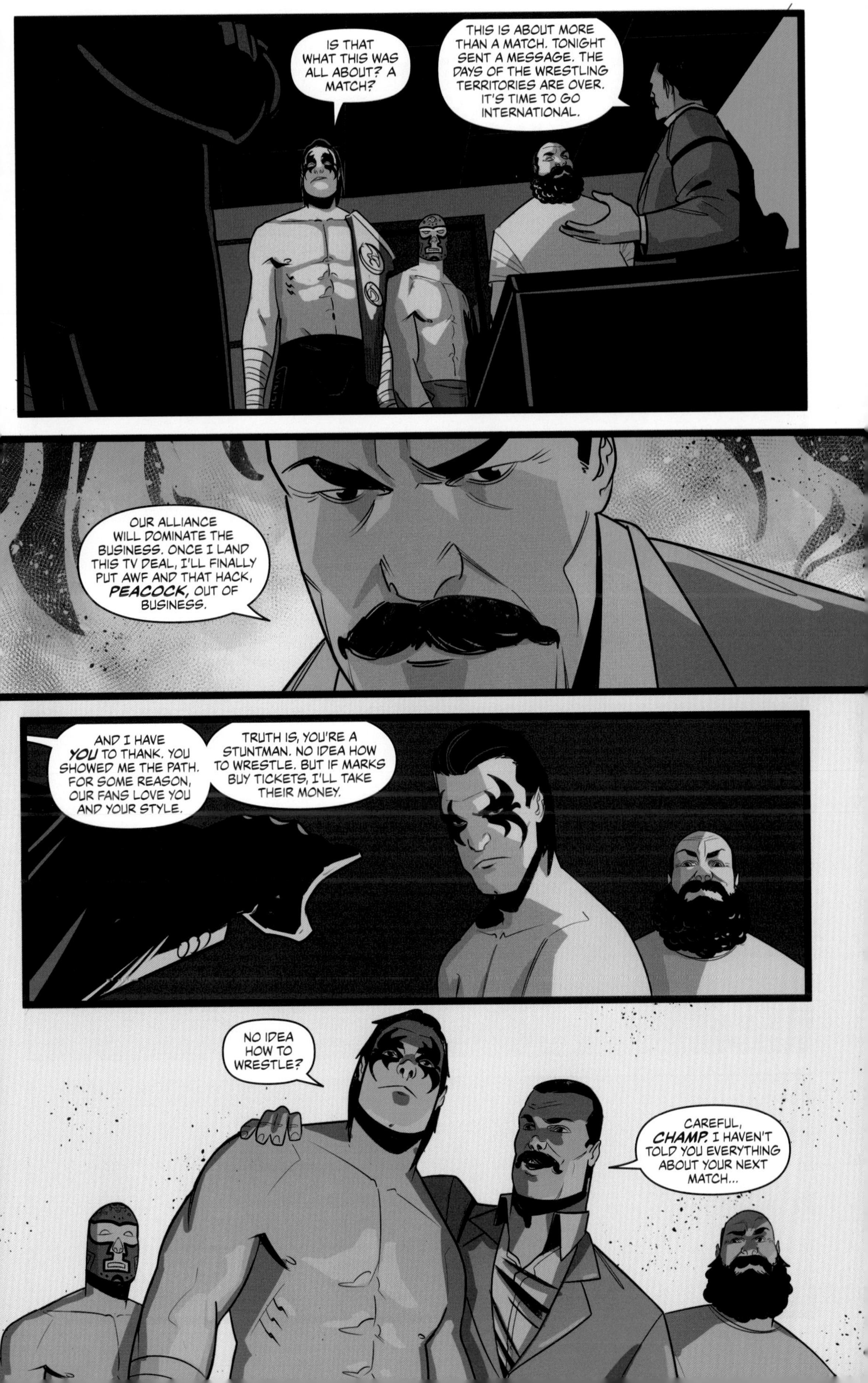
IS THAT WHAT THIS WAS ALL ABOUT? A MATCH?
THIS IS ABOUT MORE THAN A MATCH. TONIGHT SENT A MESSAGE. THE DAYS OF THE WRESTLING TERRITORIES ARE OVER. IT'S TIME TO GO INTERNATIONAL.
OUR ALLIANCE WILL DOMINATE THE BUSINESS. ONCE I LAND THIS TV DEAL, I'LL FINALLY PUT AWF AND THAT HACK, ***PEACOCK,*** OUT OF BUSINESS.
AND I HAVE ***YOU*** TO THANK. YOU SHOWED ME THE PATH. FOR SOME REASON, OUR FANS LOVE YOU AND YOUR STYLE.
TRUTH IS, YOU'RE A STUNTMAN. NO IDEA HOW TO WRESTLE. BUT IF MARKS BUY TICKETS, I'LL TAKE THEIR MONEY.
NO IDEA HOW TO WRESTLE?
CAREFUL, ***CHAMP.*** I HAVEN'T TOLD YOU EVERYTHING ABOUT YOUR NEXT MATCH...

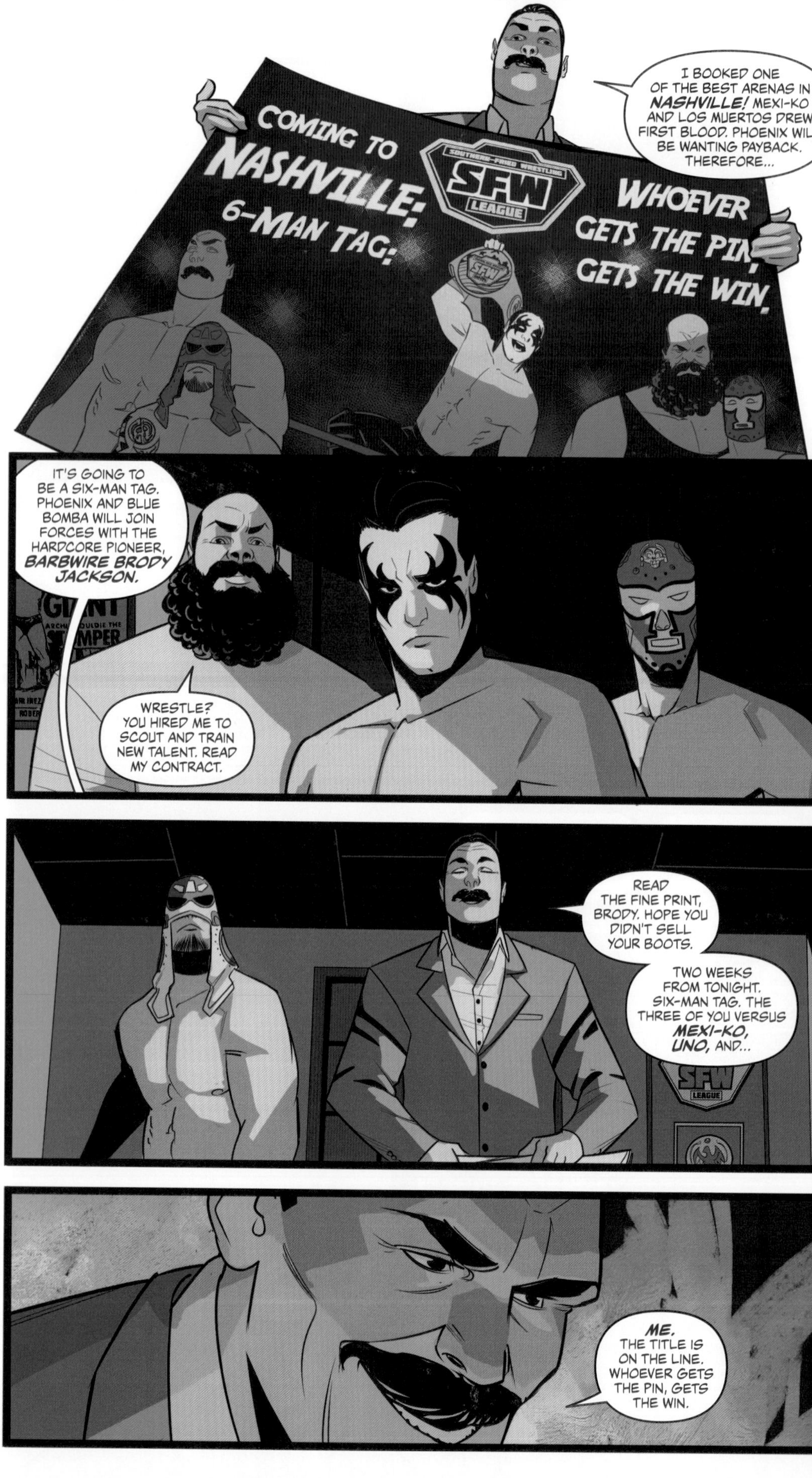

COMING TO NASHVILLE:
SOUTHERN-FRIED WRESTLING SFW LEAGUE
6-MAN TAG:
WHOEVER GETS THE PIN, GETS THE WIN.
I BOOKED ONE OF THE BEST ARENAS IN NASHVILLE! MEXI-KO AND LOS MUERTOS DREW FIRST BLOOD. PHOENIX WILL BE WANTING PAYBACK. THEREFORE...
IT'S GOING TO BE A SIX-MAN TAG. PHOENIX AND BLUE BOMBA WILL JOIN FORCES WITH THE HARDCORE PIONEER, BARBWIRE BRODY JACKSON.
WRESTLE? YOU HIRED ME TO SCOUT AND TRAIN NEW TALENT. READ MY CONTRACT.
READ THE FINE PRINT, BRODY. HOPE YOU DIDN'T SELL YOUR BOOTS.
TWO WEEKS FROM TONIGHT. SIX-MAN TAG. THE THREE OF YOU VERSUS MEXI-KO, UNO, AND...
SFW LEAGUE
ME. THE TITLE IS ON THE LINE. WHOEVER GETS THE PIN, GETS THE WIN.

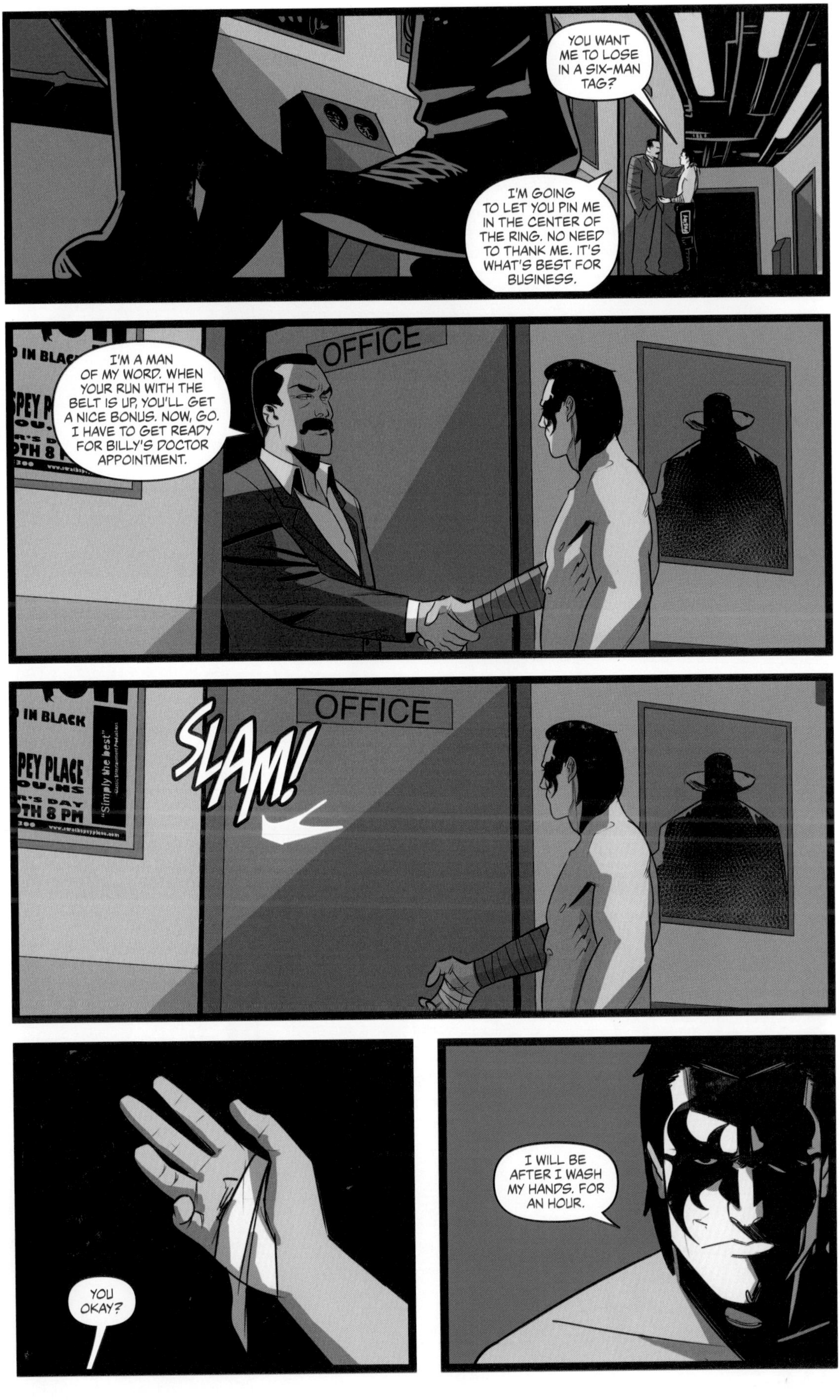
YOU WANT ME TO LOSE IN A SIX-MAN TAG?
I'M GOING TO LET YOU PIN ME IN THE CENTER OF THE RING. NO NEED TO THANK ME. IT'S WHAT'S BEST FOR BUSINESS.
OFFICE
I'M A MAN OF MY WORD. WHEN YOUR RUN WITH THE BELT IS UP, YOU'LL GET A NICE BONUS. NOW, GO. I HAVE TO GET READY FOR BILLY'S DOCTOR APPOINTMENT.
OFFICE
"Simply the best"
SLAM!
YOU OKAY?
I WILL BE AFTER I WASH MY HANDS. FOR AN HOUR.

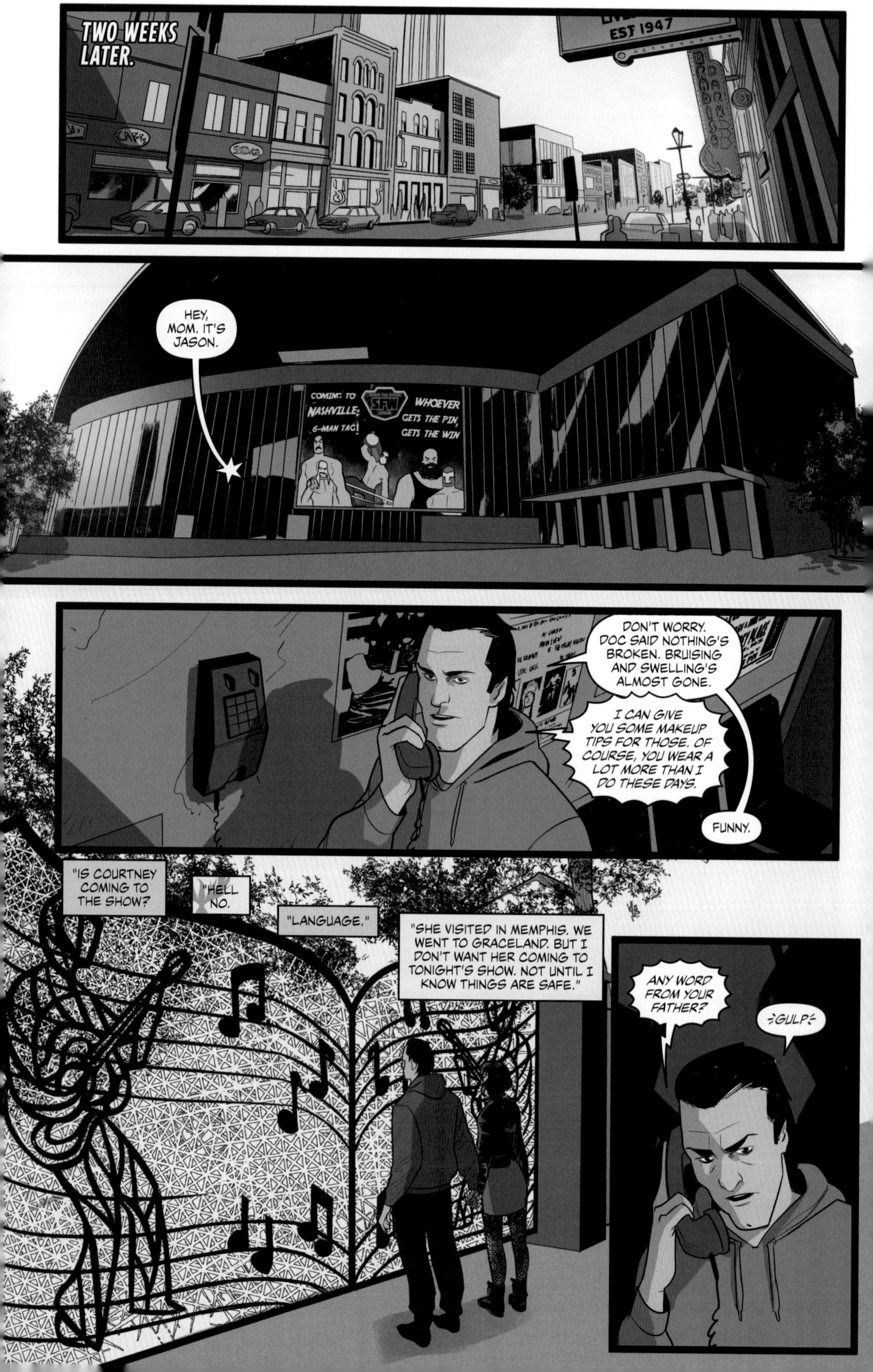
TWO WEEKS LATER.
EST 1947
HEY, MOM. IT'S JASON.
COMING TO NASHVILLE: 6-MAN TAG!
SFW
WHOEVER GETS THE PIN, GETS THE WIN
DON'T WORRY. DOC SAID NOTHING'S BROKEN. BRUISING AND SWELLING'S ALMOST GONE.
I CAN GIVE YOU SOME MAKEUP TIPS FOR THOSE. OF COURSE, YOU WEAR A LOT MORE THAN I DO THESE DAYS.
FUNNY.
"IS COURTNEY COMING TO THE SHOW?
"HELL NO.
"LANGUAGE."
"SHE VISITED IN MEMPHIS. WE WENT TO GRACELAND. BUT I DON'T WANT HER COMING TO TONIGHT'S SHOW. NOT UNTIL I KNOW THINGS ARE SAFE."
ANY WORD FROM YOUR FATHER?
GULP

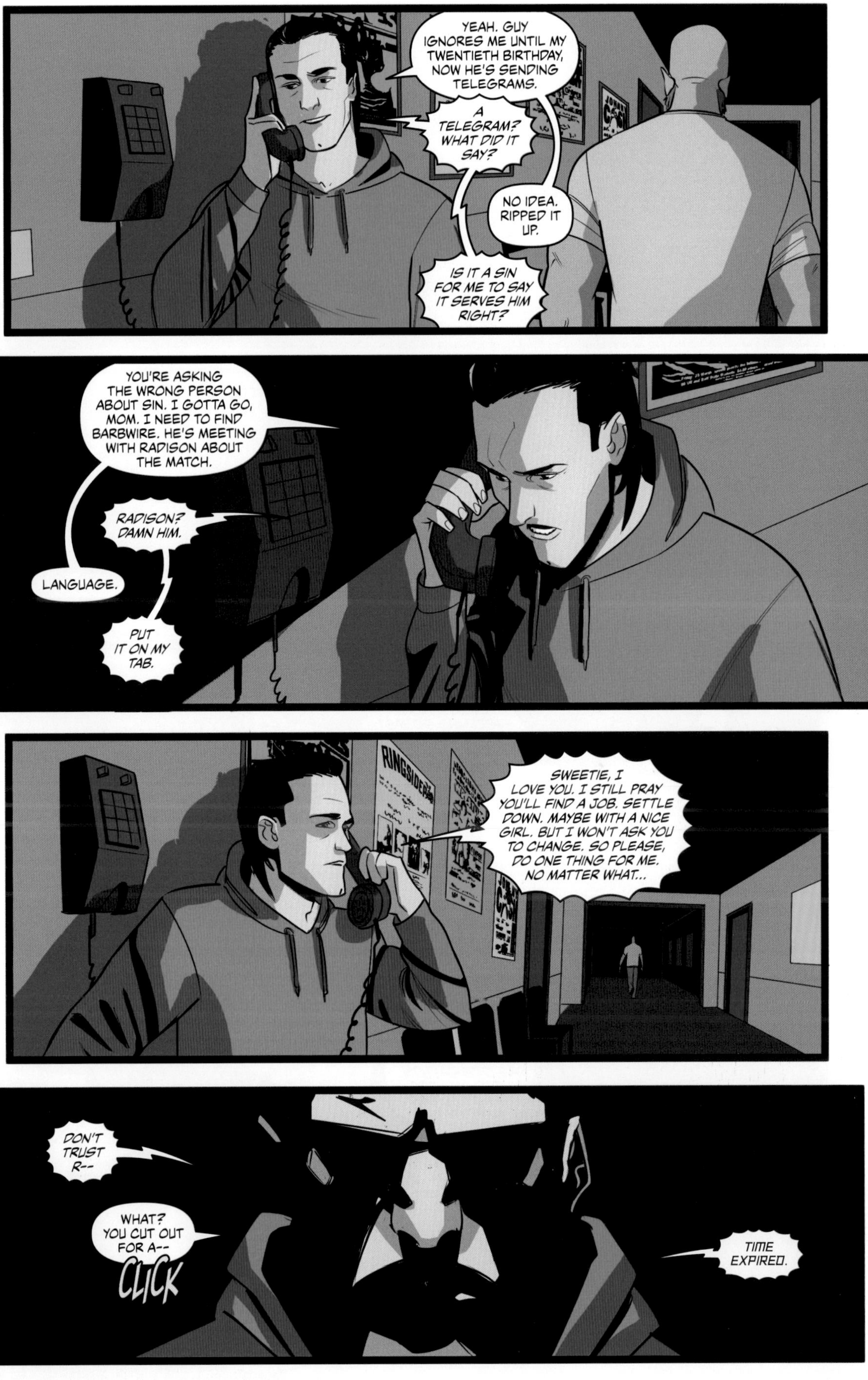
YEAH. GUY IGNORES ME UNTIL MY TWENTIETH BIRTHDAY, NOW HE'S SENDING TELEGRAMS.
A TELEGRAM? WHAT DID IT SAY?
NO IDEA. RIPPED IT UP.
IS IT A SIN FOR ME TO SAY IT SERVES HIM RIGHT?
YOU'RE ASKING THE WRONG PERSON ABOUT SIN. I GOTTA GO, MOM. I NEED TO FIND BARBWIRE. HE'S MEETING WITH RADISON ABOUT THE MATCH.
RADISON? DAMN HIM.
LANGUAGE.
PUT IT ON MY TAB.
SWEETIE, I LOVE YOU. I STILL PRAY YOU'LL FIND A JOB. SETTLE DOWN. MAYBE WITH A NICE GIRL. BUT I WON'T ASK YOU TO CHANGE. SO PLEASE, DO ONE THING FOR ME. NO MATTER WHAT...
DON'T TRUST R--
WHAT? YOU CUT OUT FOR A--
CLICK
TIME EXPIRED.

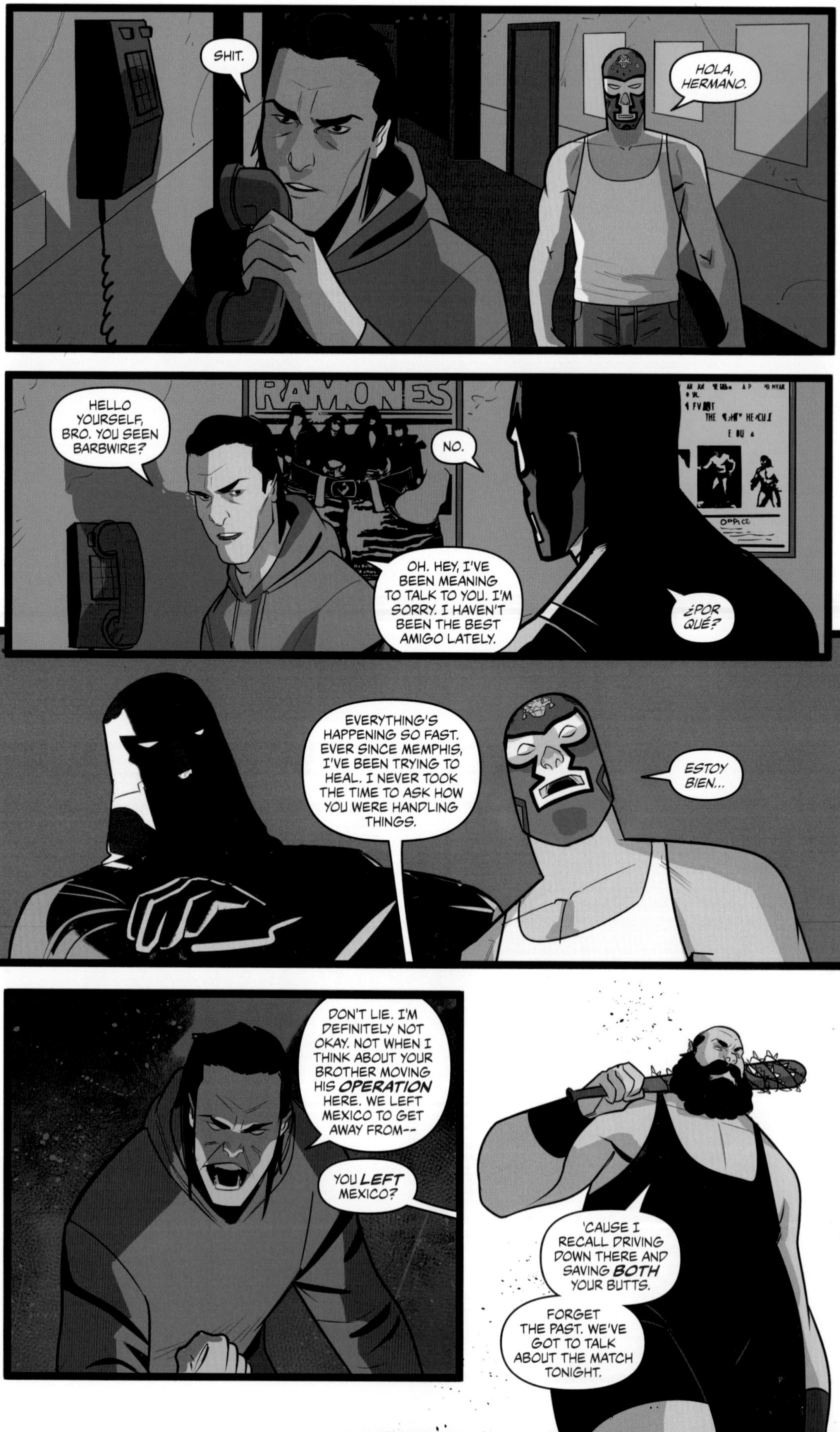
SHIT.
HOLA, HERMANO.
HELLO YOURSELF, BRO. YOU SEEN BARBWIRE?
RAMONES
NO.
OH. HEY, I'VE BEEN MEANING TO TALK TO YOU. I'M SORRY. I HAVEN'T BEEN THE BEST AMIGO LATELY.
¿POR QUÉ?
EVERYTHING'S HAPPENING SO FAST. EVER SINCE MEMPHIS, I'VE BEEN TRYING TO HEAL. I NEVER TOOK THE TIME TO ASK HOW YOU WERE HANDLING THINGS.
ESTOY BIEN...
DON'T LIE. I'M DEFINITELY NOT OKAY. NOT WHEN I THINK ABOUT YOUR BROTHER MOVING HIS *OPERATION* HERE. WE LEFT MEXICO TO GET AWAY FROM--
YOU *LEFT* MEXICO?
'CAUSE I RECALL DRIVING DOWN THERE AND SAVING *BOTH* YOUR BUTTS.
FORGET THE PAST. WE'VE GOT TO TALK ABOUT THE MATCH TONIGHT.

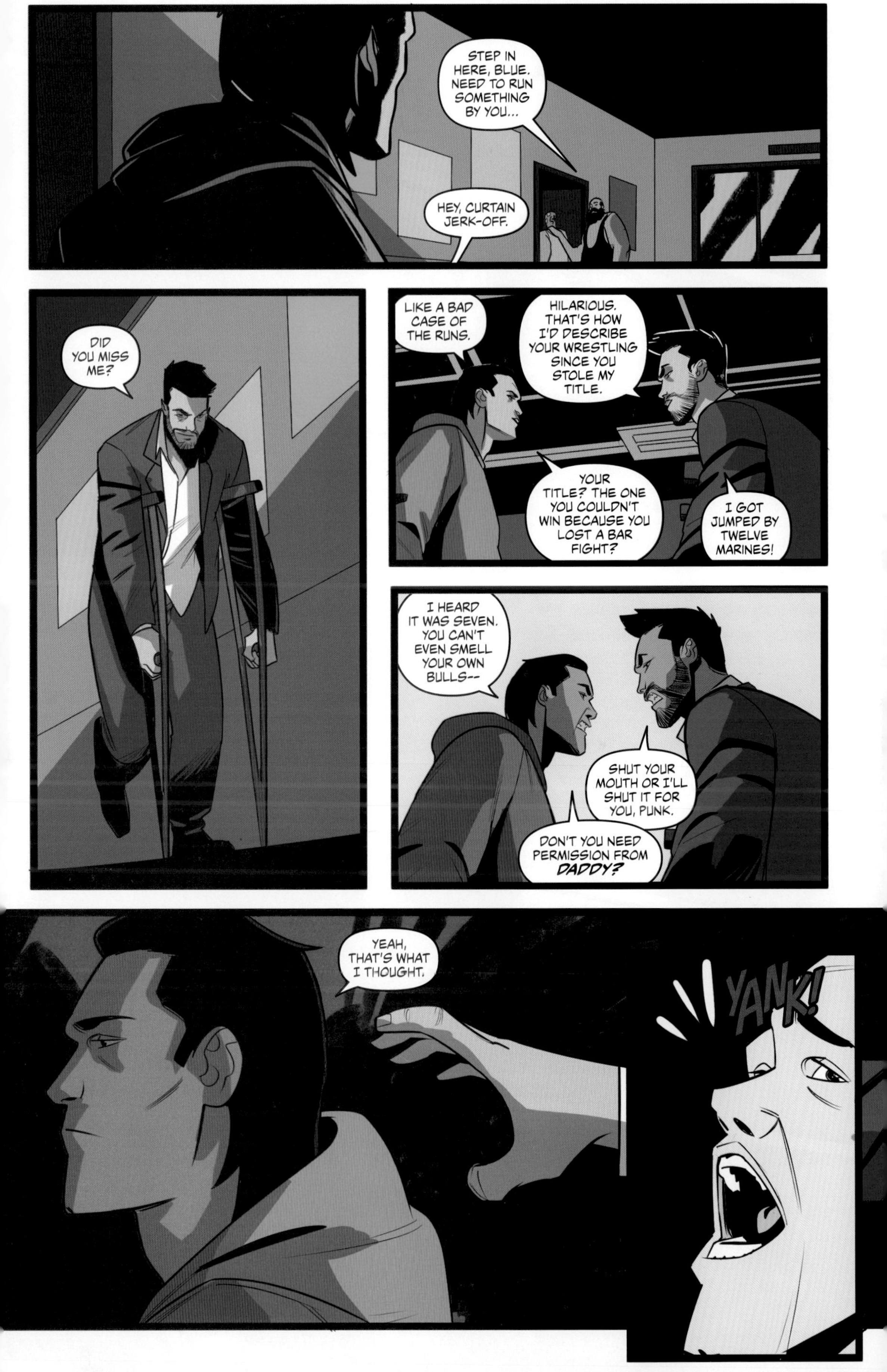
STEP IN HERE, BLUE. NEED TO RUN SOMETHING BY YOU...
HEY, CURTAIN JERK-OFF.
DID YOU MISS ME?
LIKE A BAD CASE OF THE RUNS.
HILARIOUS. THAT'S HOW I'D DESCRIBE YOUR WRESTLING SINCE YOU STOLE MY TITLE.
YOUR TITLE? THE ONE YOU COULDN'T WIN BECAUSE YOU LOST A BAR FIGHT?
I GOT JUMPED BY TWELVE MARINES!
I HEARD IT WAS SEVEN. YOU CAN'T EVEN SMELL YOUR OWN BULLS--
SHUT YOUR MOUTH OR I'LL SHUT IT FOR YOU, PUNK.
DON'T YOU NEED PERMISSION FROM DADDY?
YEAH, THAT'S WHAT I THOUGHT.
YANK!

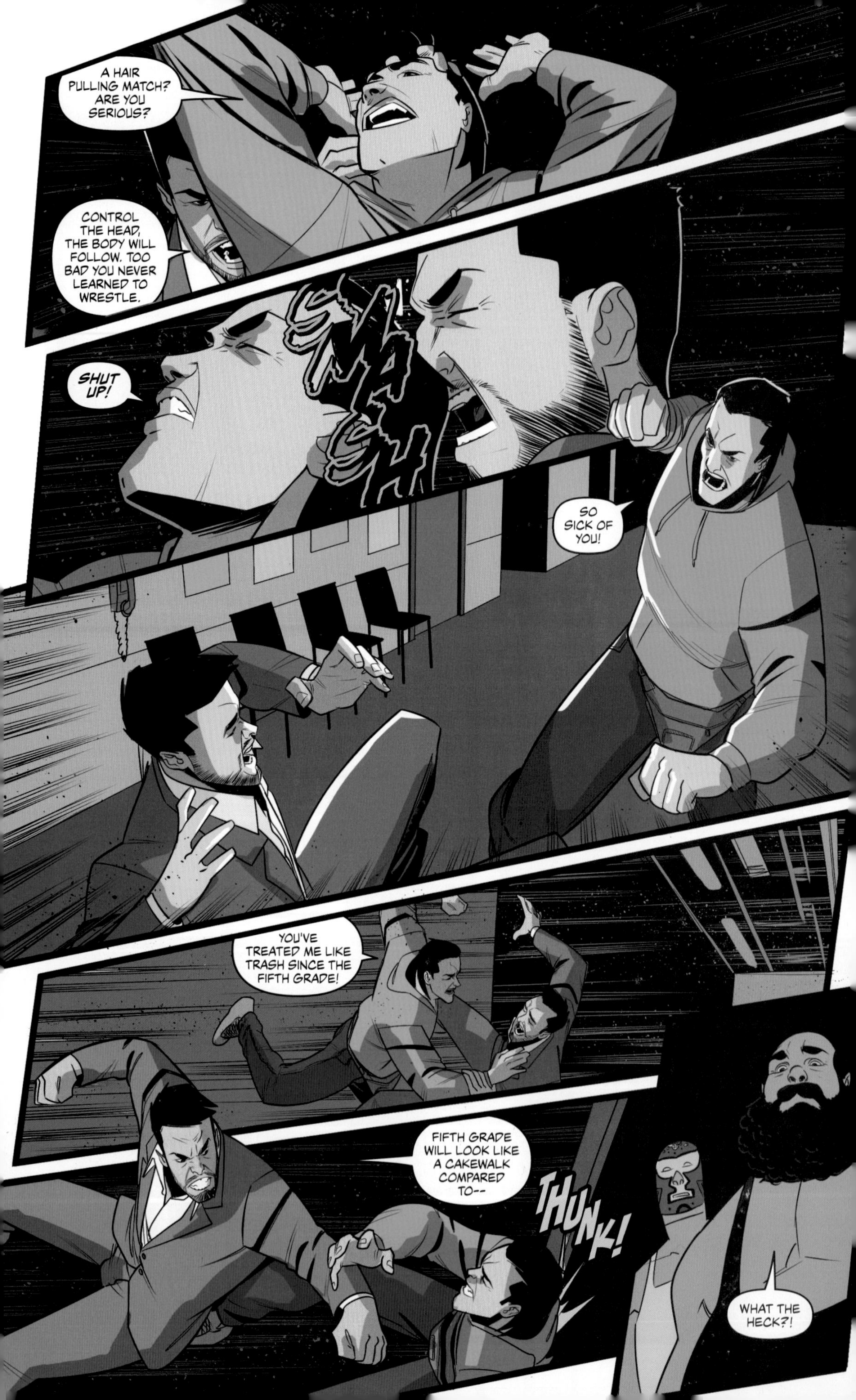
A HAIR PULLING MATCH? ARE YOU SERIOUS?
CONTROL THE HEAD, THE BODY WILL FOLLOW. TOO BAD YOU NEVER LEARNED TO WRESTLE.
SMASH
SHUT UP!
SO SICK OF YOU!
YOU'VE TREATED ME LIKE TRASH SINCE THE FIFTH GRADE!
FIFTH GRADE WILL LOOK LIKE A CAKEWALK COMPARED TO--
THUNK!
WHAT THE HECK?!

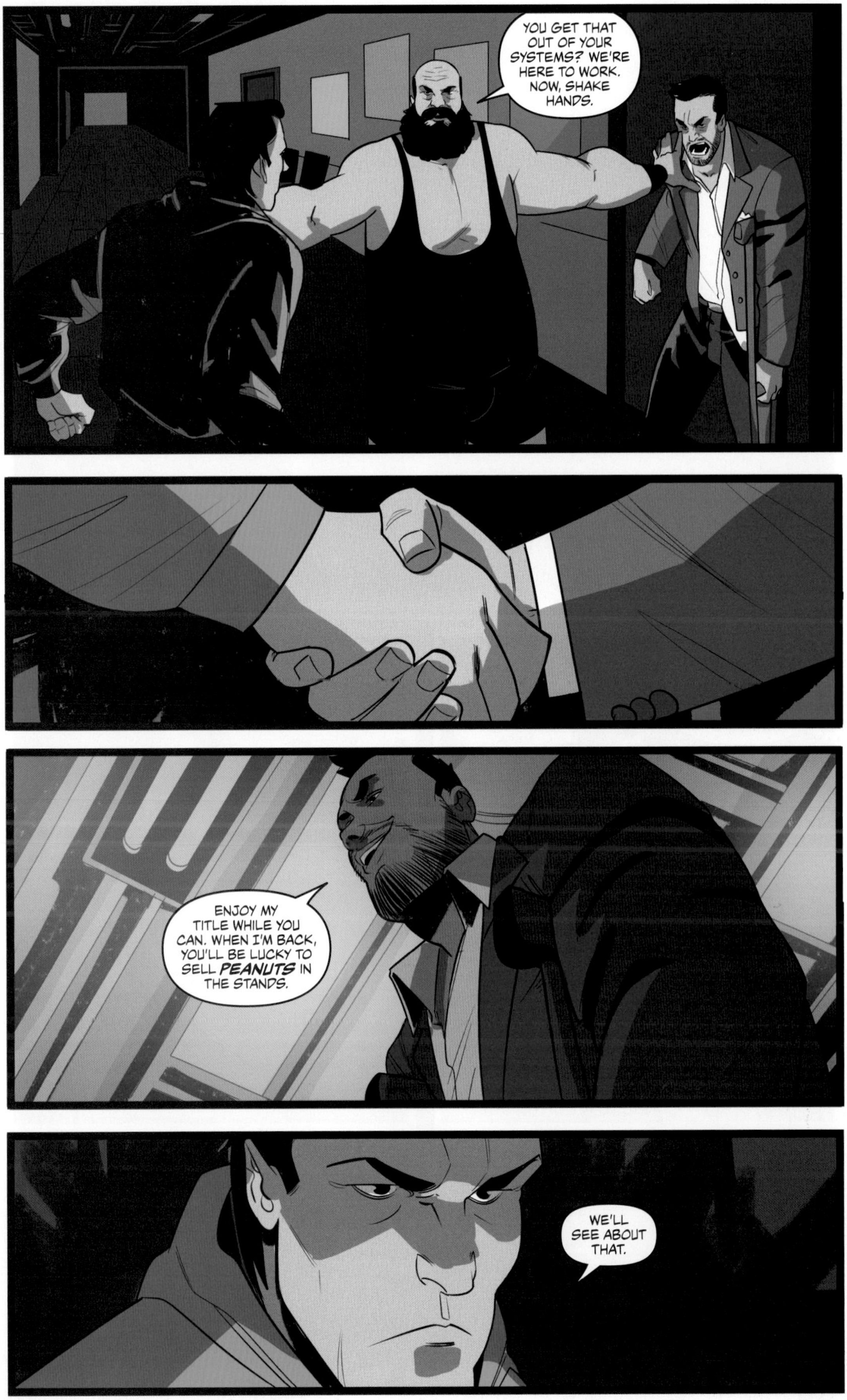
YOU GET THAT OUT OF YOUR SYSTEMS? WE'RE HERE TO WORK. NOW, SHAKE HANDS.
ENJOY MY TITLE WHILE YOU CAN. WHEN I'M BACK, YOU'LL BE LUCKY TO SELL PEANUTS IN THE STANDS.
WE'LL SEE ABOUT THAT.

NASHVILLE, TENNESSEE! RADISON'S CHAMPIONSHIP CHICKEN IS PROUD TO DELIVER YOUR MAIN EVENT OF THE EVENING.
IN THIS CORNER, HAILING FROM MEXICO CITY, MEXICO-- UNO!
BOO!
HISS!
¡GRACIAS A TODOS!
THE MEXICAN HEAVYWEIGHT CHAMPION, A DESCENDANT OF TRIBAL WARRIORS... MEXI-KO!
I SWEAR BY THE BLOOD OF THE AZTECS, YOU WILL DON THE CRIMSON MASK.
BOO!
COWARD!
YOU SUCKER-PUNCHED PHOENIX!
A WRESTLER WHO NEEDS NO INTRODUCTION, THE CHAIRMAN OF THE BOARD AND OWNER OF SOUTHERN-FRIED WRESTLING-- RAMBLIN' RICKY RADISON!
BOO!
WHY'D YOU DO IT, RICKY? WHY?!
THEY'LL BE FACING OFF AGAINST BLUE BOMBA, THE LEGENDARY BARBWIRE BRODY JACKSON, AND YOUR SFW WORLD HEAVYWEIGHT CHAMPION-- PHOENIX!
I WILL RISE! I WILL RISE!

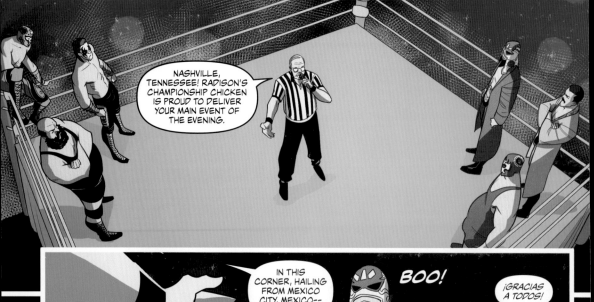

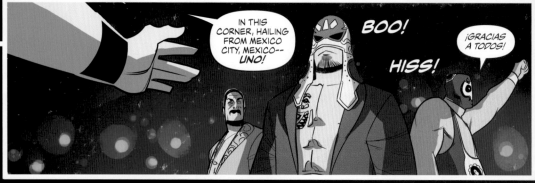

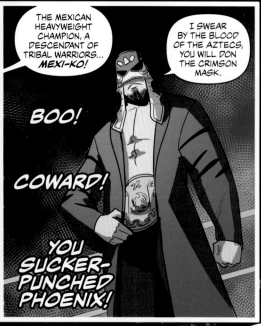

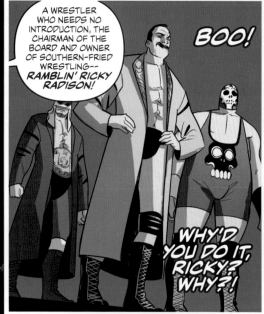

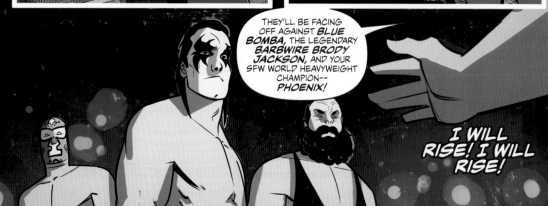

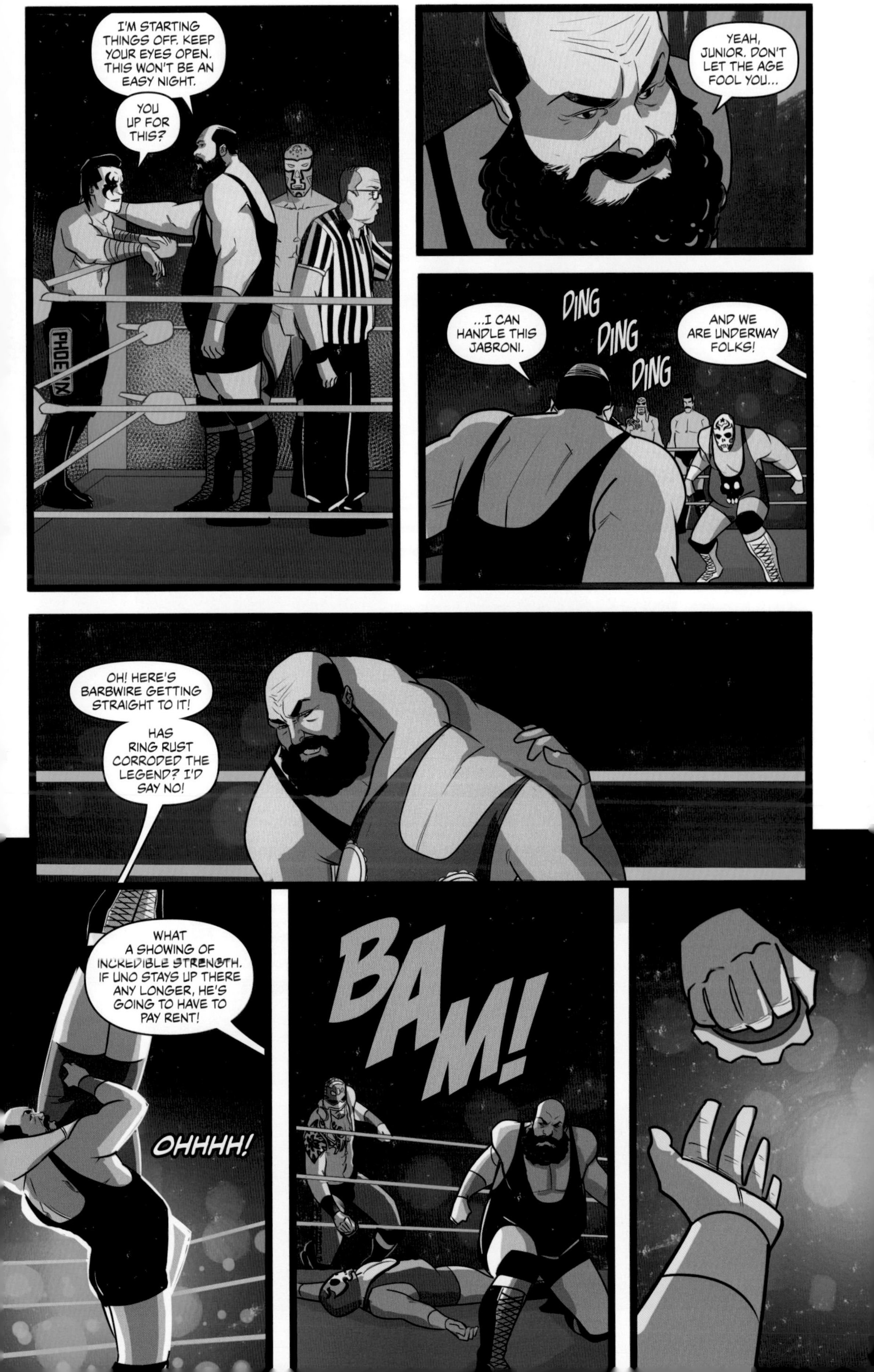
I'M STARTING THINGS OFF. KEEP YOUR EYES OPEN. THIS WON'T BE AN EASY NIGHT.
YOU UP FOR THIS?
PHOENIX
YEAH, JUNIOR. DON'T LET THE AGE FOOL YOU...
...I CAN HANDLE THIS JABRONI.
DING
DING
DING
AND WE ARE UNDERWAY FOLKS!
OH! HERE'S BARBWIRE GETTING STRAIGHT TO IT!
HAS RING RUST CORRODED THE LEGEND? I'D SAY NO!
WHAT A SHOWING OF INCREDIBLE STRENGTH. IF UNO STAYS UP THERE ANY LONGER, HE'S GOING TO HAVE TO PAY RENT!
OHHHH!
BAM!

BUT UNO IS NOT DONE YET!

BARBWIRE!

BARBWIRE!

OUCH! WHAT A HAYMAKER!

OHHHH!

CRUNCH

IT'S LIGHTS OUT FOR BARBWIRE. HIS PARTNERS HAVE A BONE TO PICK WITH UNO!

OOMPH!

LOOKS LIKE HE'S HAD ENOUGH!

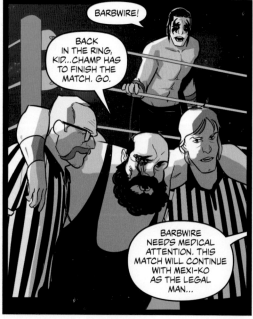

BARBWIRE!

BACK IN THE RING, KID...CHAMP HAS TO FINISH THE MATCH. GO.

BARBWIRE NEEDS MEDICAL ATTENTION. THIS MATCH WILL CONTINUE WITH MEXI-KO AS THE LEGAL MAN...

AGAINST HIS BROTHER, BLUE BOMBA.

STAY BEHIND THE ROPES!

WATCH HIM. BE CAREFUL.

FAMILY TIES WON'T HELP THE HIGH-FLYER AGAINST HIS MONSTER SIBLING.

WHAT A MISMATCH. BLUE BOMBA NEEDS TO USE HIS SPEED AND UNORTHODOX MOVESET TO GET THE BIG MAN OFF HIS FEET.

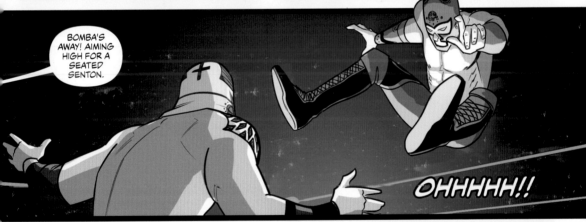

BOMBA'S AWAY! AIMING HIGH FOR A SEATED SENTON.

OHHHHH!!

OUCH! NOW MEXI-KO HAS BOMBA IN HIS GRASP AND HE'S ABOUT TO DELIVER A TOMBSTONE PILEDRIVER.

ESCOGISTE MAL A TUS AMIGOS, HERMANITO. *

*YOU CHOSE YOUR FRIENDS POORLY, LITTLE BROTHER.

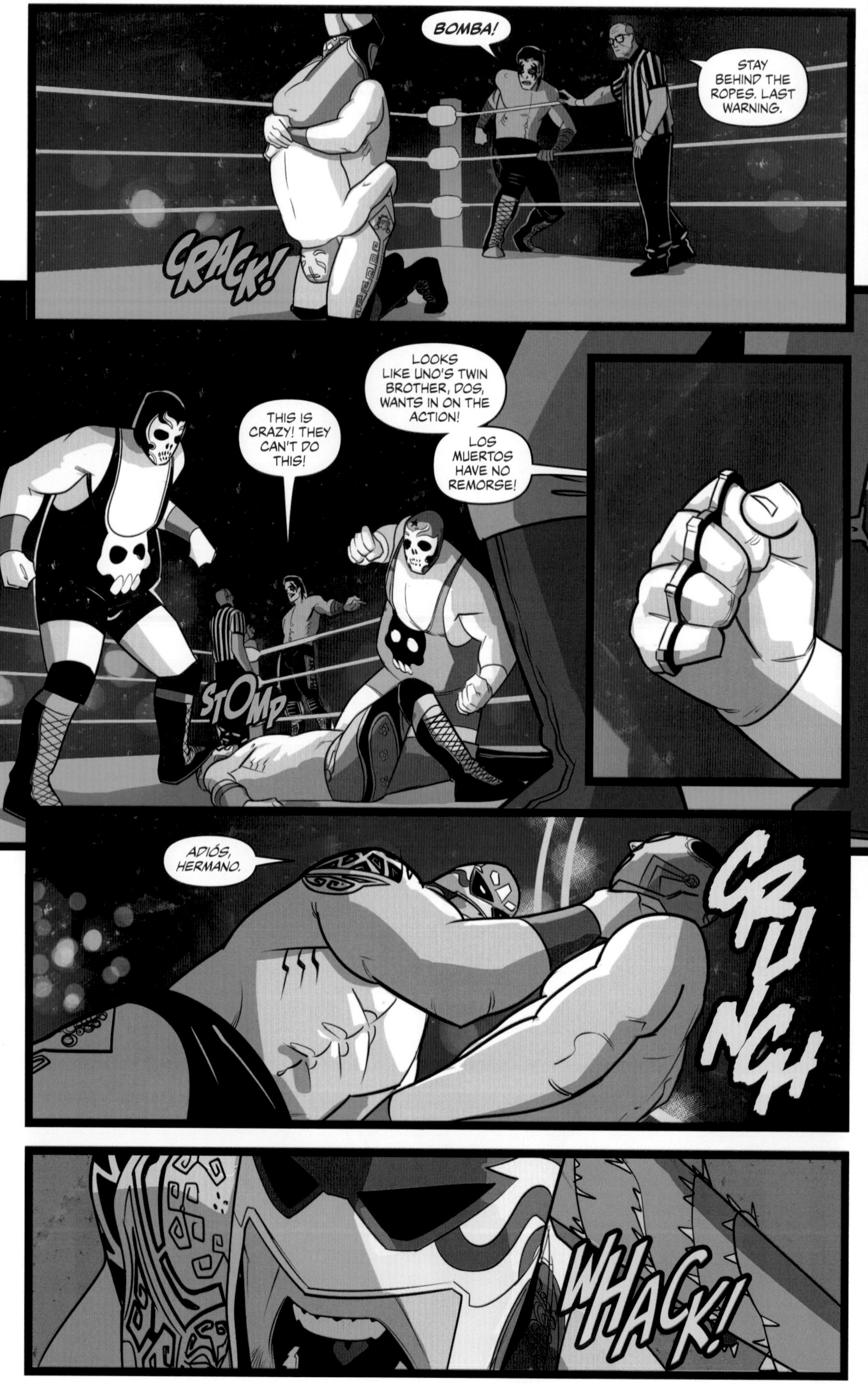
BOMBA!
STAY BEHIND THE ROPES. LAST WARNING.
CRACK!
THIS IS CRAZY! THEY CAN'T DO THIS!
LOOKS LIKE UNO'S TWIN BROTHER, DOS, WANTS IN ON THE ACTION!
LOS MUERTOS HAVE NO REMORSE!
STOMP
ADIÓS, HERMANO.
CRUNCH
WHACK!

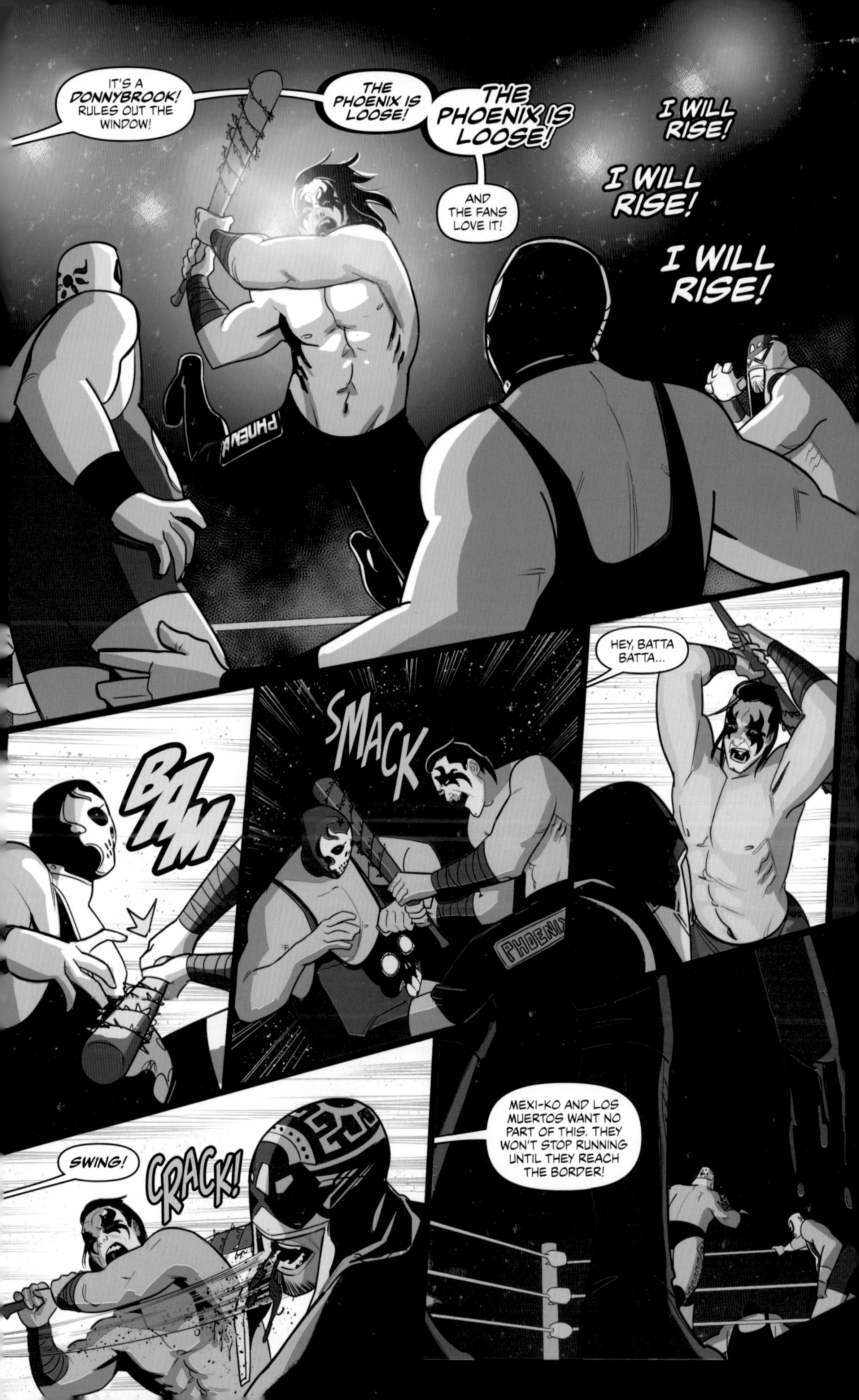
IT'S A DONNYBROOK! RULES OUT THE WINDOW!
THE PHOENIX IS LOOSE!
THE PHOENIX IS LOOSE!
AND THE FANS LOVE IT!
I WILL RISE!
I WILL RISE!
I WILL RISE!
PHOENIX
BAM
SMACK
PHOENIX
HEY, BATTA BATTA...
SWING!
CRACK!
MEXI-KO AND LOS MUERTOS WANT NO PART OF THIS. THEY WON'T STOP RUNNING UNTIL THEY REACH THE BORDER!

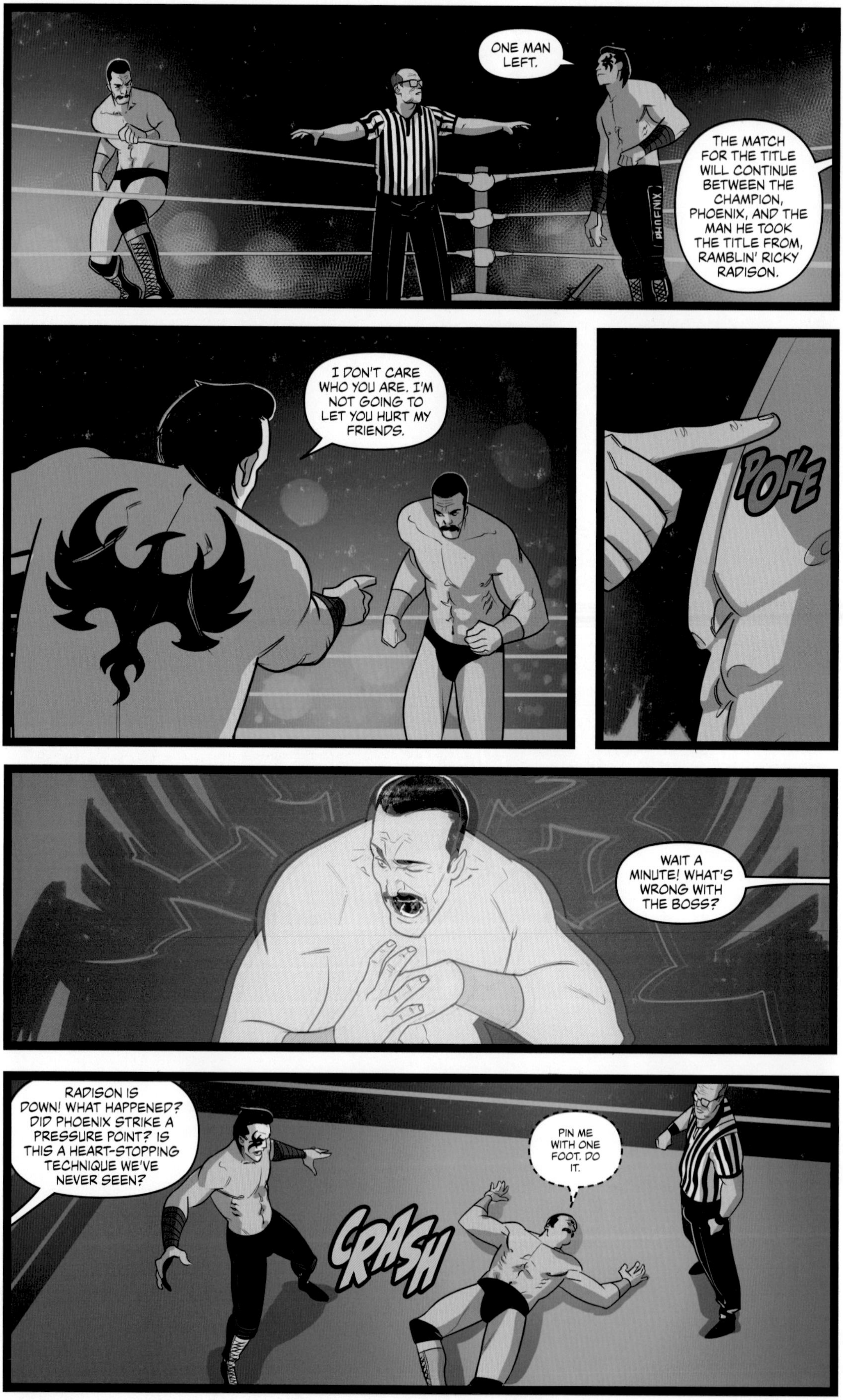
ONE MAN LEFT.
THE MATCH FOR THE TITLE WILL CONTINUE BETWEEN THE CHAMPION, PHOENIX, AND THE MAN HE TOOK THE TITLE FROM, RAMBLIN' RICKY RADISON.
I DON'T CARE WHO YOU ARE. I'M NOT GOING TO LET YOU HURT MY FRIENDS.
POKE
WAIT A MINUTE! WHAT'S WRONG WITH THE BOSS?
RADISON IS DOWN! WHAT HAPPENED? DID PHOENIX STRIKE A PRESSURE POINT? IS THIS A HEART-STOPPING TECHNIQUE WE'VE NEVER SEEN?
PIN ME WITH ONE FOOT. DO IT.
CRASH

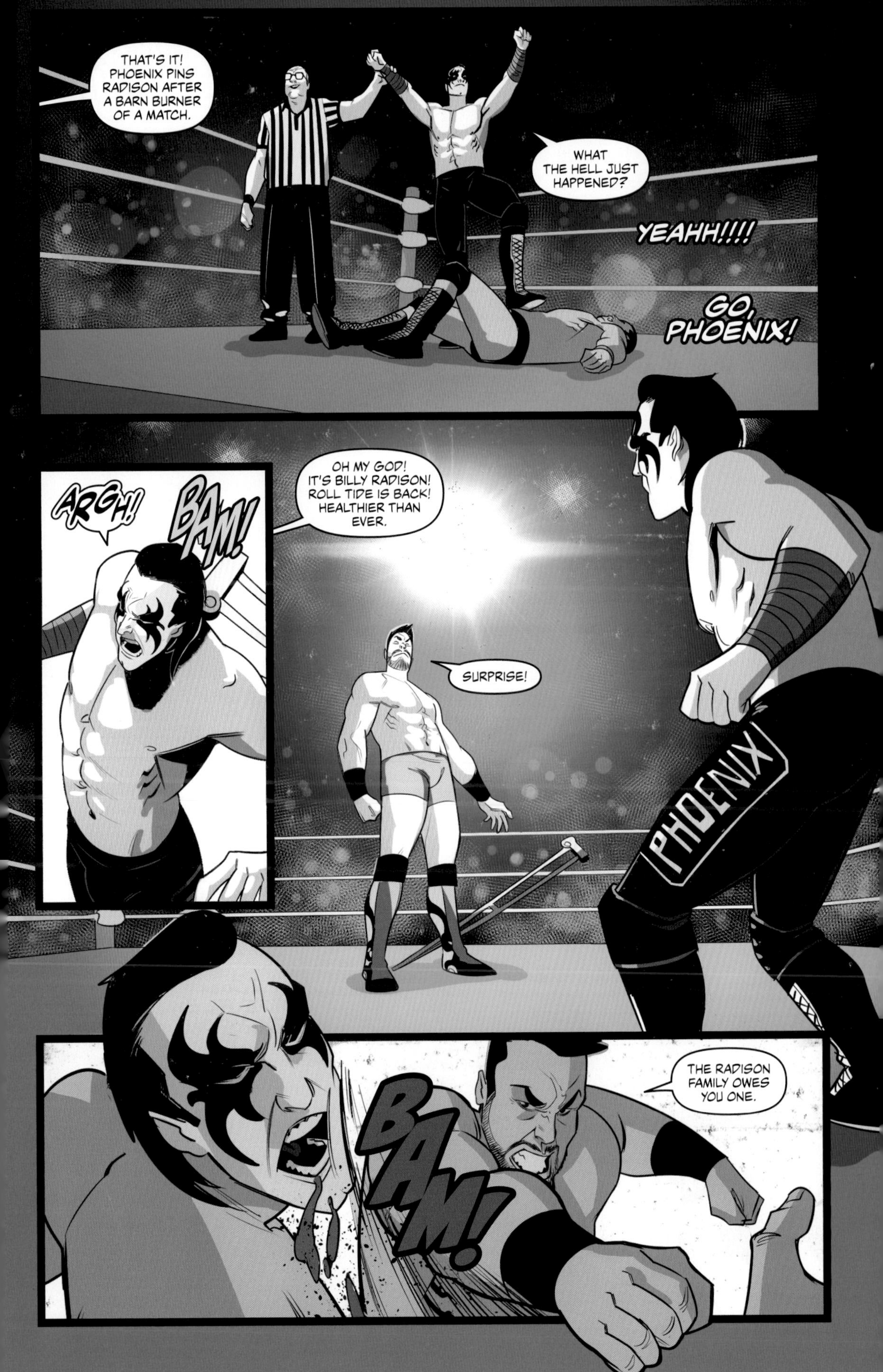
THAT'S IT! PHOENIX PINS RADISON AFTER A BARN BURNER OF A MATCH.
WHAT THE HELL JUST HAPPENED?
YEAHH!!!!
GO, PHOENIX!
ARGH!
BAM!
OH MY GOD! IT'S BILLY RADISON! ROLL TIDE IS BACK! HEALTHIER THAN EVER.
SURPRISE!
PHOENIX
THE RADISON FAMILY OWES YOU ONE.
BAM!

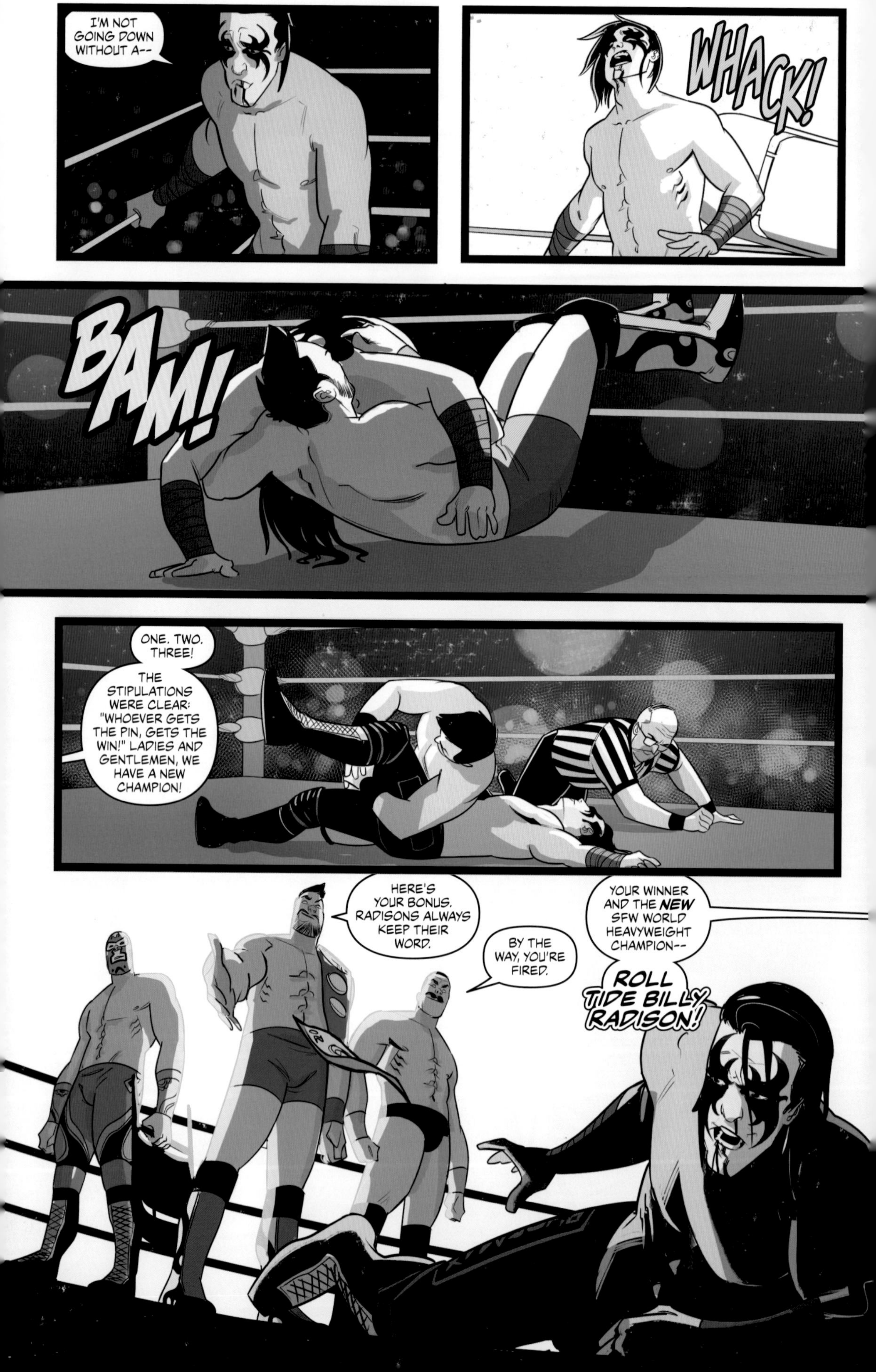
I'M NOT GOING DOWN WITHOUT A--
WHACK!
BAM!
ONE. TWO. THREE!
THE STIPULATIONS WERE CLEAR: "WHOEVER GETS THE PIN, GETS THE WIN!" LADIES AND GENTLEMEN, WE HAVE A NEW CHAMPION!
HERE'S YOUR BONUS. RADISONS ALWAYS KEEP THEIR WORD.
BY THE WAY, YOU'RE FIRED.
YOUR WINNER AND THE NEW SFW WORLD HEAVYWEIGHT CHAMPION--
ROLL TIDE BILLY RADISON!

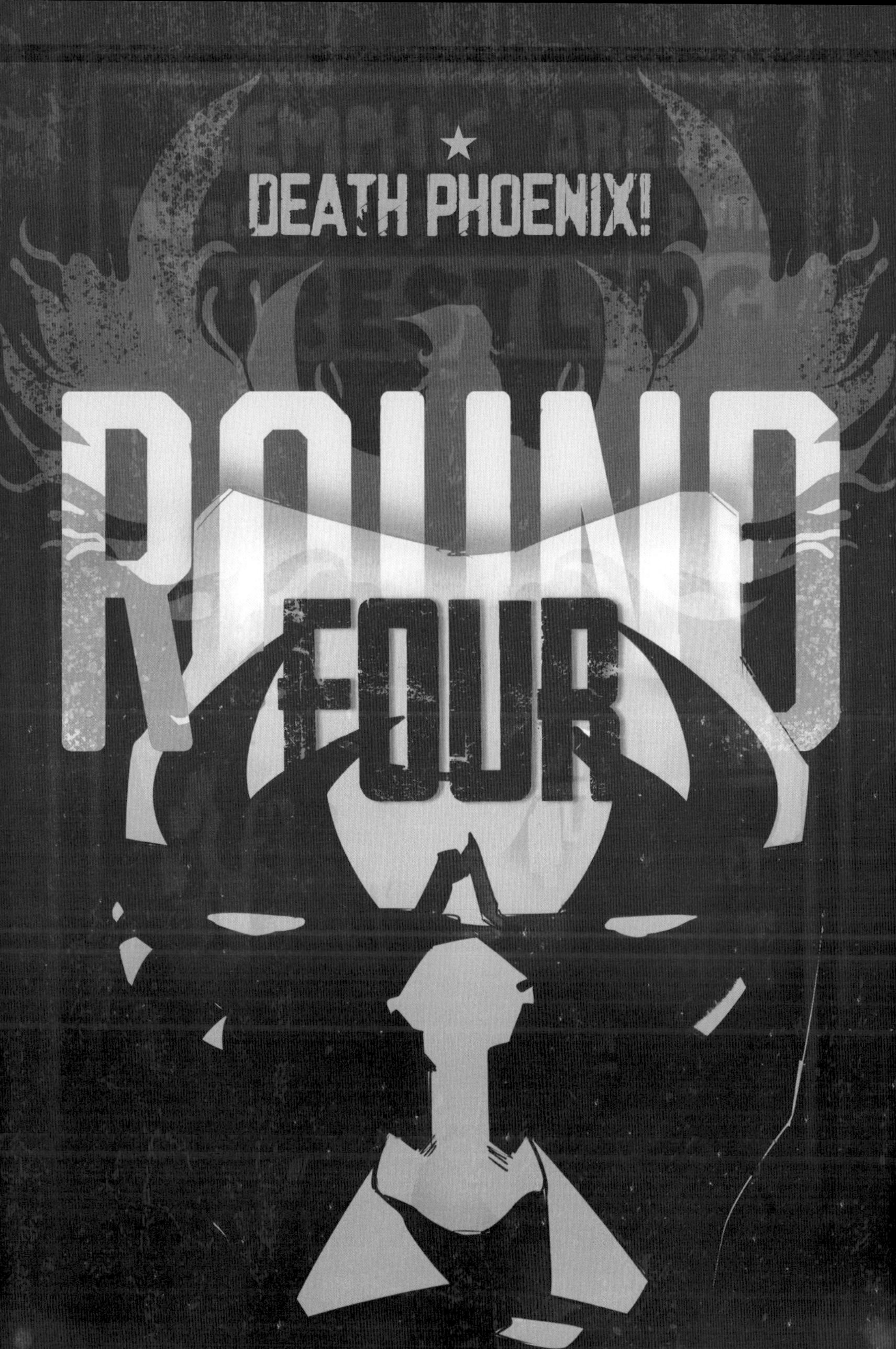
DEATH PHOENIX!
ROUND
FOUR

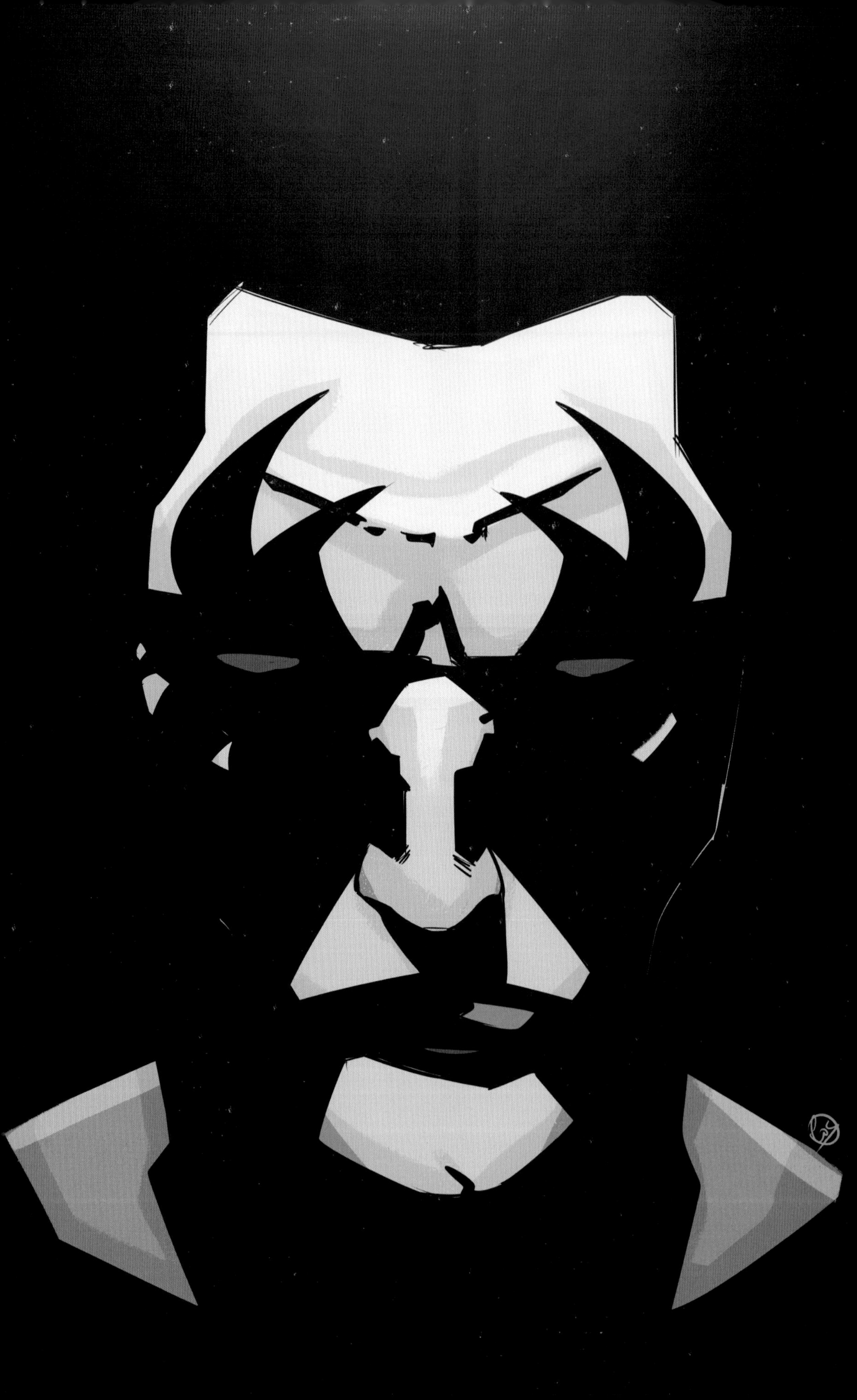

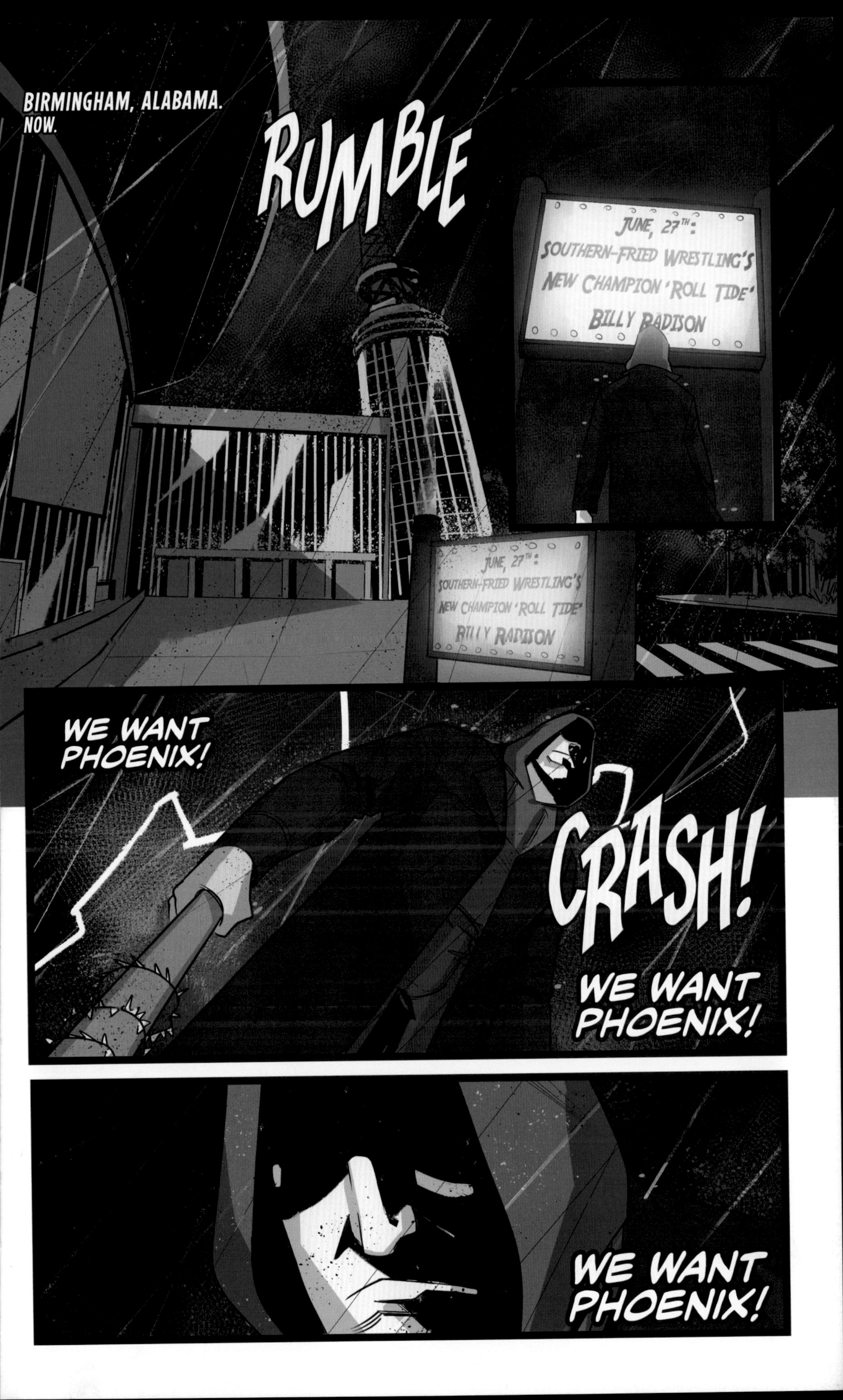
BIRMINGHAM, ALABAMA. NOW.
RUMBLE
JUNE, 27TH:
SOUTHERN-FRIED WRESTLING'S
NEW CHAMPION 'ROLL TIDE'
BILLY RADISON
JUNE, 27TH:
SOUTHERN-FRIED WRESTLING'S
NEW CHAMPION 'ROLL TIDE'
BILLY RADISON
WE WANT PHOENIX!
CRASH!
WE WANT PHOENIX!
WE WANT PHOENIX!

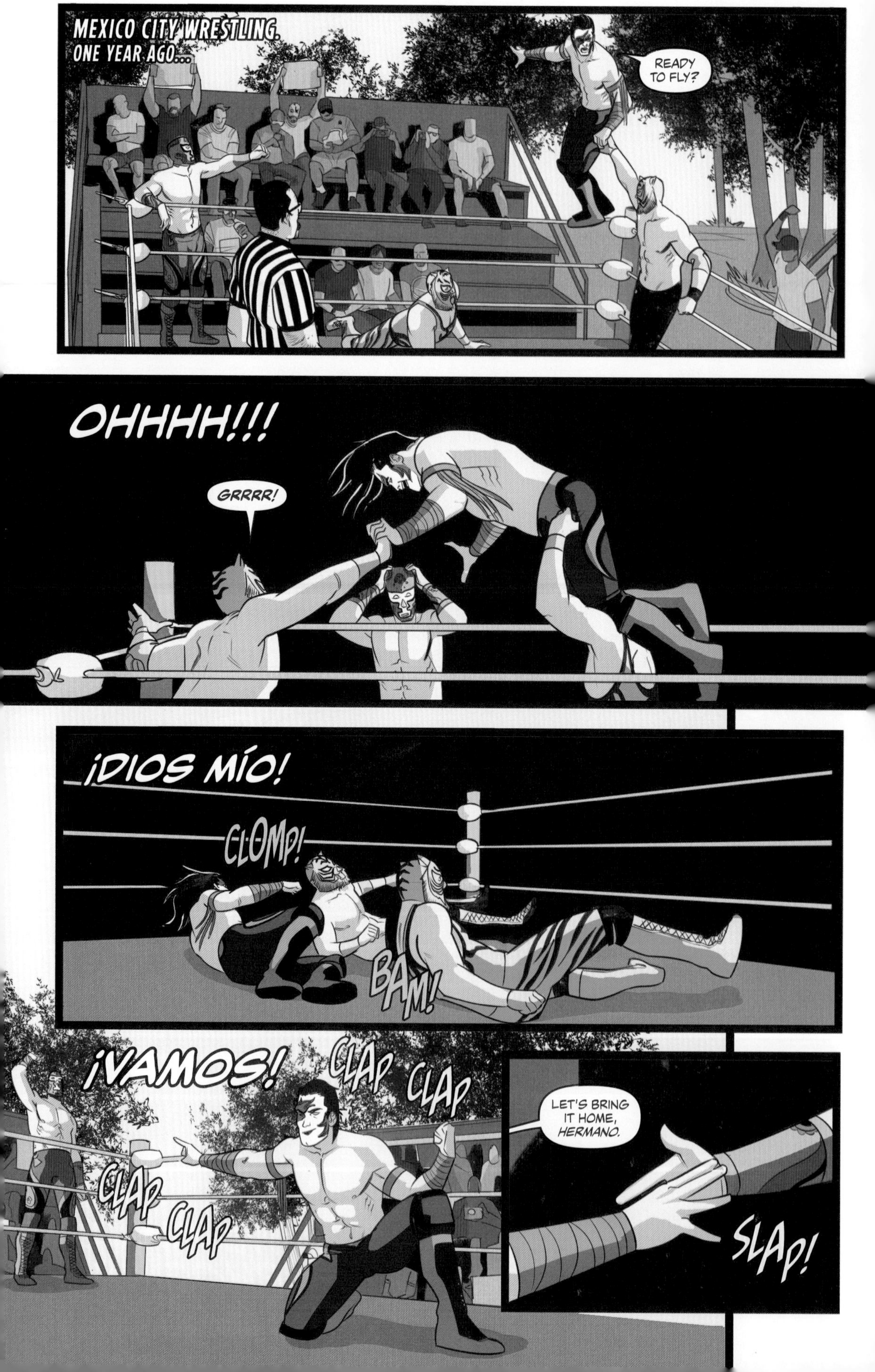
MEXICO CITY WRESTLING.
ONE YEAR AGO...
READY TO FLY?
OHHHH!!!
GRRRR!
¡DIOS MÍO!
CLOMP!
BAM!
¡VAMOS!
CLAP
CLAP
CLAP
CLAP
LET'S BRING IT HOME, HERMANO.
SLAP!

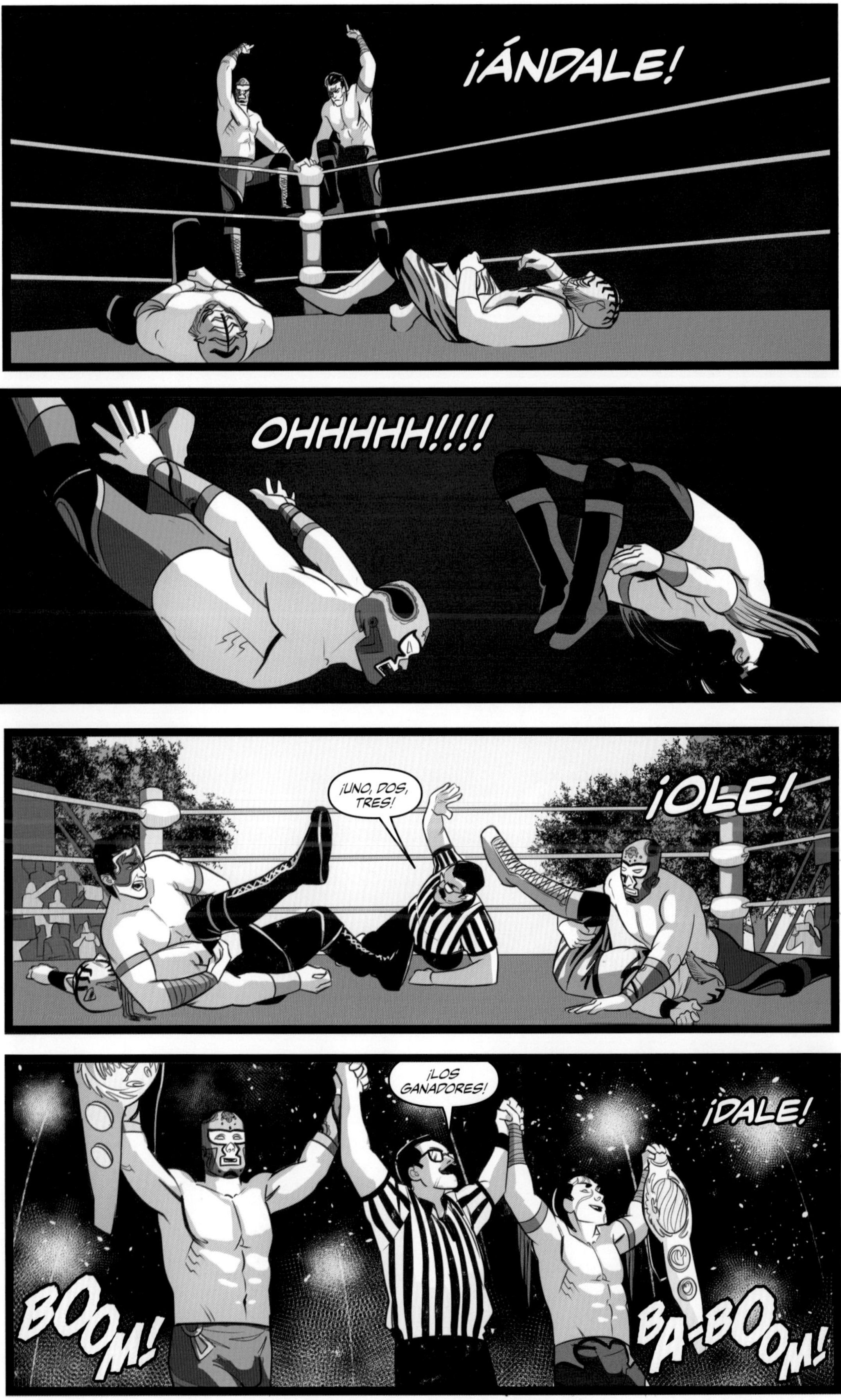
¡ÁNDALE!
OHHHHH!!!!
¡UNO, DOS, TRES!
¡OLE!
¡LOS GANADORES!
¡DALE!
BOOM!
BA-BOOM!

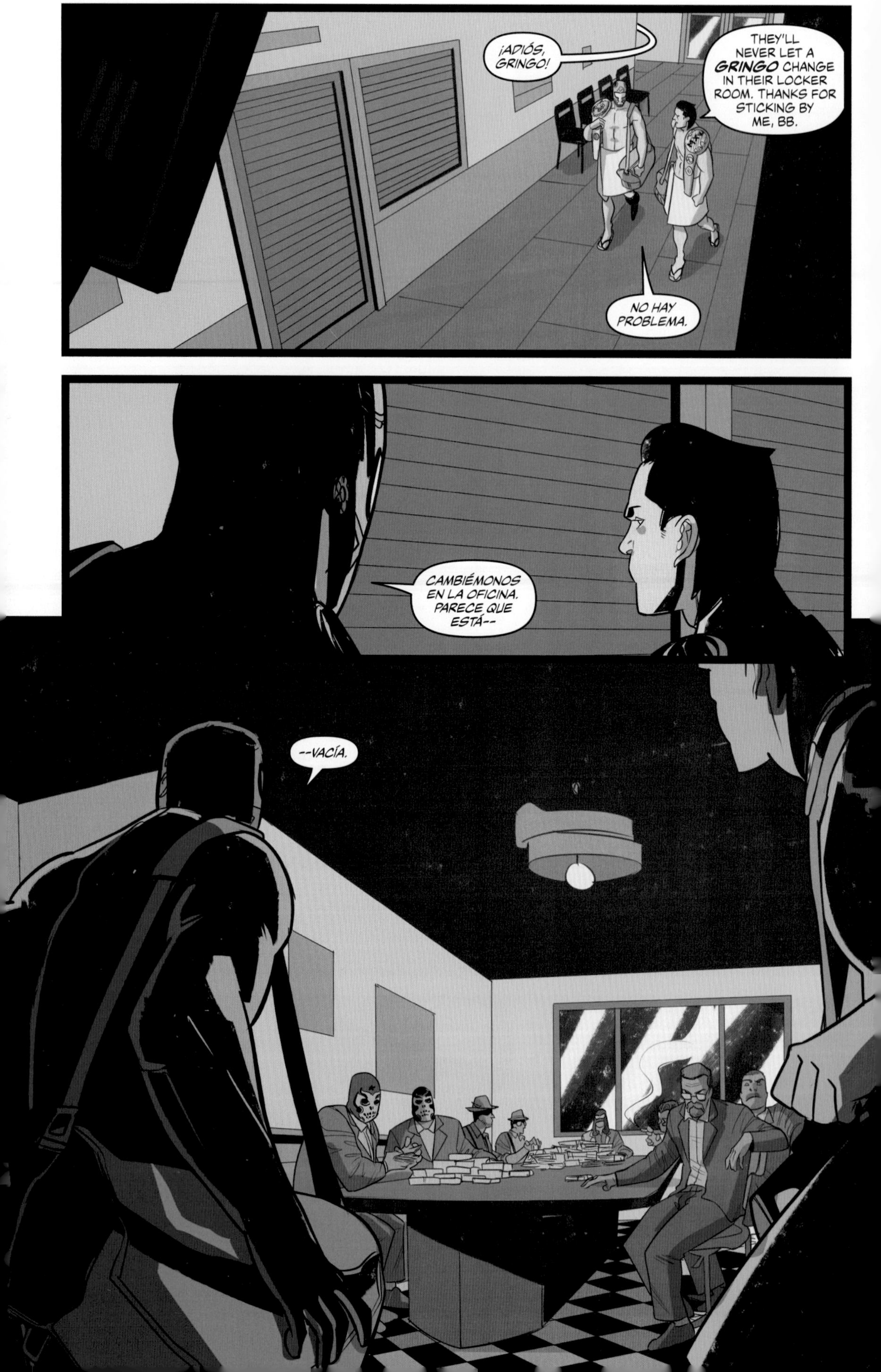
¡ADIÓS, GRINGO!
THEY'LL NEVER LET A GRINGO CHANGE IN THEIR LOCKER ROOM. THANKS FOR STICKING BY ME, BB.
NO HAY PROBLEMA.
CAMBIÉMONOS EN LA OFICINA. PARECE QUE ESTÁ--
--VACÍA.

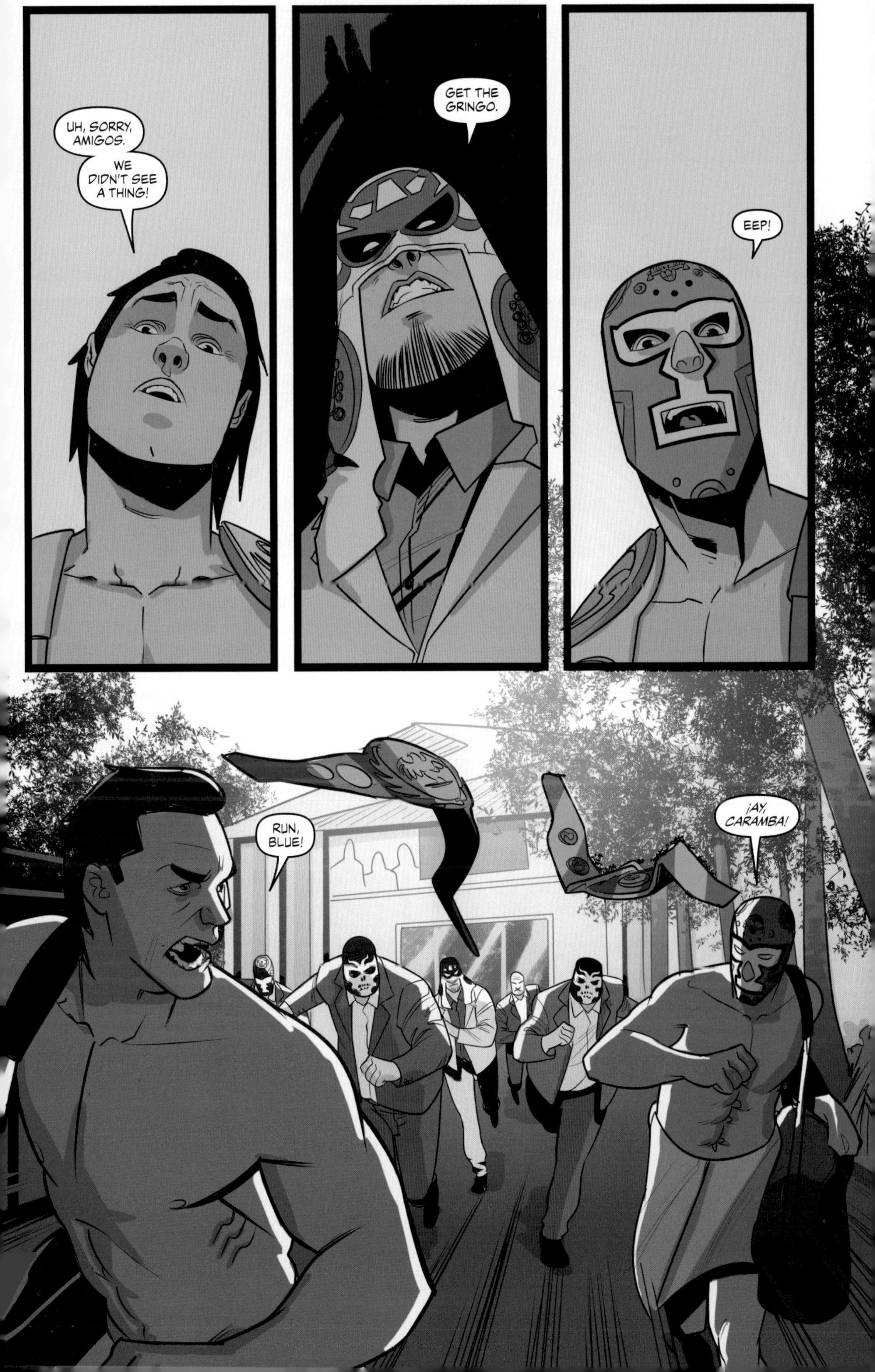
UH, SORRY, AMIGOS.
WE DIDN'T SEE A THING!
GET THE GRINGO.
EEP!
RUN, BLUE!
¡AY, CARAMBA!

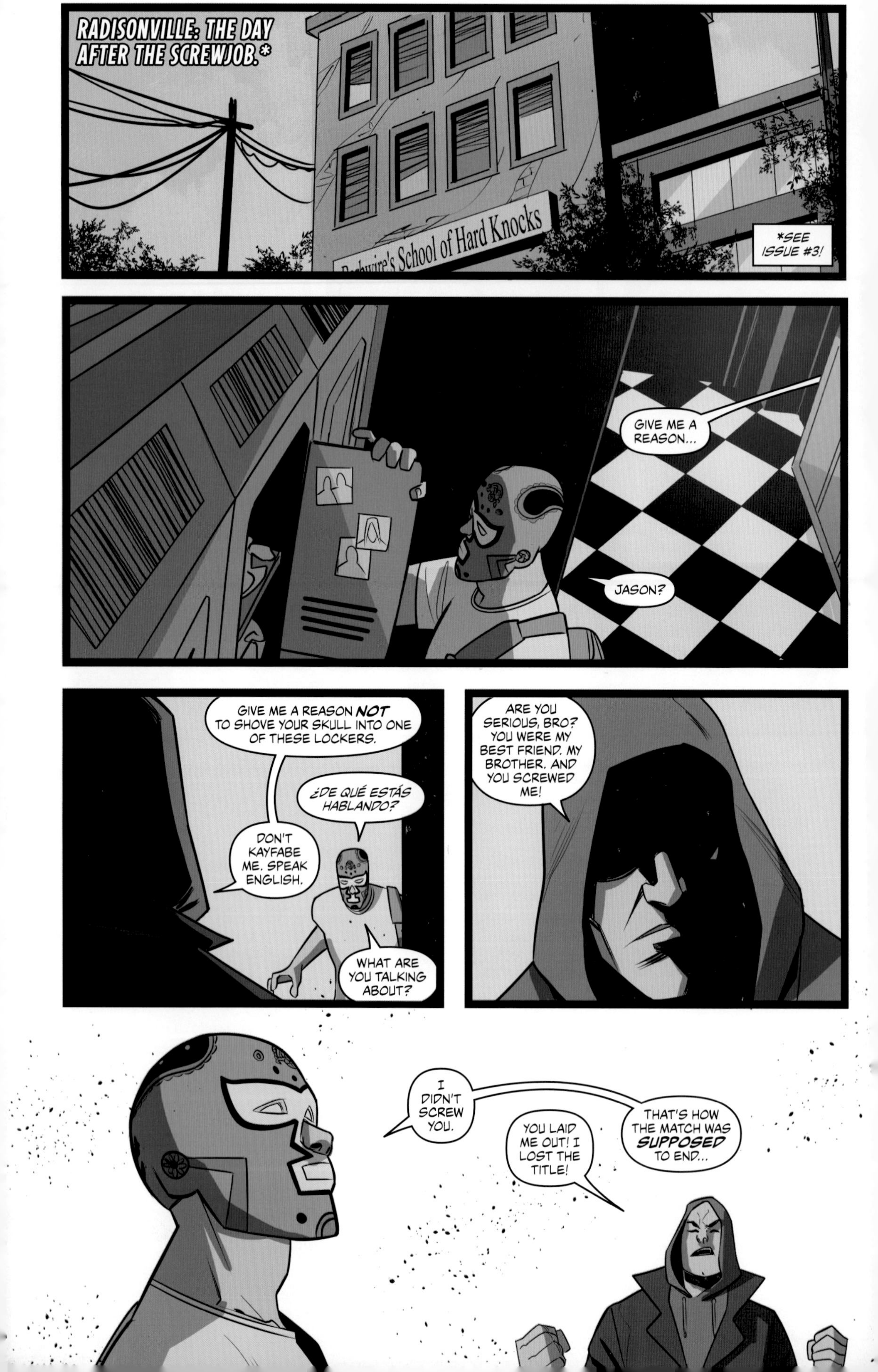
RADISONVILLE: THE DAY AFTER THE SCREWJOB.*
Dashwire's School of Hard Knocks
*SEE ISSUE #3!
GIVE ME A REASON...
JASON?
GIVE ME A REASON NOT TO SHOVE YOUR SKULL INTO ONE OF THESE LOCKERS.
¿DE QUÉ ESTÁS HABLANDO?
DON'T KAYFABE ME. SPEAK ENGLISH.
WHAT ARE YOU TALKING ABOUT?
ARE YOU SERIOUS, BRO? YOU WERE MY BEST FRIEND. MY BROTHER. AND YOU SCREWED ME!
I DIDN'T SCREW YOU.
THAT'S HOW THE MATCH WAS SUPPOSED TO END...
YOU LAID ME OUT! I LOST THE TITLE!

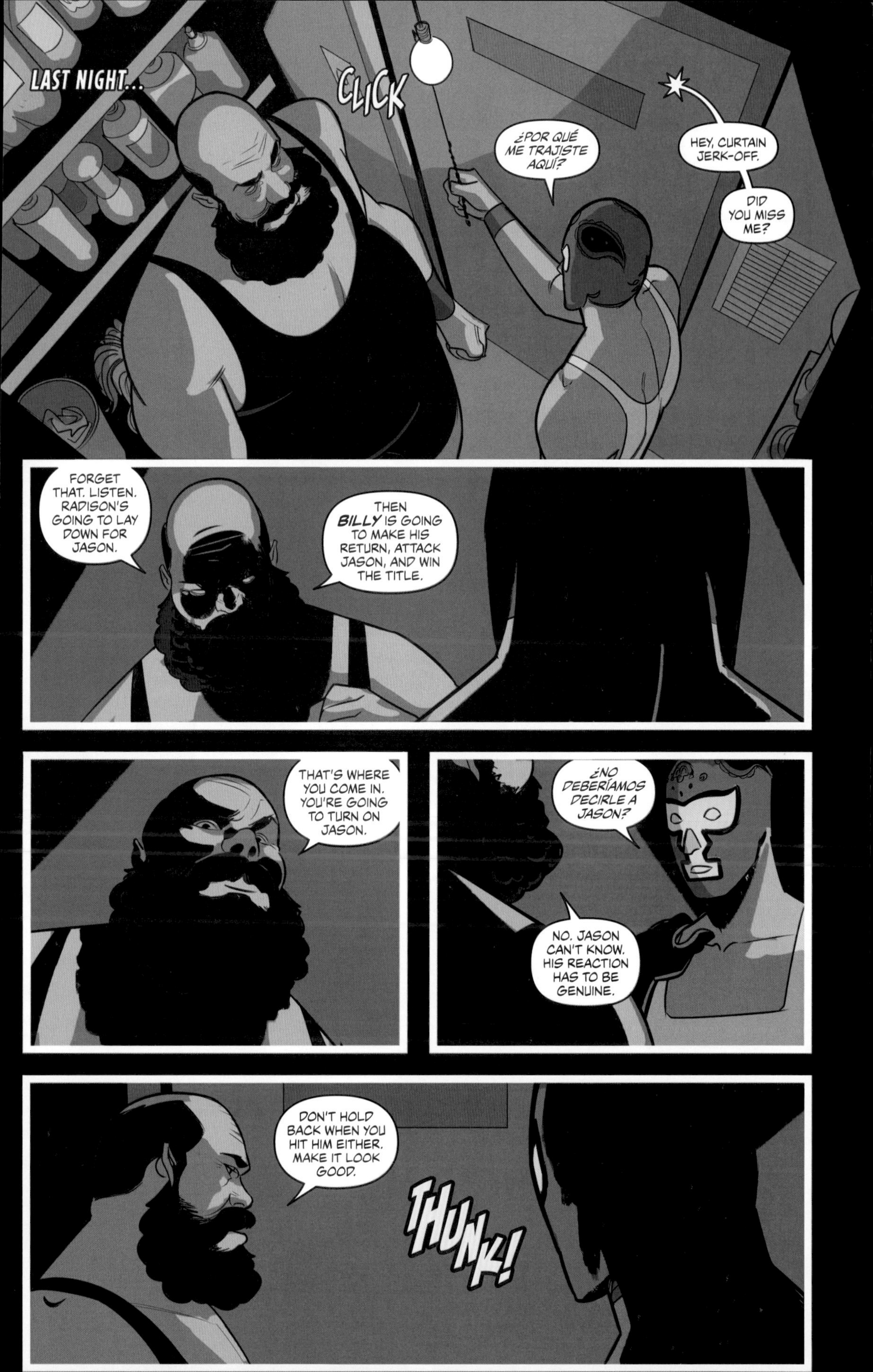

LAST NIGHT...
CLICK
¿POR QUÉ ME TRAJISTE AQUÍ?
HEY, CURTAIN JERK-OFF.
DID YOU MISS ME?
FORGET THAT. LISTEN. RADISON'S GOING TO LAY DOWN FOR JASON.
THEN BILLY IS GOING TO MAKE HIS RETURN, ATTACK JASON, AND WIN THE TITLE.
THAT'S WHERE YOU COME IN. YOU'RE GOING TO TURN ON JASON.
¿NO DEBERÍAMOS DECIRLE A JASON?
NO. JASON CAN'T KNOW. HIS REACTION HAS TO BE GENUINE.
DON'T HOLD BACK WHEN YOU HIT HIM EITHER. MAKE IT LOOK GOOD.
THUNK!

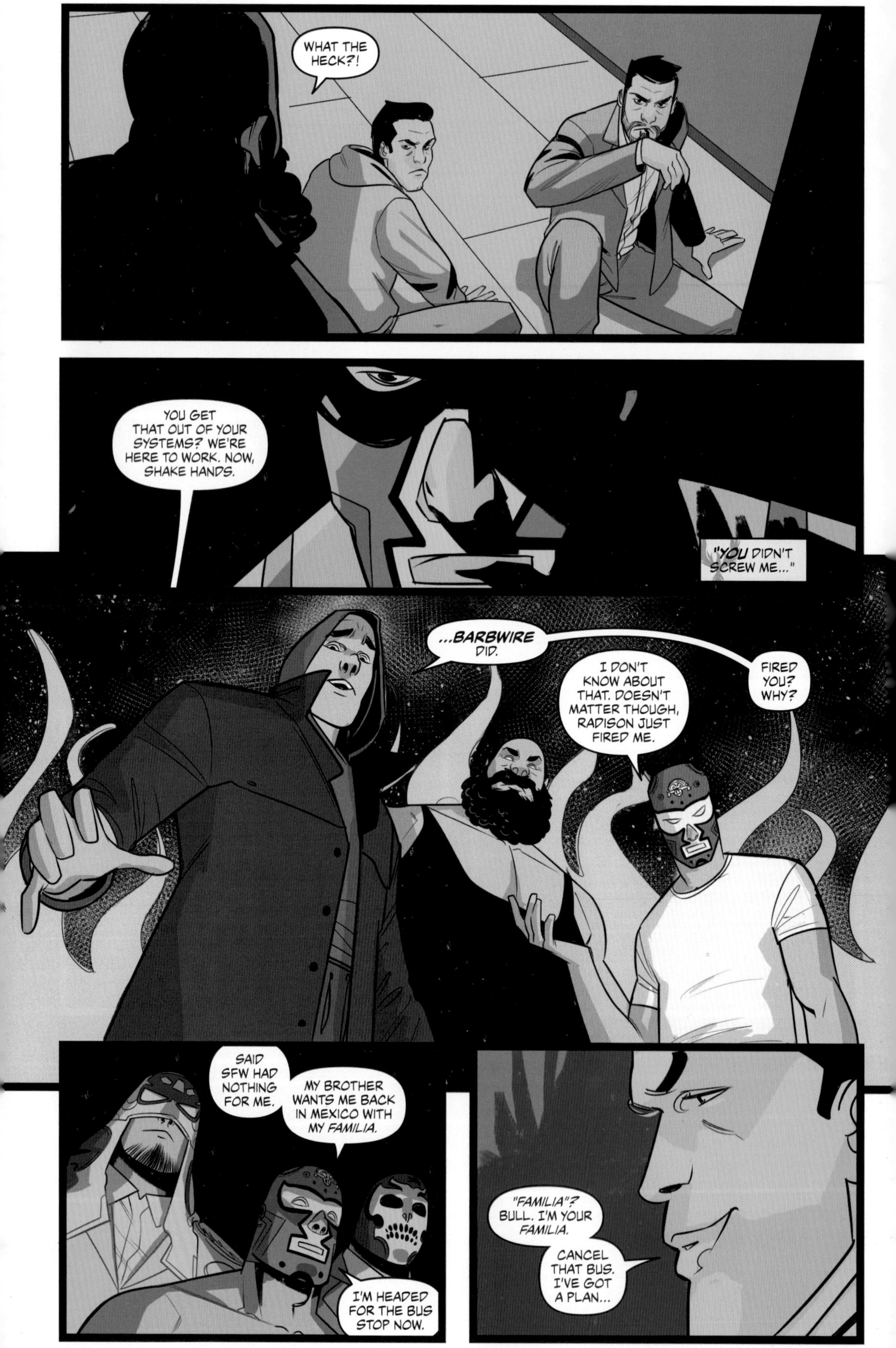
WHAT THE HECK?!
YOU GET THAT OUT OF YOUR SYSTEMS? WE'RE HERE TO WORK. NOW, SHAKE HANDS.
"YOU DIDN'T SCREW ME..."
...BARBWIRE DID.
FIRED YOU? WHY?
I DON'T KNOW ABOUT THAT. DOESN'T MATTER THOUGH, RADISON JUST FIRED ME.
SAID SFW HAD NOTHING FOR ME.
MY BROTHER WANTS ME BACK IN MEXICO WITH MY FAMILIA.
I'M HEADED FOR THE BUS STOP NOW.
"FAMILIA"? BULL. I'M YOUR FAMILIA.
CANCEL THAT BUS. I'VE GOT A PLAN...

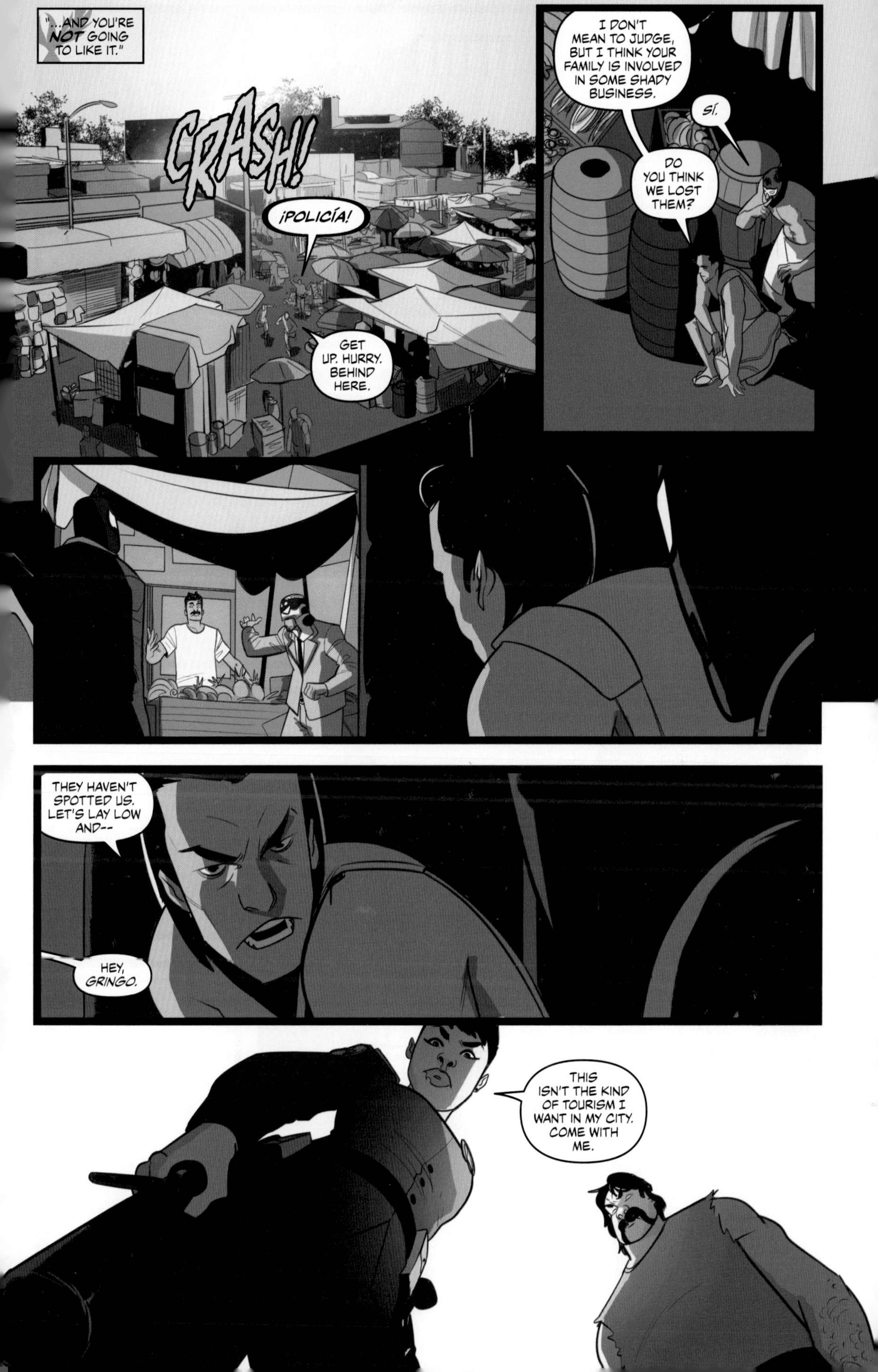
"...AND YOU'RE NOT GOING TO LIKE IT."
CRASH!
¡POLICÍA!
GET UP. HURRY. BEHIND HERE.
I DON'T MEAN TO JUDGE, BUT I THINK YOUR FAMILY IS INVOLVED IN SOME SHADY BUSINESS.
SÍ.
DO YOU THINK WE LOST THEM?
THEY HAVEN'T SPOTTED US. LET'S LAY LOW AND--
HEY, GRINGO.
THIS ISN'T THE KIND OF TOURISM I WANT IN MY CITY. COME WITH ME.

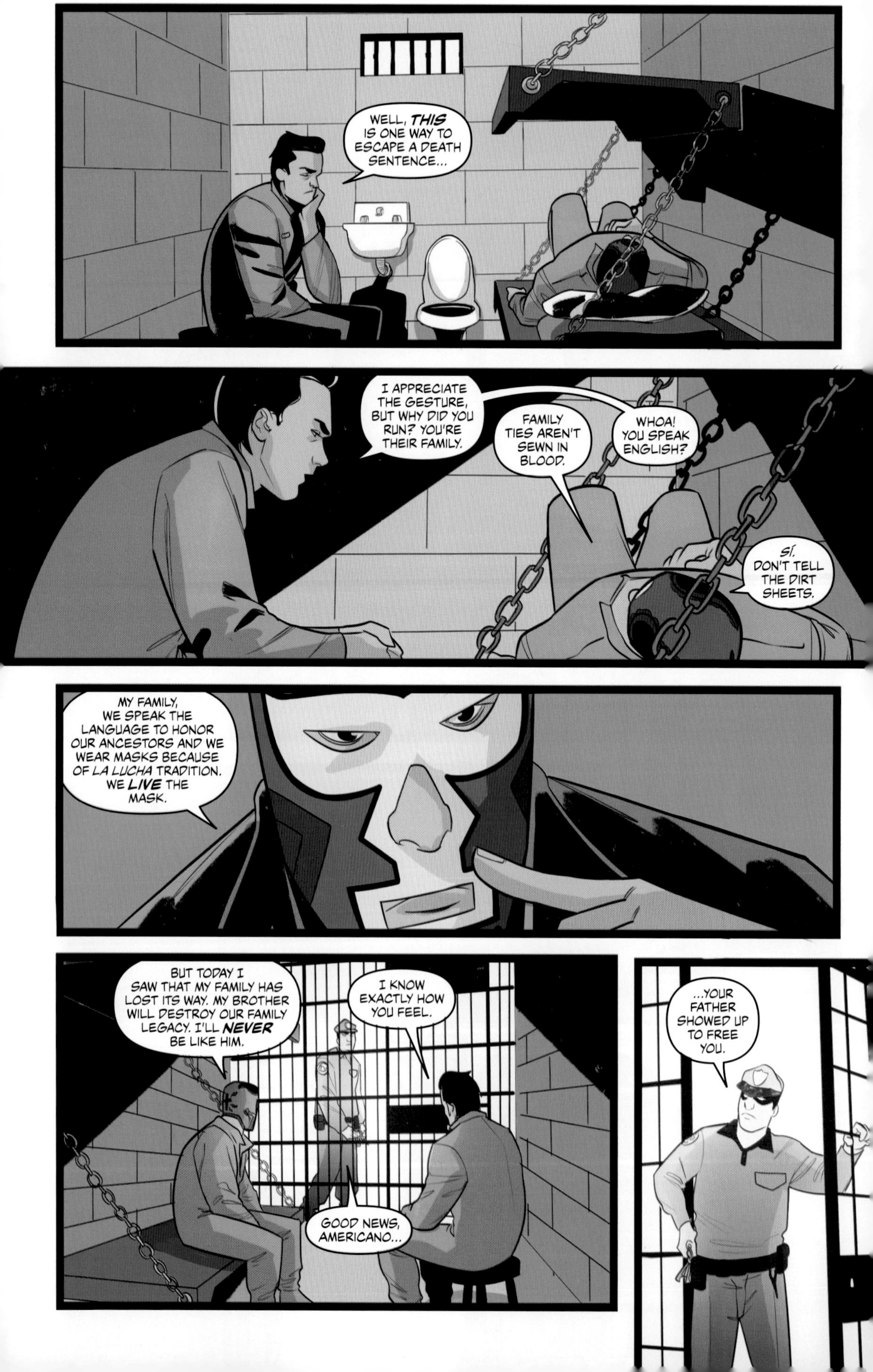
WELL, THIS IS ONE WAY TO ESCAPE A DEATH SENTENCE...
I APPRECIATE THE GESTURE, BUT WHY DID YOU RUN? YOU'RE THEIR FAMILY.
FAMILY TIES AREN'T SEWN IN BLOOD.
WHOA! YOU SPEAK ENGLISH?
SÍ. DON'T TELL THE DIRT SHEETS.
MY FAMILY, WE SPEAK THE LANGUAGE TO HONOR OUR ANCESTORS AND WE WEAR MASKS BECAUSE OF LA LUCHA TRADITION. WE LIVE THE MASK.
BUT TODAY I SAW THAT MY FAMILY HAS LOST ITS WAY. MY BROTHER WILL DESTROY OUR FAMILY LEGACY. I'LL NEVER BE LIKE HIM.
I KNOW EXACTLY HOW YOU FEEL.
GOOD NEWS, AMERICANO...
...YOUR FATHER SHOWED UP TO FREE YOU.

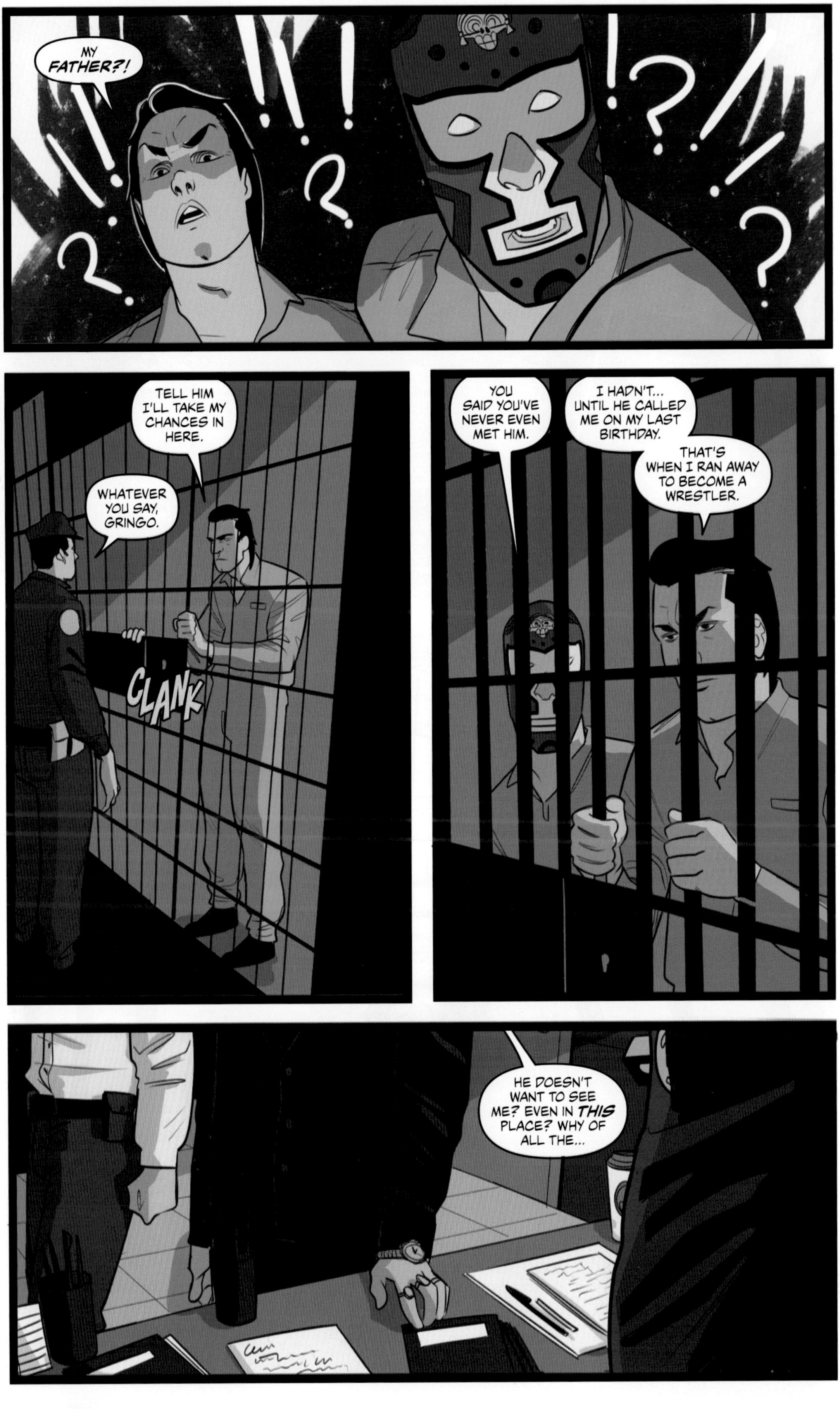
MY FATHER?!
TELL HIM I'LL TAKE MY CHANCES IN HERE.
WHATEVER YOU SAY, GRINGO.
CLANK
YOU SAID YOU'VE NEVER EVEN MET HIM.
I HADN'T... UNTIL HE CALLED ME ON MY LAST BIRTHDAY.
THAT'S WHEN I RAN AWAY TO BECOME A WRESTLER.
HE DOESN'T WANT TO SEE ME? EVEN IN THIS PLACE? WHY OF ALL THE...

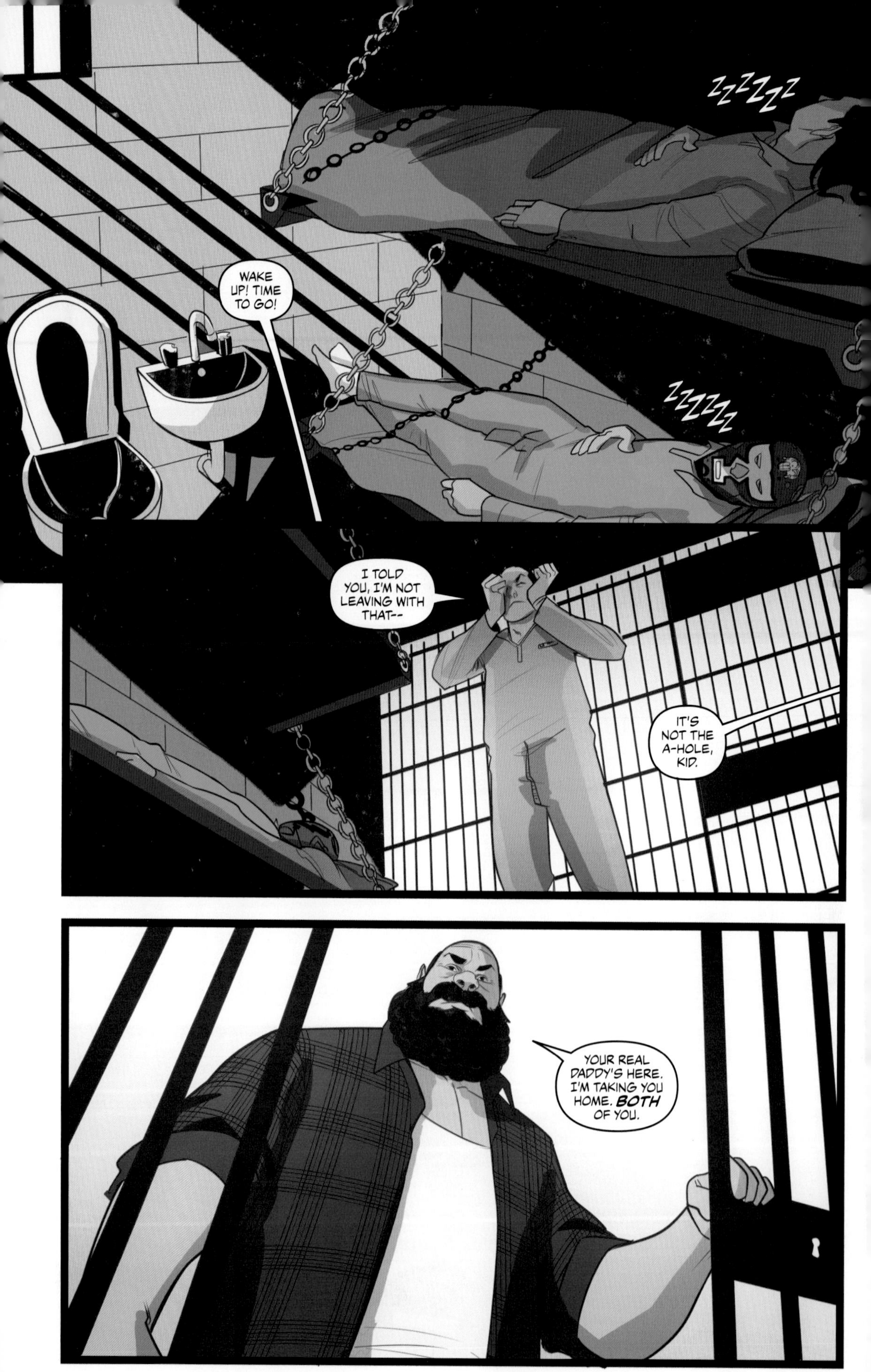
ZZZZZZ
WAKE UP! TIME TO GO!
ZZZZZZ
I TOLD YOU, I'M NOT LEAVING WITH THAT--
IT'S NOT THE A-HOLE, KID.
YOUR REAL DADDY'S HERE. I'M TAKING YOU HOME. *BOTH* OF YOU.

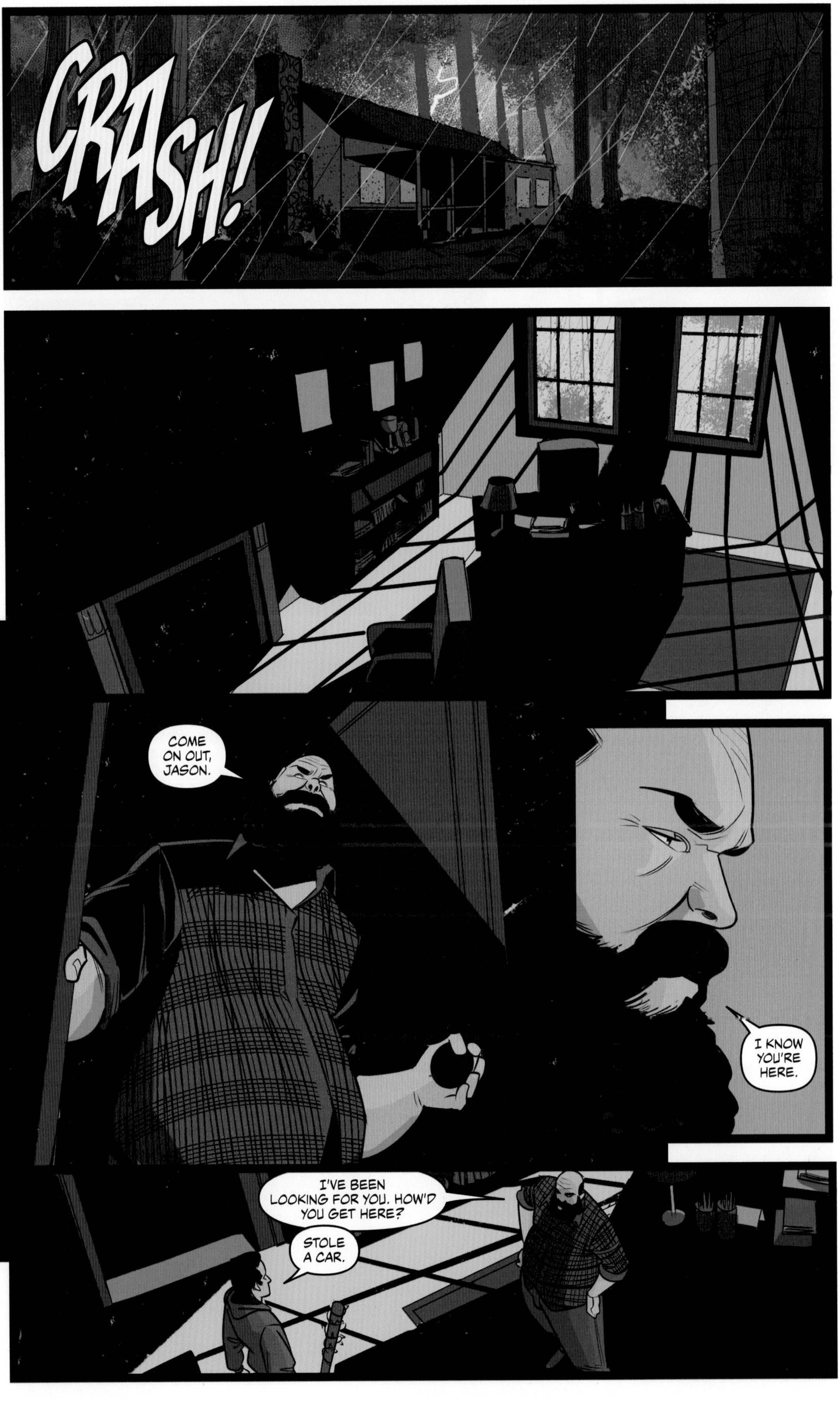
CRASH!
COME ON OUT, JASON.
I KNOW YOU'RE HERE.
I'VE BEEN LOOKING FOR YOU. HOW'D YOU GET HERE?
STOLE A CAR.

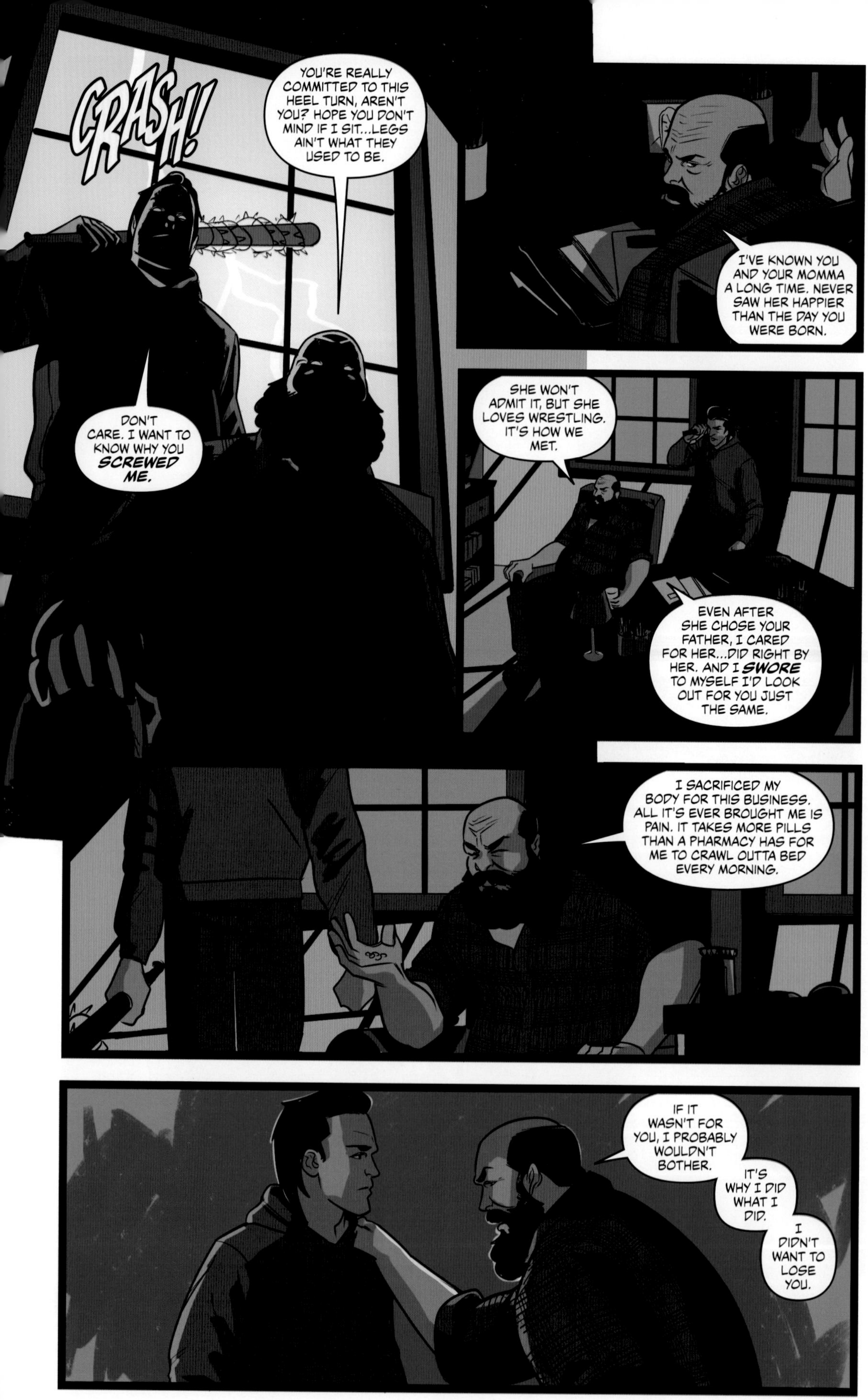
CRASH!
YOU'RE REALLY COMMITTED TO THIS HEEL TURN, AREN'T YOU? HOPE YOU DON'T MIND IF I SIT...LEGS AIN'T WHAT THEY USED TO BE.
DON'T CARE. I WANT TO KNOW WHY YOU SCREWED ME.
I'VE KNOWN YOU AND YOUR MOMMA A LONG TIME. NEVER SAW HER HAPPIER THAN THE DAY YOU WERE BORN.
SHE WON'T ADMIT IT, BUT SHE LOVES WRESTLING. IT'S HOW WE MET.
EVEN AFTER SHE CHOSE YOUR FATHER, I CARED FOR HER...DID RIGHT BY HER. AND I SWORE TO MYSELF I'D LOOK OUT FOR YOU JUST THE SAME.
I SACRIFICED MY BODY FOR THIS BUSINESS. ALL IT'S EVER BROUGHT ME IS PAIN. IT TAKES MORE PILLS THAN A PHARMACY HAS FOR ME TO CRAWL OUTTA BED EVERY MORNING.
IF IT WASN'T FOR YOU, I PROBABLY WOULDN'T BOTHER.
IT'S WHY I DID WHAT I DID.
I DIDN'T WANT TO LOSE YOU.

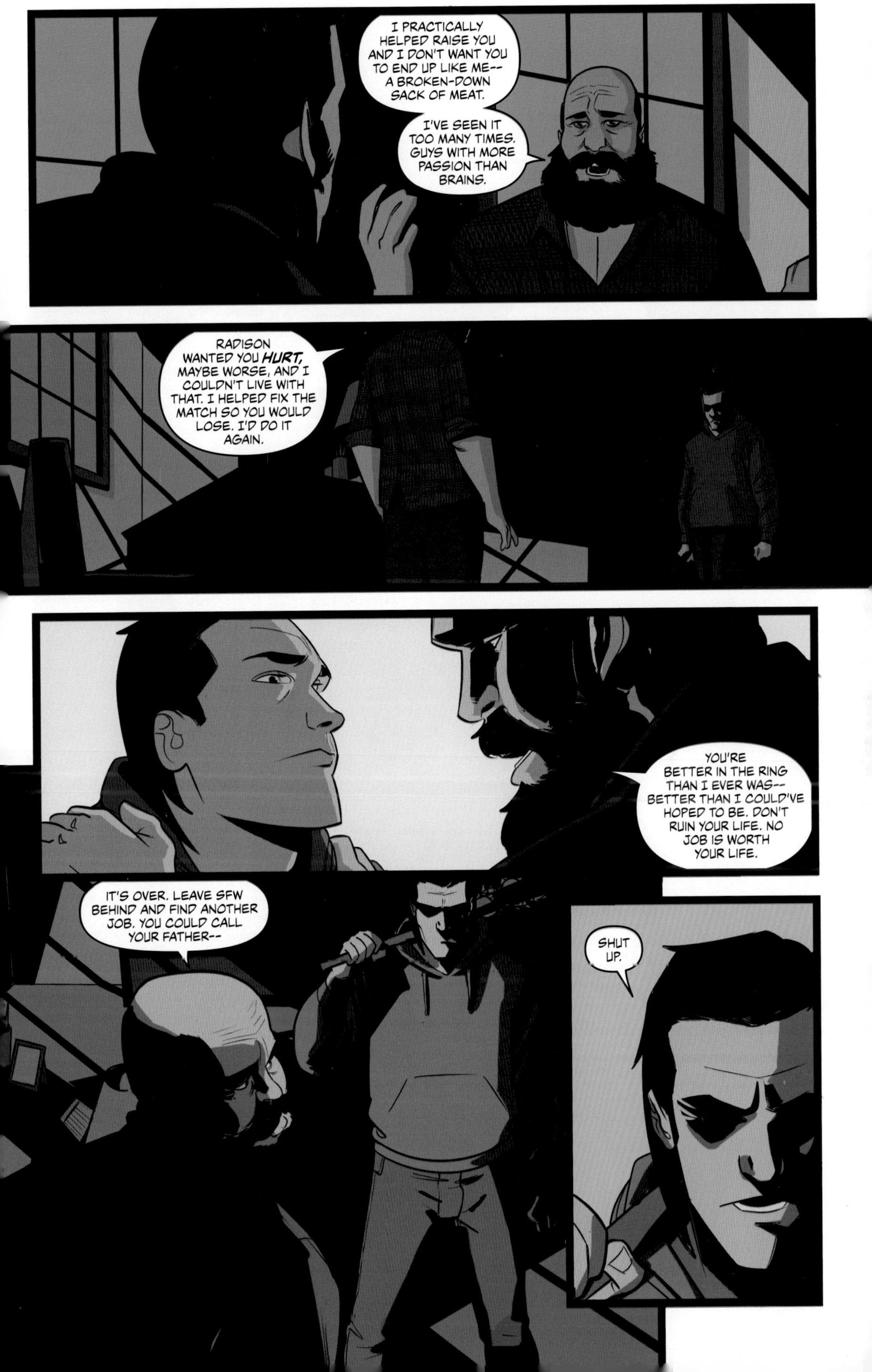
I PRACTICALLY HELPED RAISE YOU AND I DON'T WANT YOU TO END UP LIKE ME-- A BROKEN-DOWN SACK OF MEAT.
I'VE SEEN IT TOO MANY TIMES. GUYS WITH MORE PASSION THAN BRAINS.
RADISON WANTED YOU **HURT,** MAYBE WORSE, AND I COULDN'T LIVE WITH THAT. I HELPED FIX THE MATCH SO YOU WOULD LOSE. I'D DO IT AGAIN.
YOU'RE BETTER IN THE RING THAN I EVER WAS-- BETTER THAN I COULD'VE HOPED TO BE. DON'T RUIN YOUR LIFE. NO JOB IS WORTH YOUR LIFE.
IT'S OVER. LEAVE SFW BEHIND AND FIND ANOTHER JOB. YOU COULD CALL YOUR FATHER--
SHUT UP.

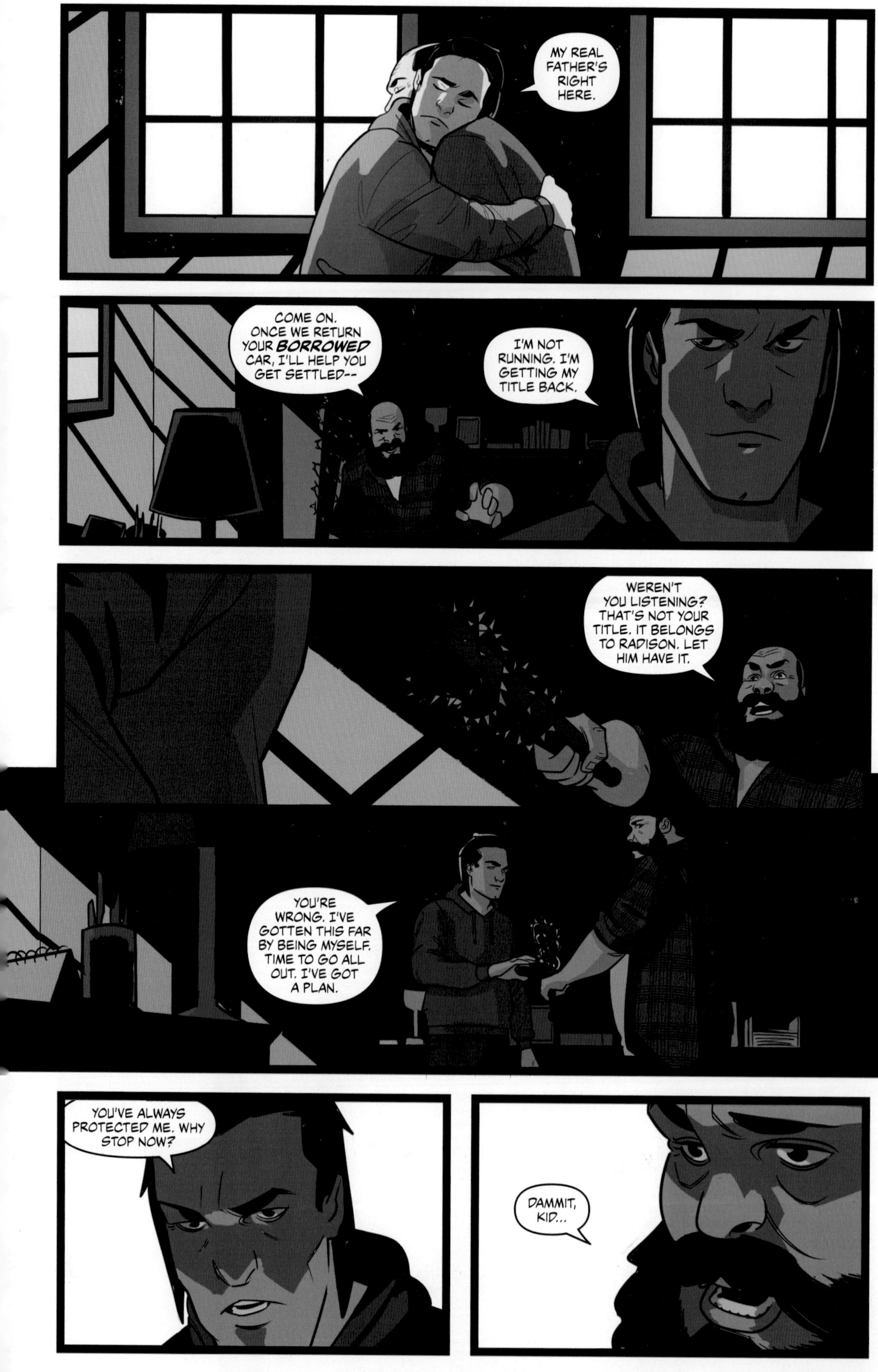

MY REAL FATHER'S RIGHT HERE.
COME ON. ONCE WE RETURN YOUR BORROWED CAR, I'LL HELP YOU GET SETTLED--
I'M NOT RUNNING. I'M GETTING MY TITLE BACK.
WEREN'T YOU LISTENING? THAT'S NOT YOUR TITLE. IT BELONGS TO RADISON. LET HIM HAVE IT.
YOU'RE WRONG. I'VE GOTTEN THIS FAR BY BEING MYSELF. TIME TO GO ALL OUT. I'VE GOT A PLAN.
YOU'VE ALWAYS PROTECTED ME. WHY STOP NOW?
DAMMIT, KID...

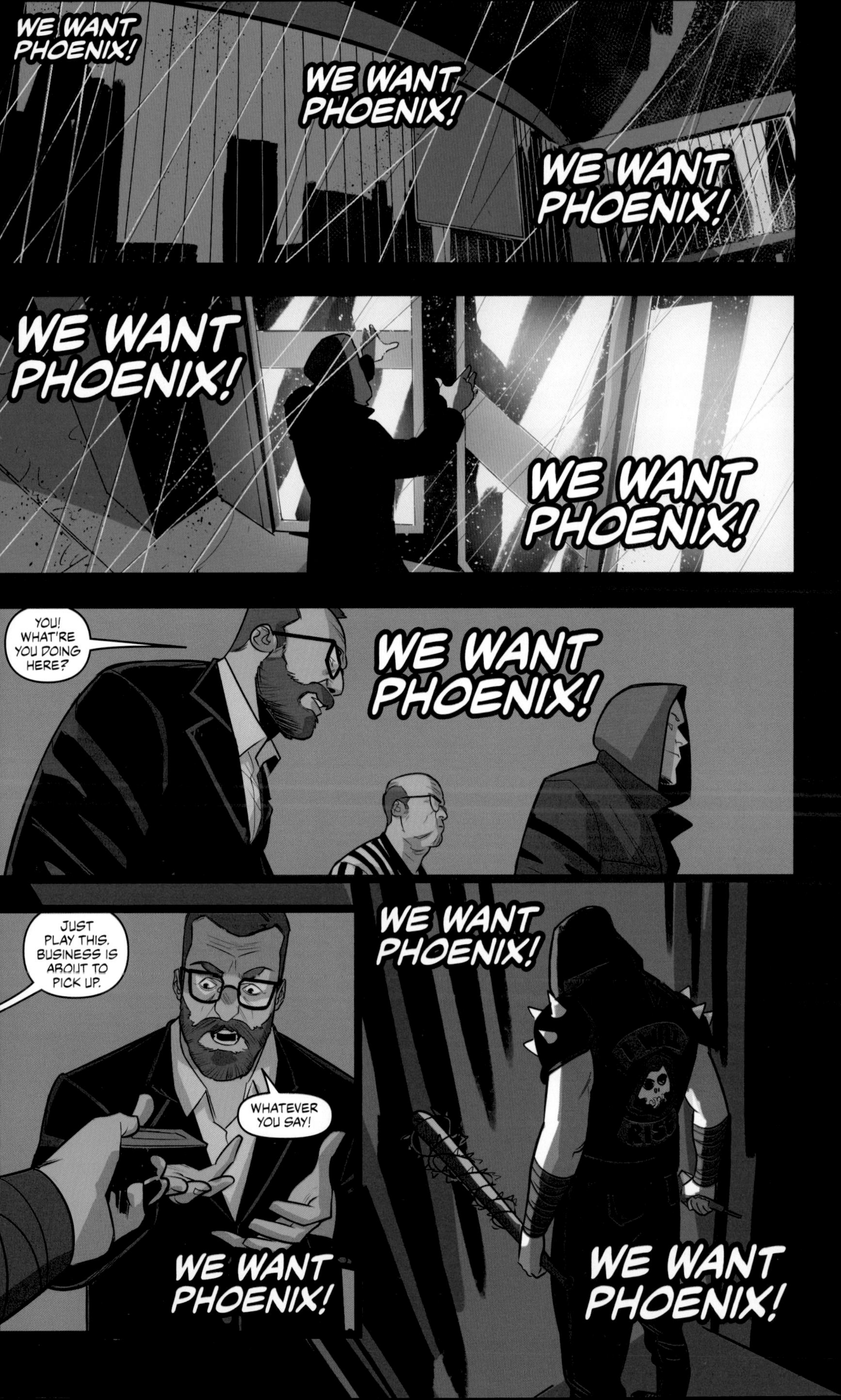
WE WANT PHOENIX!
WE WANT PHOENIX!
WE WANT PHOENIX!
WE WANT PHOENIX!
WE WANT PHOENIX!
YOU! WHAT'RE YOU DOING HERE?
WE WANT PHOENIX!
JUST PLAY THIS. BUSINESS IS ABOUT TO PICK UP.
WHATEVER YOU SAY!
WE WANT PHOENIX!
WE WANT PHOENIX!
WE WANT PHOENIX!

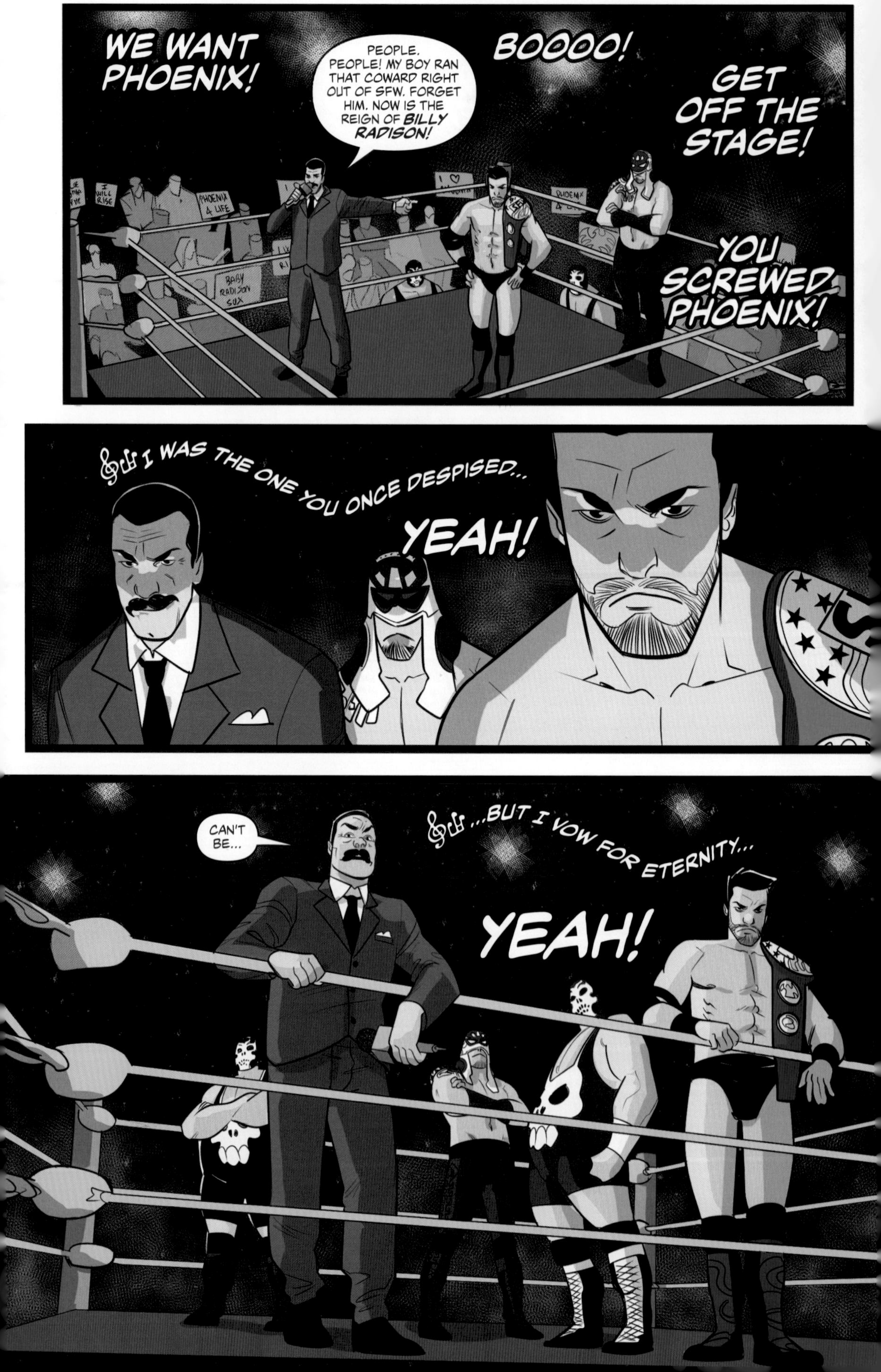
WE WANT PHOENIX!
PEOPLE. PEOPLE! MY BOY RAN THAT COWARD RIGHT OUT OF SFW. FORGET HIM. NOW IS THE REIGN OF BILLY RADISON!
BOOOO!
GET OFF THE STAGE!
I WILL RISE
PHOENIX 4 LIFE
BABY RADISON SUX
YOU SCREWED PHOENIX!
I WAS THE ONE YOU ONCE DESPISED...
YEAH!
CAN'T BE...
...BUT I VOW FOR ETERNITY...
YEAH!

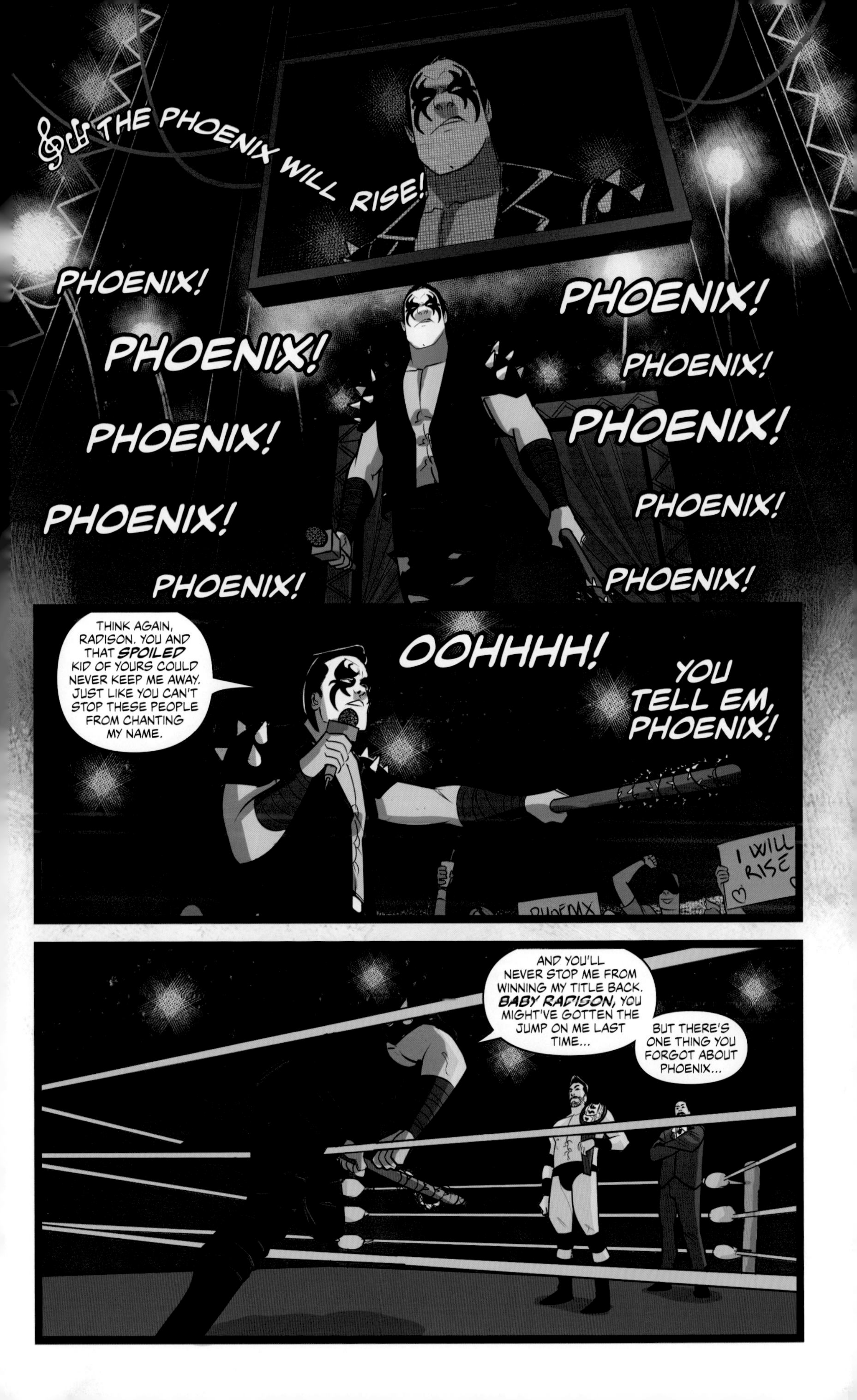
THE PHOENIX WILL RISE!
PHOENIX!
PHOENIX!
PHOENIX!
PHOENIX!
PHOENIX!
PHOENIX!
PHOENIX!
PHOENIX!
PHOENIX!
PHOENIX!
THINK AGAIN, RADISON. YOU AND THAT SPOILED KID OF YOURS COULD NEVER KEEP ME AWAY. JUST LIKE YOU CAN'T STOP THESE PEOPLE FROM CHANTING MY NAME.
OOHHHH!
YOU TELL EM, PHOENIX!
I WILL RISE
AND YOU'LL NEVER STOP ME FROM WINNING MY TITLE BACK. BABY RADISON, YOU MIGHT'VE GOTTEN THE JUMP ON ME LAST TIME...
BUT THERE'S ONE THING YOU FORGOT ABOUT PHOENIX...

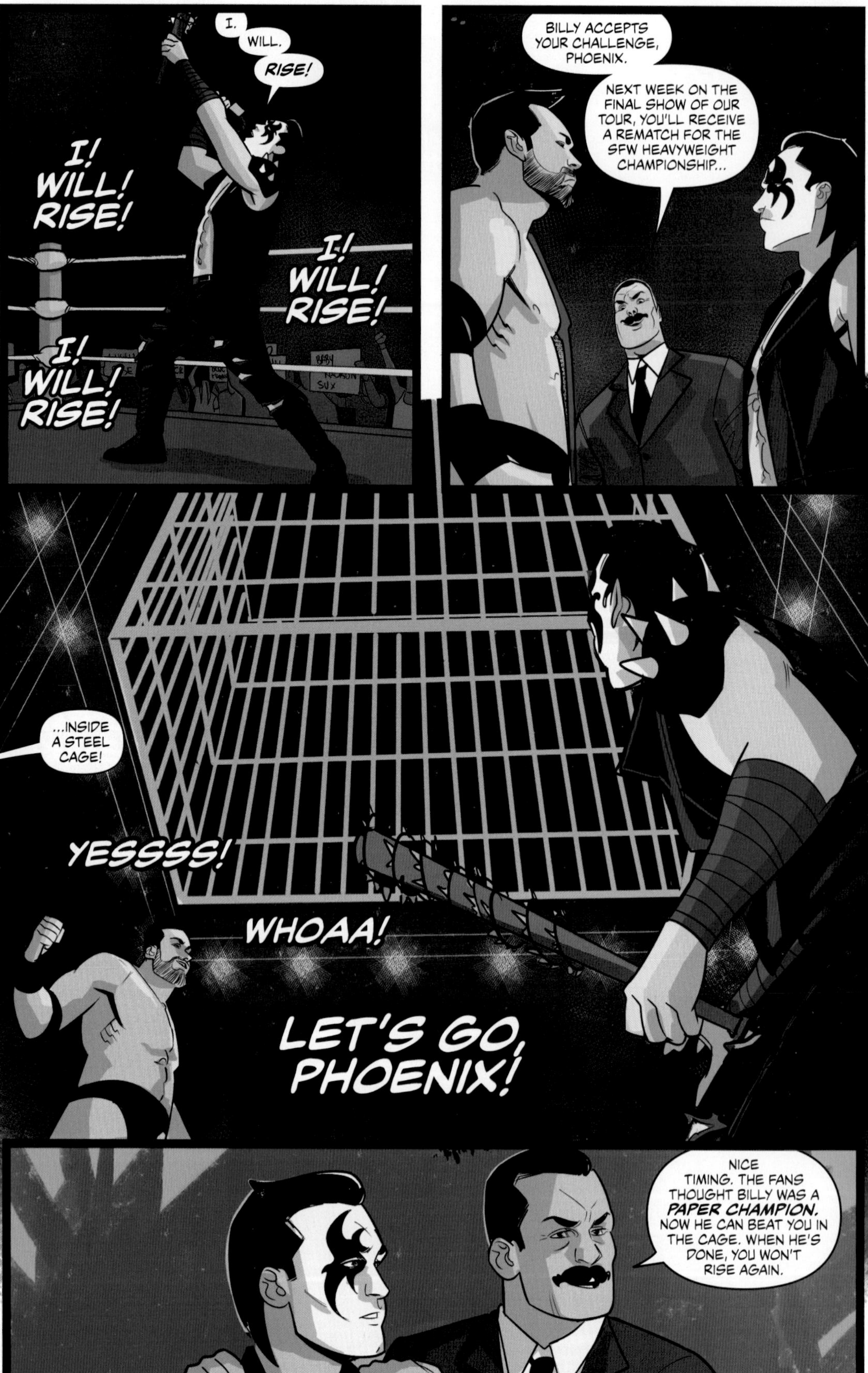
I.
WILL.
RISE!
I! WILL! RISE!
I! WILL! RISE!
I! WILL! RISE!
BILLY ACCEPTS YOUR CHALLENGE, PHOENIX.
NEXT WEEK ON THE FINAL SHOW OF OUR TOUR, YOU'LL RECEIVE A REMATCH FOR THE SFW HEAVYWEIGHT CHAMPIONSHIP...
...INSIDE A STEEL CAGE!
YESSSSS!
WHOAA!
LET'S GO, PHOENIX!
NICE TIMING. THE FANS THOUGHT BILLY WAS A ***PAPER CHAMPION.*** NOW HE CAN BEAT YOU IN THE CAGE. WHEN HE'S DONE, YOU WON'T RISE AGAIN.

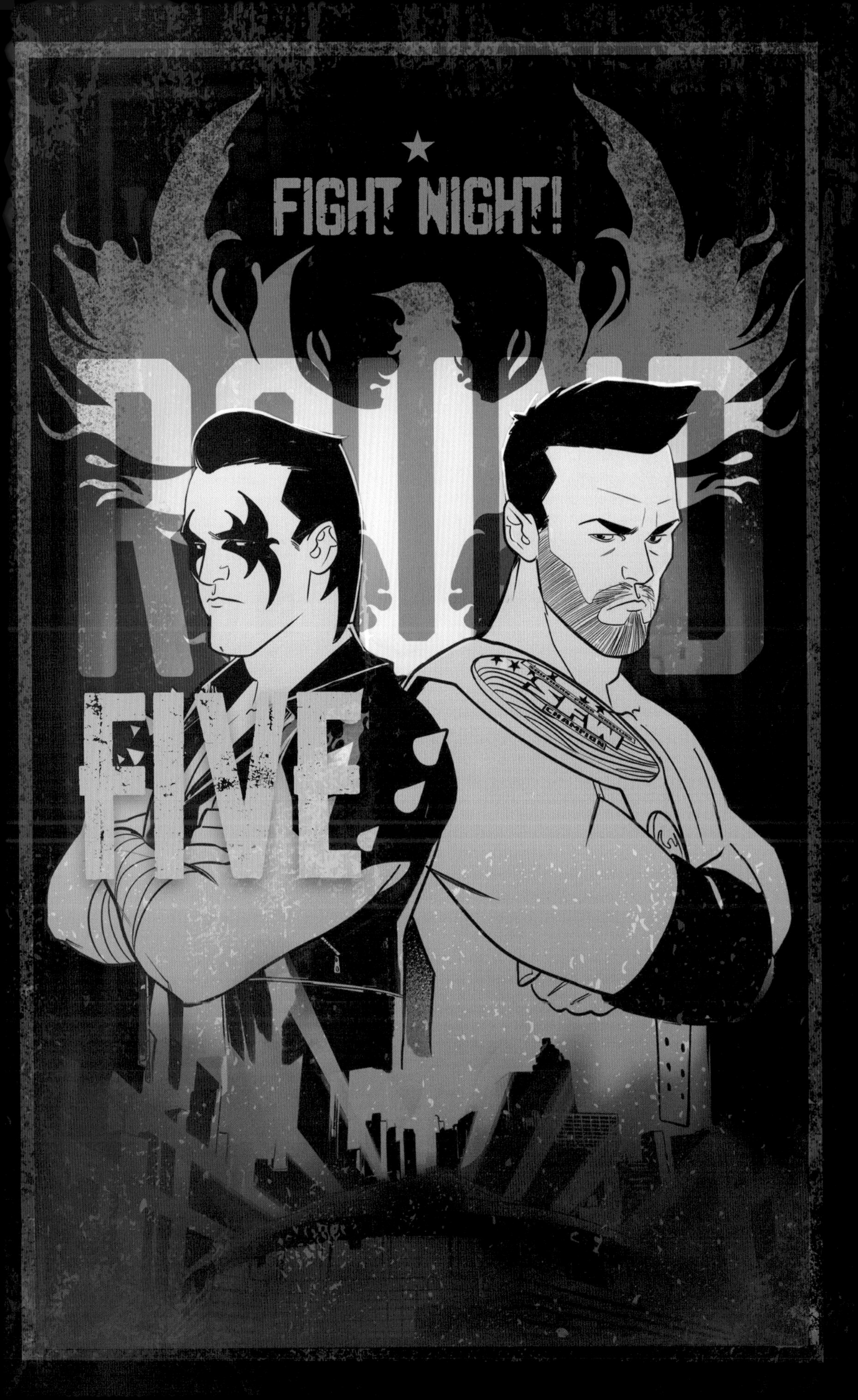
FIGHT NIGHT!
FIVE

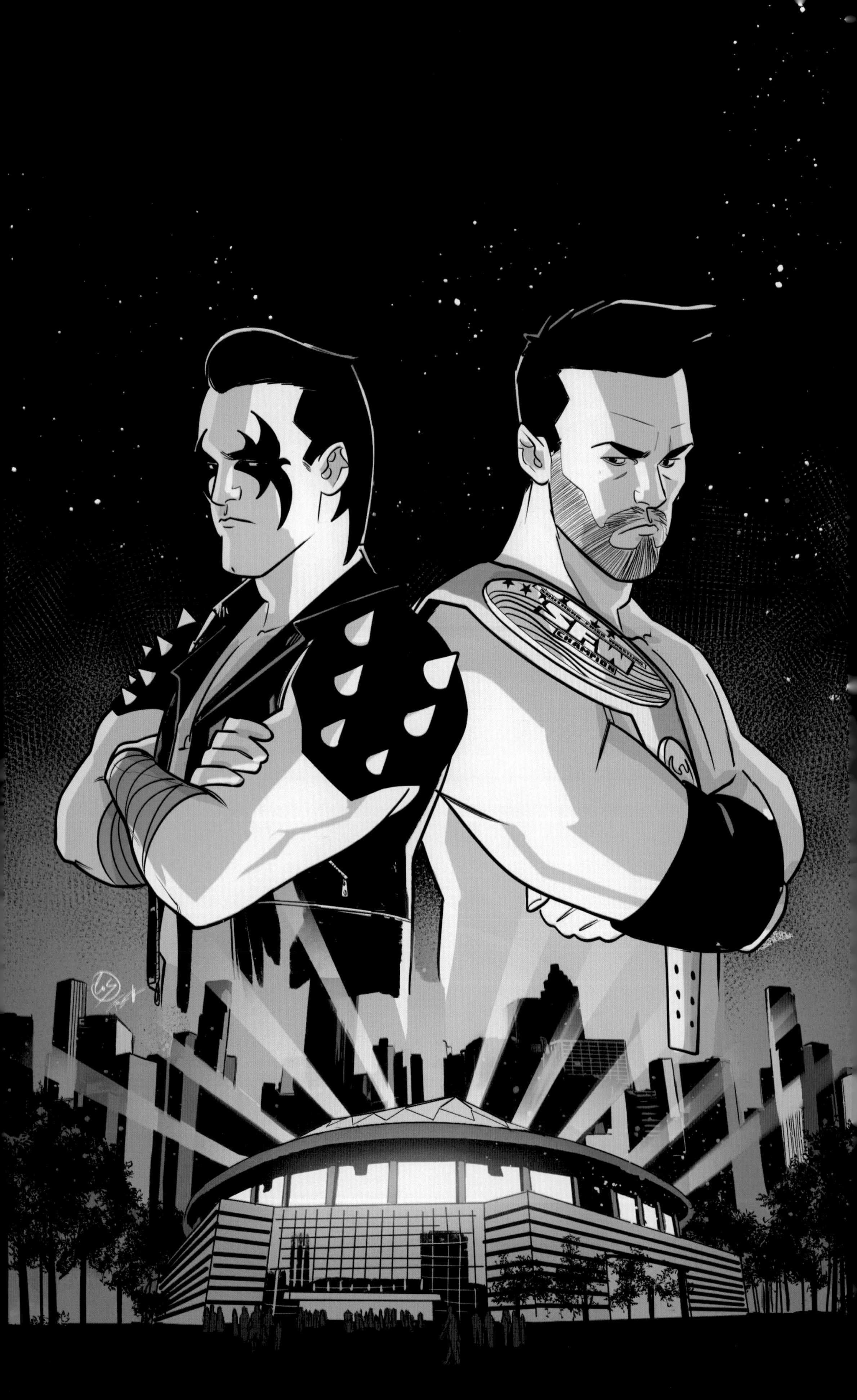
SFW
CHAMPION

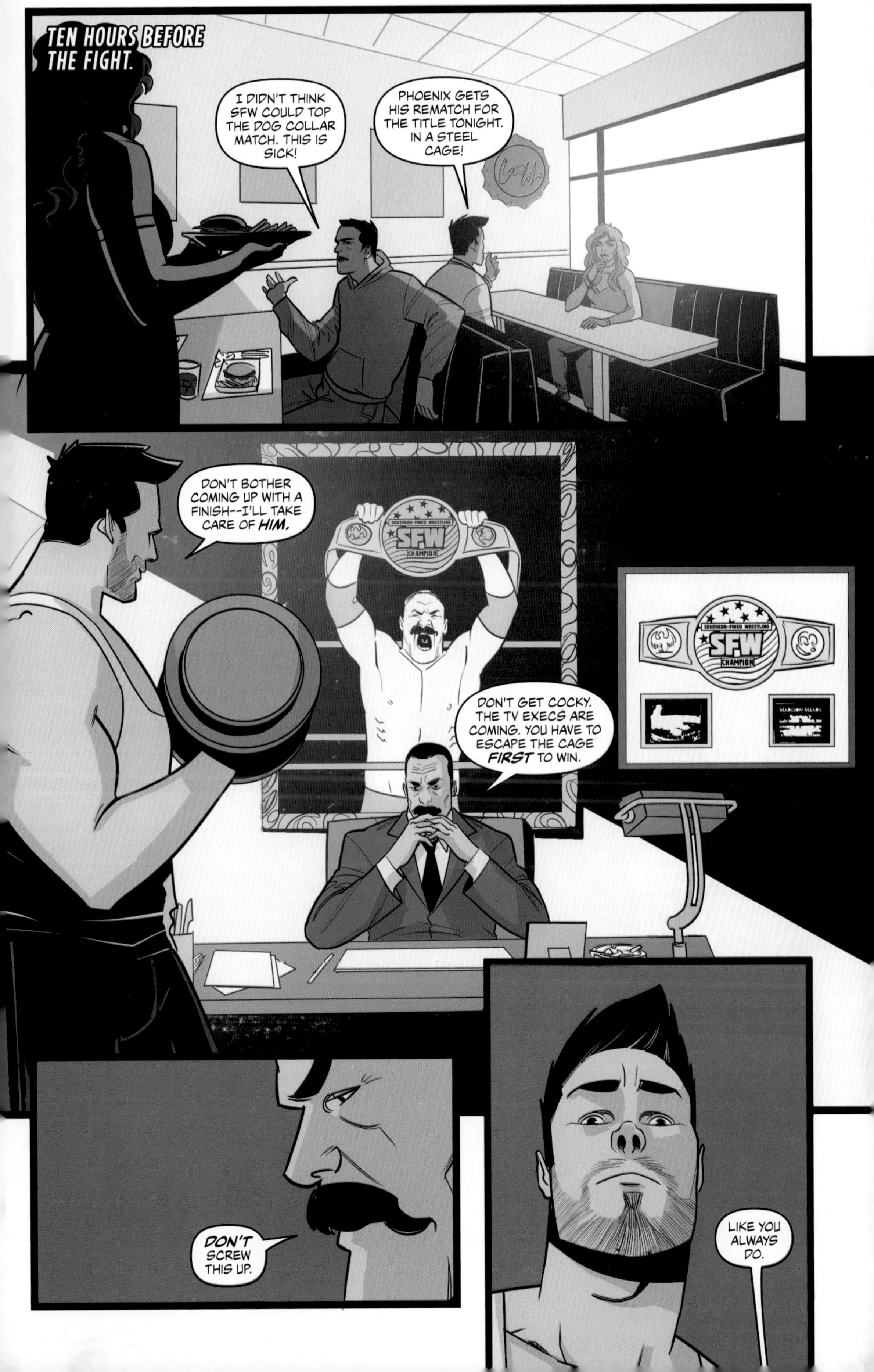
TEN HOURS BEFORE THE FIGHT.
I DIDN'T THINK SFW COULD TOP THE DOG COLLAR MATCH. THIS IS SICK!
PHOENIX GETS HIS REMATCH FOR THE TITLE TONIGHT. IN A STEEL CAGE!
DON'T BOTHER COMING UP WITH A FINISH--I'LL TAKE CARE OF HIM.
SOUTHERN-FRIED WRESTLING
SFW
CHAMPION
DON'T GET COCKY. THE TV EXECS ARE COMING. YOU HAVE TO ESCAPE THE CAGE FIRST TO WIN.
DON'T SCREW THIS UP.
LIKE YOU ALWAYS DO.

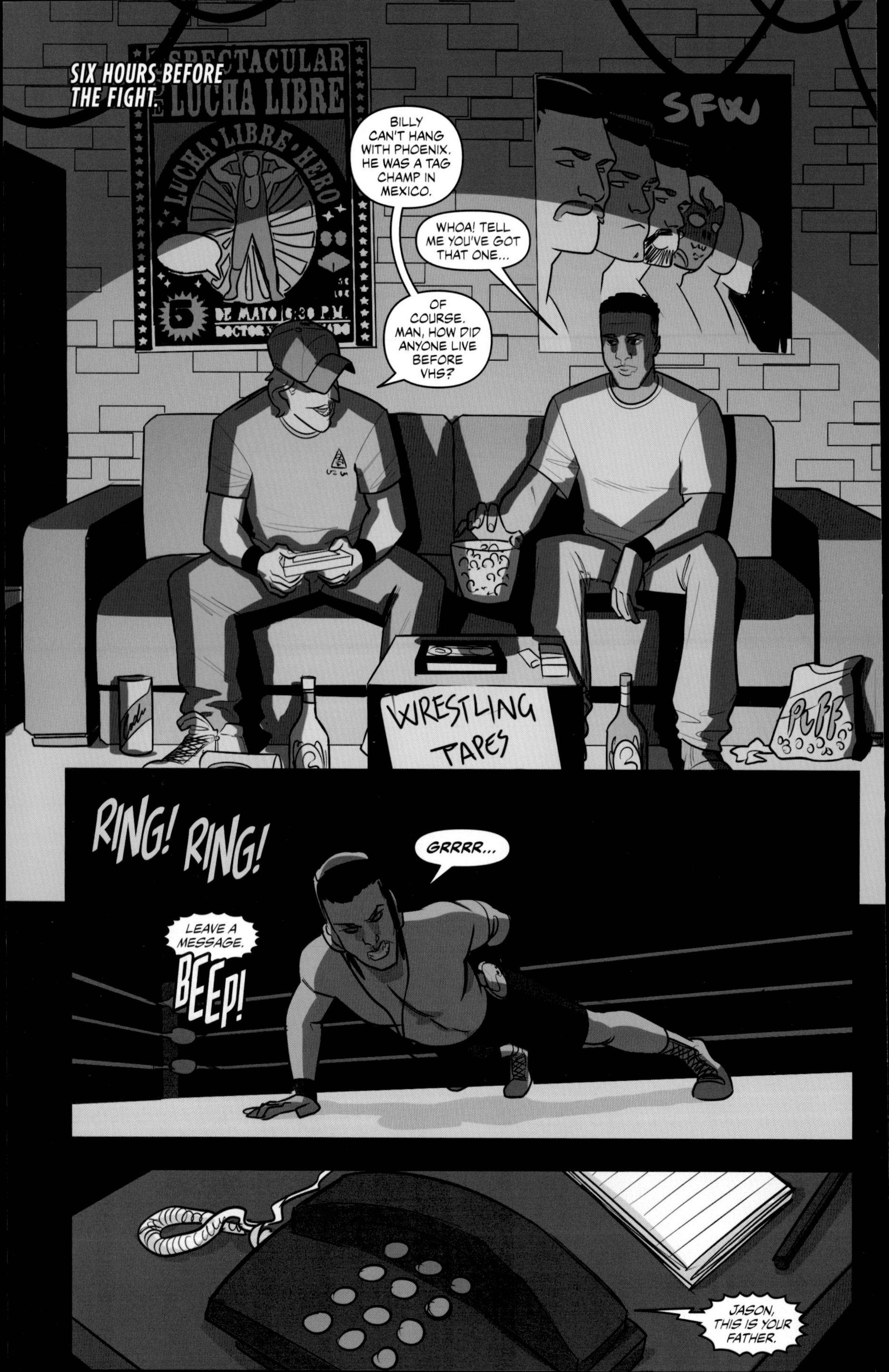
SIX HOURS BEFORE THE FIGHT.
ESPECTACULAR DE LUCHA LIBRE
LUCHA LIBRE HERO
5 DE MAYO 6:30 P.M.
SFW
BILLY CAN'T HANG WITH PHOENIX. HE WAS A TAG CHAMP IN MEXICO.
WHOA! TELL ME YOU'VE GOT THAT ONE...
OF COURSE. MAN, HOW DID ANYONE LIVE BEFORE VHS?
WRESTLING TAPES
PUFF
RING! RING!
GRRRR...
LEAVE A MESSAGE.
BEEP!
JASON, THIS IS YOUR FATHER.

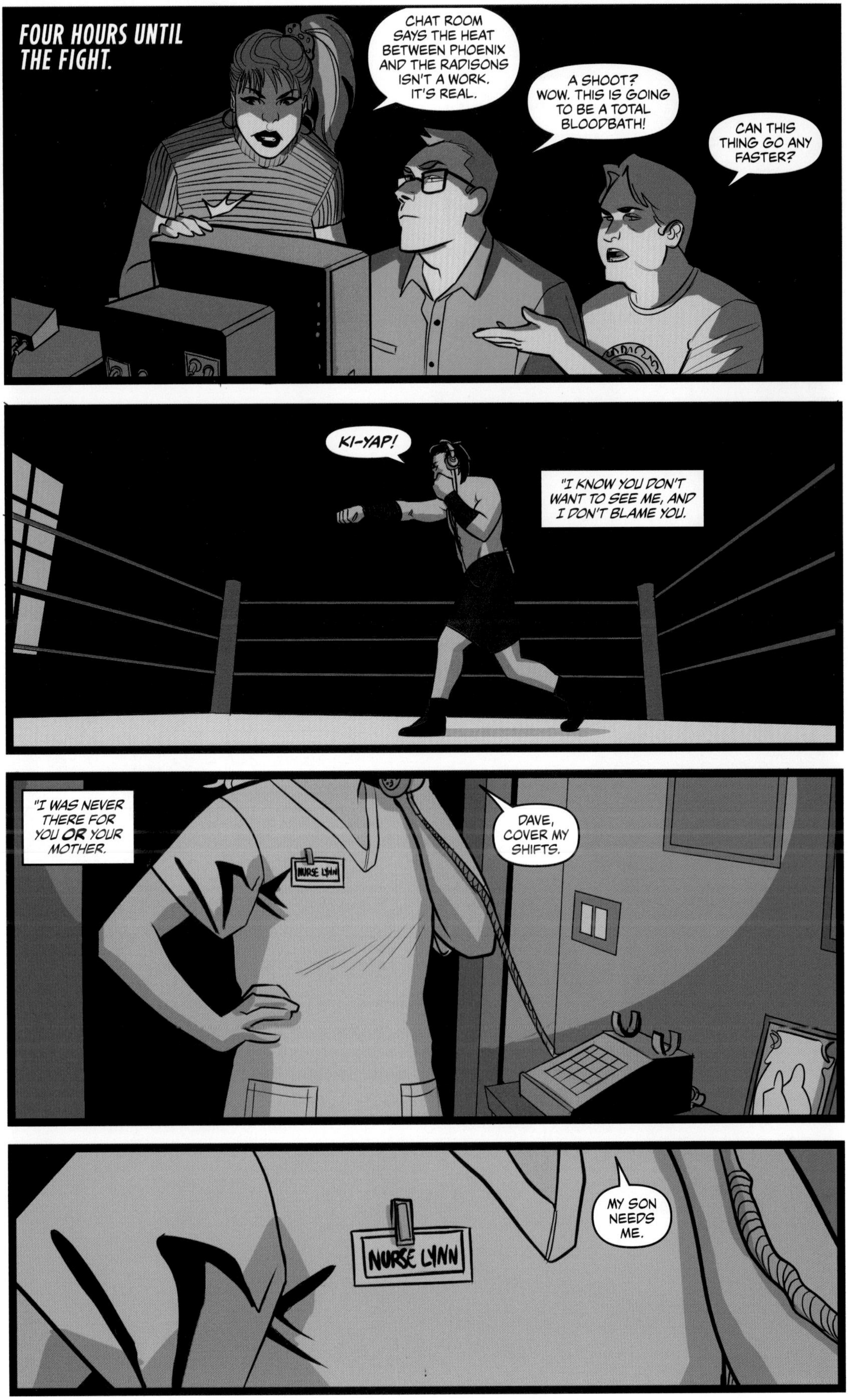
FOUR HOURS UNTIL THE FIGHT.
CHAT ROOM SAYS THE HEAT BETWEEN PHOENIX AND THE RADISONS ISN'T A WORK. IT'S REAL.
A SHOOT? WOW. THIS IS GOING TO BE A TOTAL BLOODBATH!
CAN THIS THING GO ANY FASTER?
KI-YAP!
"I KNOW YOU DON'T WANT TO SEE ME, AND I DON'T BLAME YOU.
"I WAS NEVER THERE FOR YOU OR YOUR MOTHER.
NURSE LYNN
DAVE, COVER MY SHIFTS.
NURSE LYNN
MY SON NEEDS ME.

TWO HOURS BEFORE THE FIGHT.

"I CAN'T CHANGE THE PAST...

"...BUT THAT DOESN'T MEAN WE CAN'T HAVE A **FUTURE** TOGETHER.

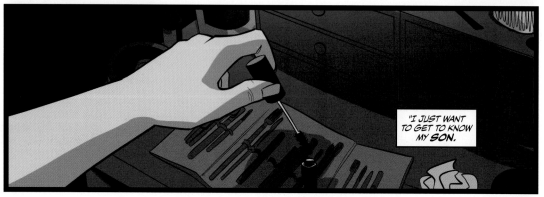

"I JUST WANT TO GET TO KNOW MY **SON.**

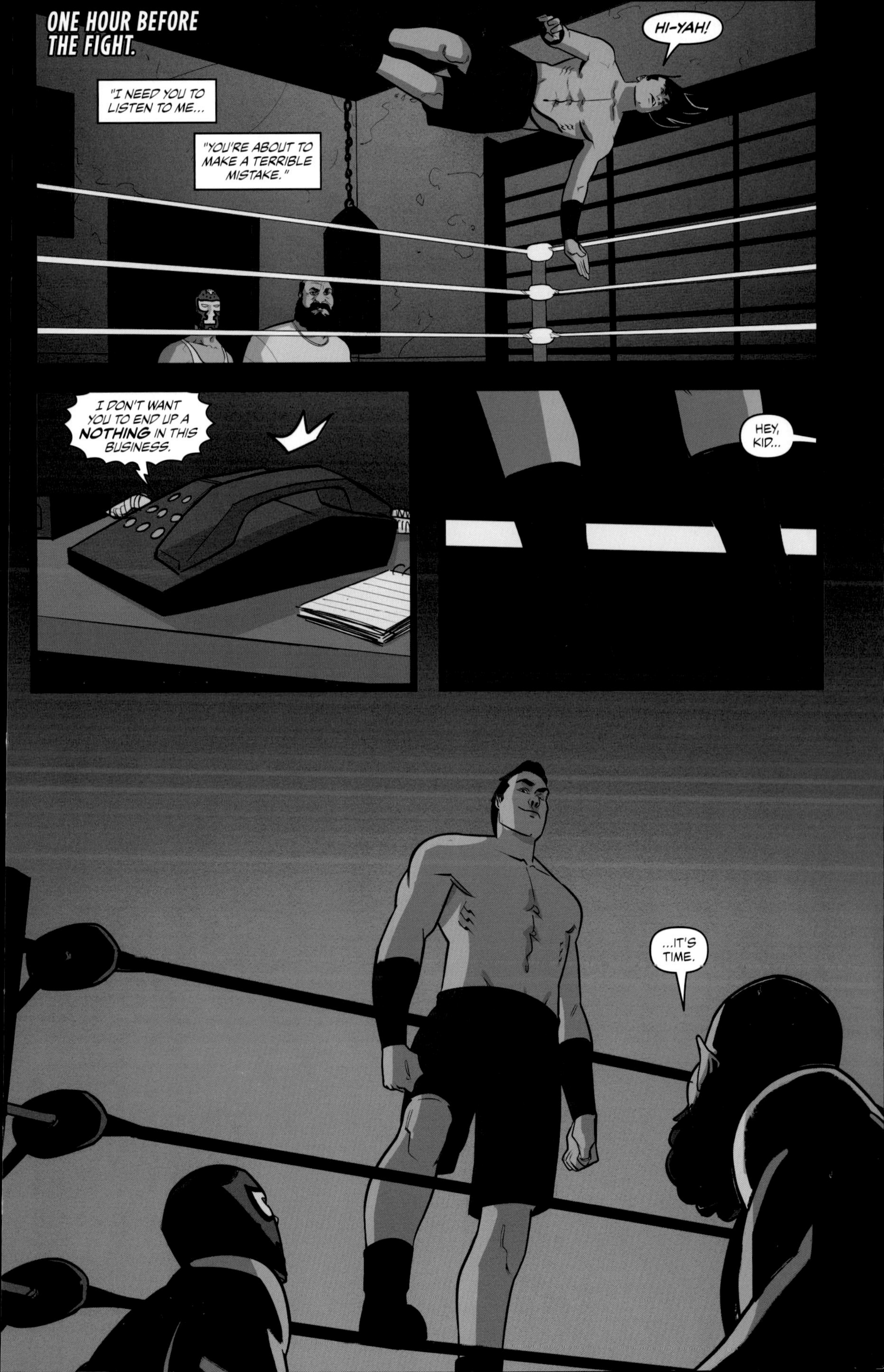
ONE HOUR BEFORE THE FIGHT.
HI-YAH!
"I NEED YOU TO LISTEN TO ME...
"YOU'RE ABOUT TO MAKE A TERRIBLE MISTAKE."
I DON'T WANT YOU TO END UP A NOTHING IN THIS BUSINESS.
HEY, KID...
...IT'S TIME.

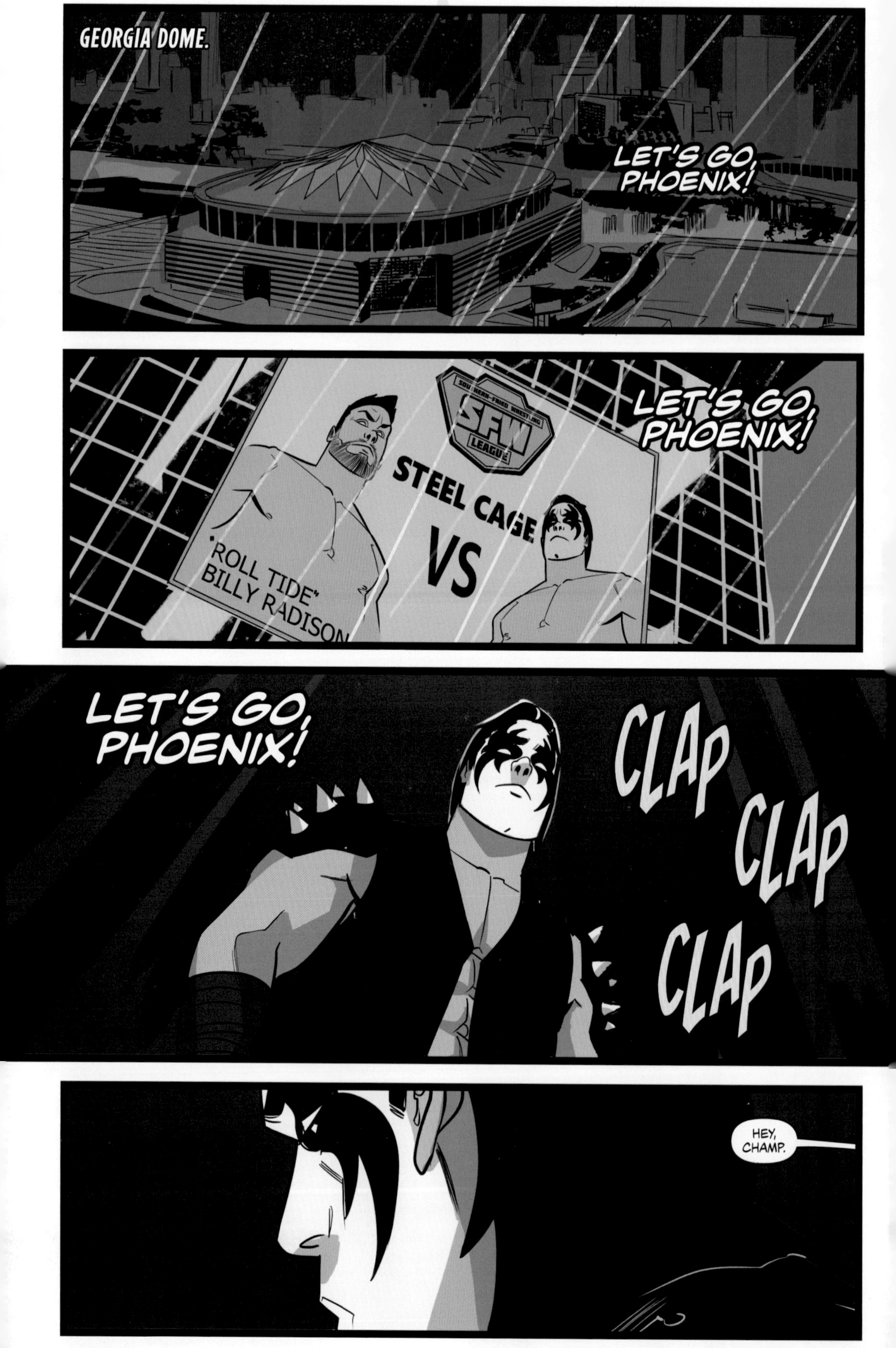
GEORGIA DOME.
LET'S GO, PHOENIX!
SOUTHERN-FRIED WRESTLING, INC.
SFW
LEAGUE
STEEL CAGE
VS
"ROLL TIDE" BILLY RADISON
LET'S GO, PHOENIX!
LET'S GO, PHOENIX!
CLAP
CLAP
CLAP
HEY, CHAMP.

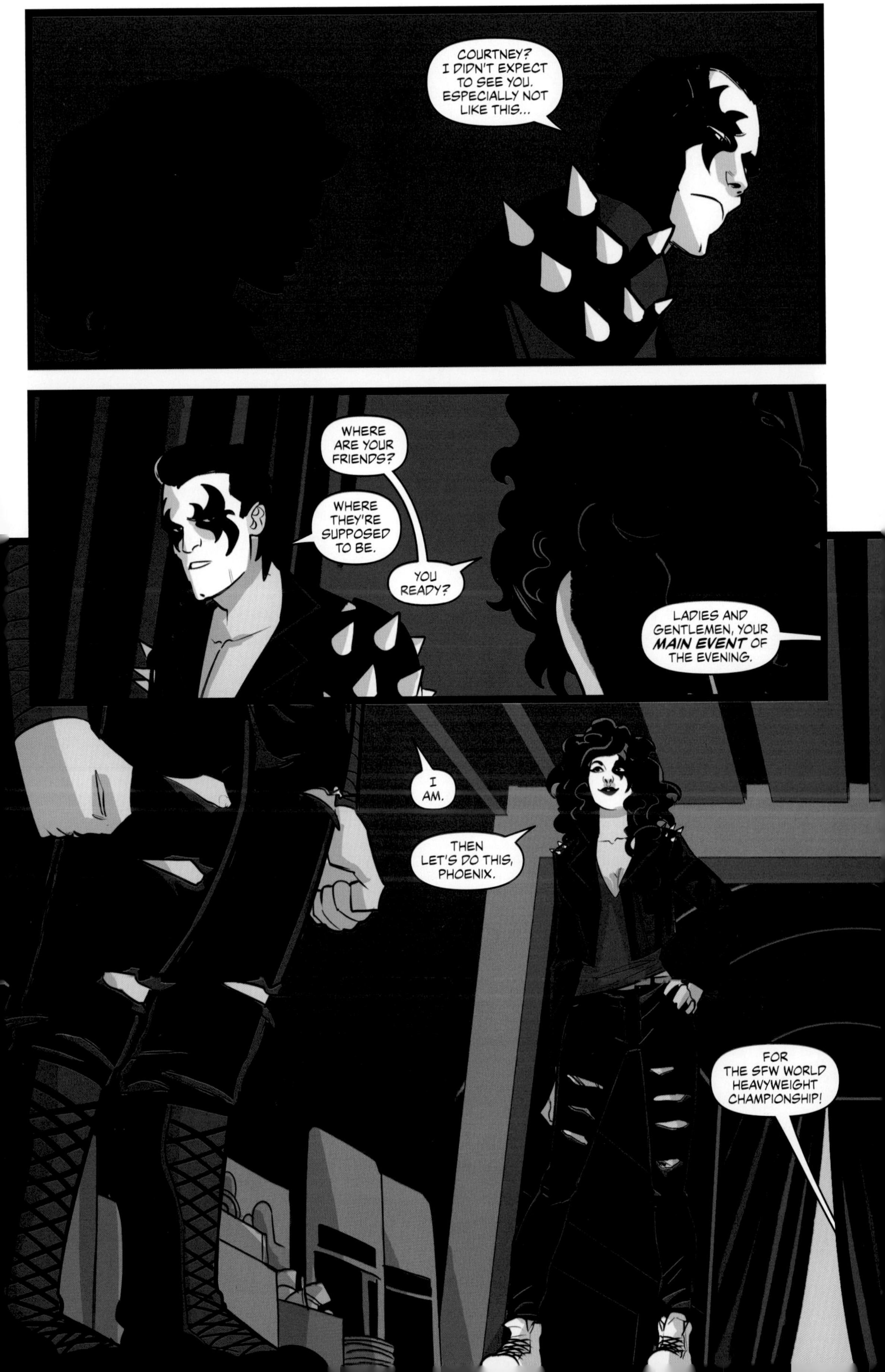
COURTNEY? I DIDN'T EXPECT TO SEE YOU. ESPECIALLY NOT LIKE THIS...
WHERE ARE YOUR FRIENDS?
WHERE THEY'RE SUPPOSED TO BE.
YOU READY?
LADIES AND GENTLEMEN, YOUR **MAIN EVENT** OF THE EVENING.
I AM.
THEN LET'S DO THIS, PHOENIX.
FOR THE SFW WORLD HEAVYWEIGHT CHAMPIONSHIP!

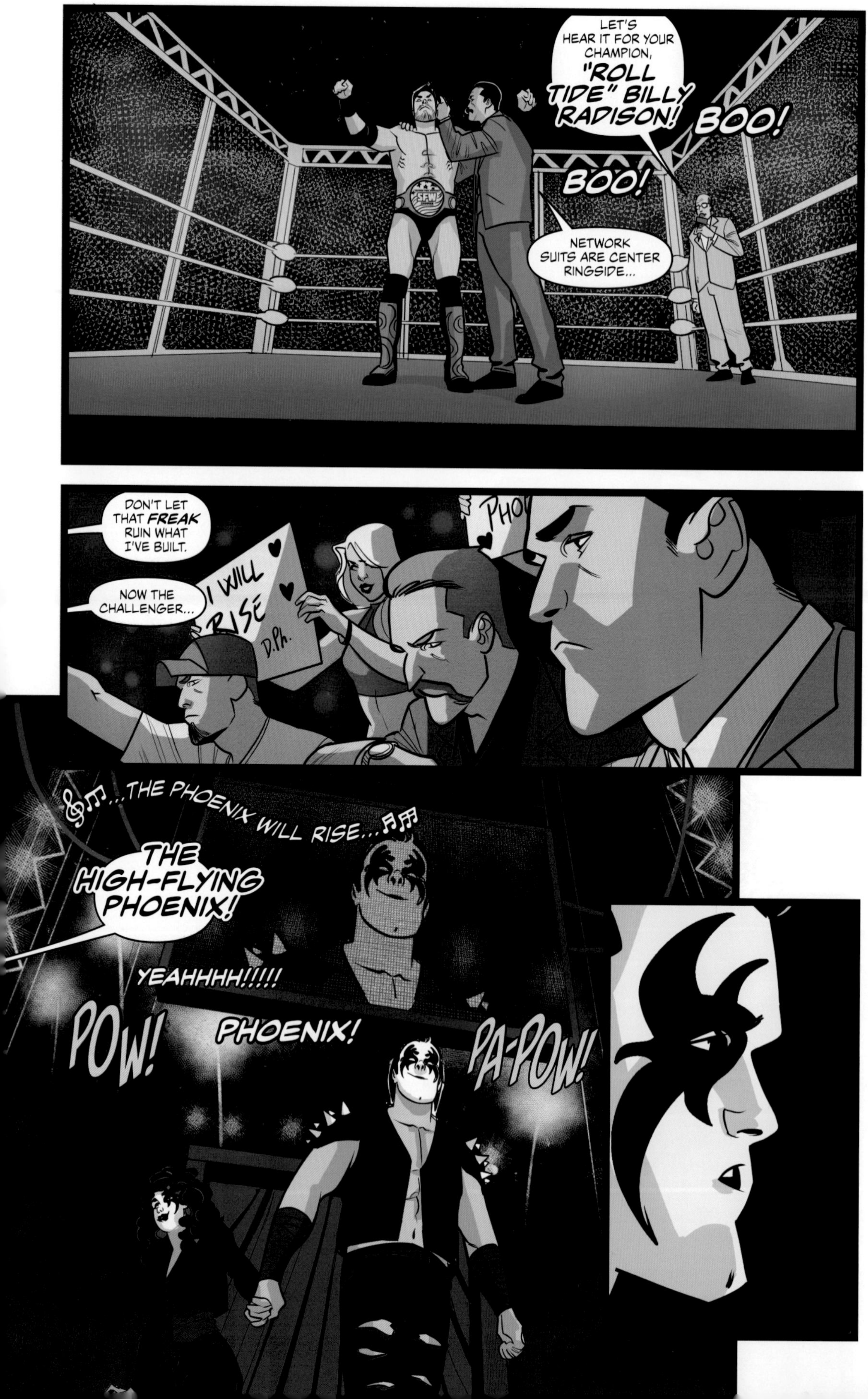
LET'S HEAR IT FOR YOUR CHAMPION, "ROLL TIDE" BILLY RADISON!
BOO!
BOO!
NETWORK SUITS ARE CENTER RINGSIDE...
DON'T LET THAT FREAK RUIN WHAT I'VE BUILT.
NOW THE CHALLENGER...
I WILL RISE D.Ph.
...THE PHOENIX WILL RISE...
THE HIGH-FLYING PHOENIX!
YEAHHHH!!!!!
POW!
PHOENIX!
PA-POW!

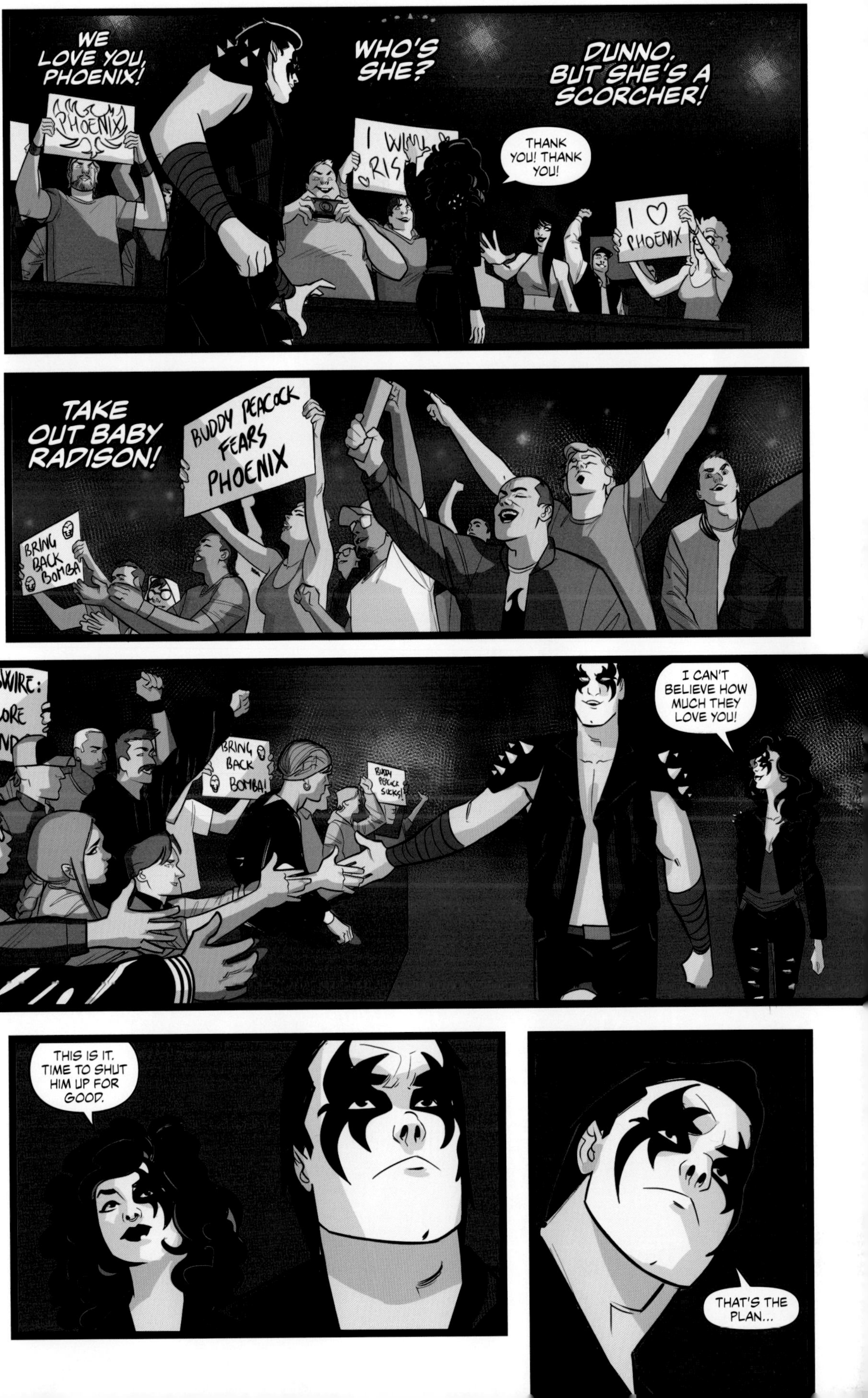
WE LOVE YOU, PHOENIX!
PHOENIX
WHO'S SHE?
DUNNO, BUT SHE'S A SCORCHER!
THANK YOU! THANK YOU!
I ♡ PHOENIX
TAKE OUT BABY RADISON!
BUDDY PEACOCK FEARS PHOENIX
BRING BACK BOMBA
BRING BACK BOMBA!
BUDDY PEACOCK SUCKS!
I CAN'T BELIEVE HOW MUCH THEY LOVE YOU!
THIS IS IT. TIME TO SHUT HIM UP FOR GOOD.
THAT'S THE PLAN...

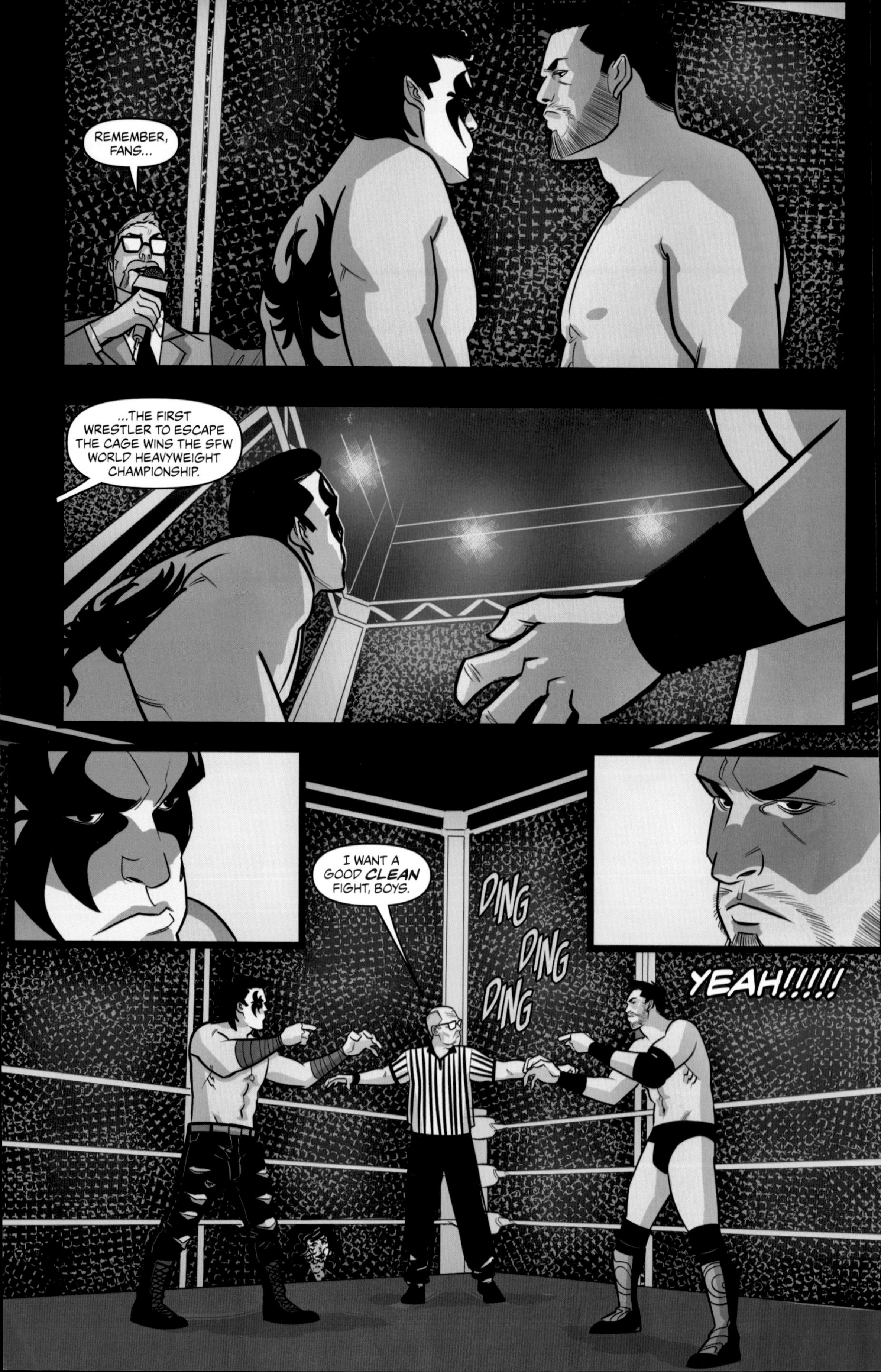
REMEMBER, FANS...
...THE FIRST WRESTLER TO ESCAPE THE CAGE WINS THE SFW WORLD HEAVYWEIGHT CHAMPIONSHIP.
I WANT A GOOD CLEAN FIGHT, BOYS.
DING DING DING
YEAH!!!!!

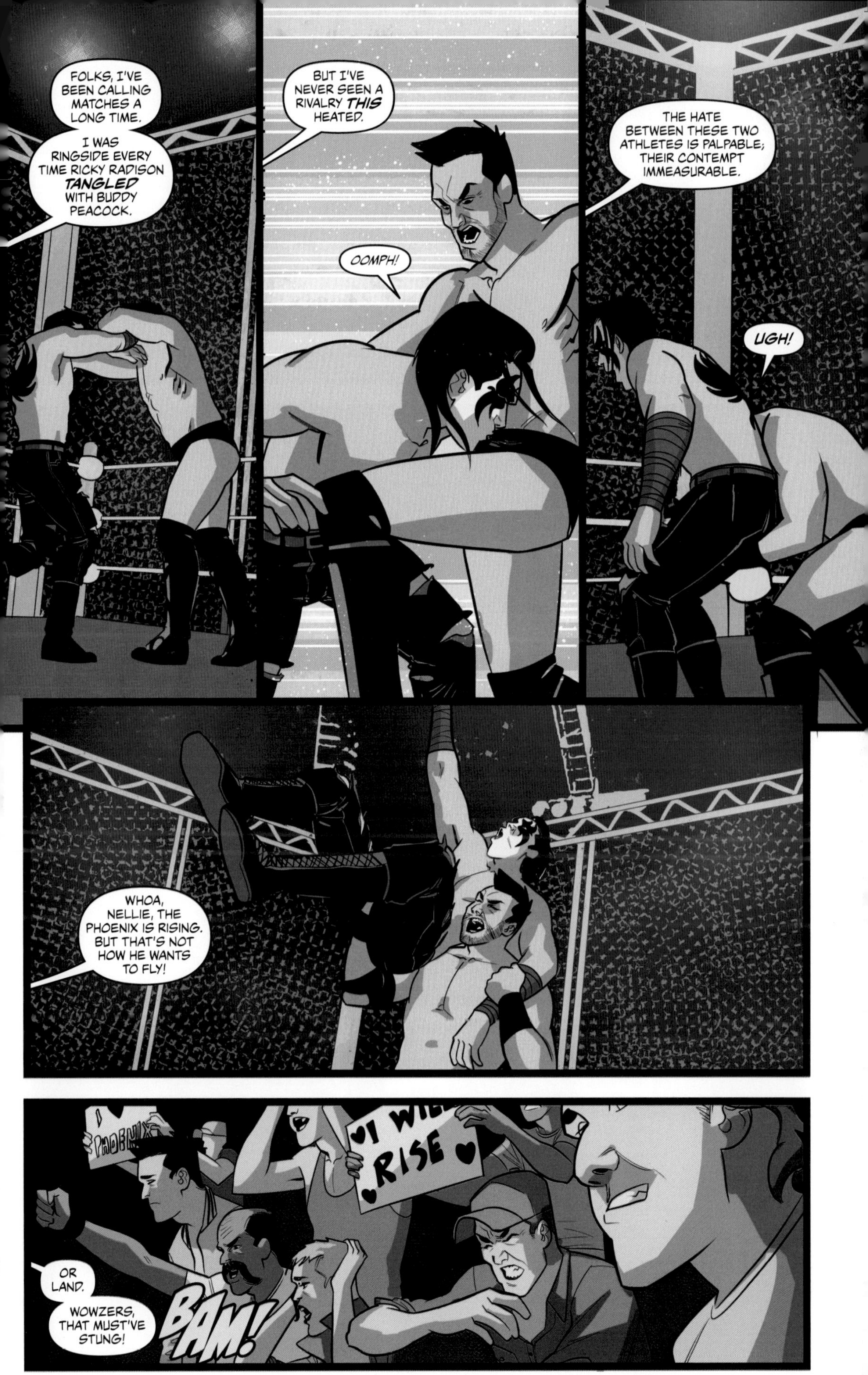
FOLKS, I'VE BEEN CALLING MATCHES A LONG TIME.
I WAS RINGSIDE EVERY TIME RICKY RADISON TANGLED WITH BUDDY PEACOCK.
BUT I'VE NEVER SEEN A RIVALRY THIS HEATED.
OOMPH!
THE HATE BETWEEN THESE TWO ATHLETES IS PALPABLE; THEIR CONTEMPT IMMEASURABLE.
UGH!
WHOA, NELLIE, THE PHOENIX IS RISING. BUT THAT'S NOT HOW HE WANTS TO FLY!
OR LAND.
WOWZERS, THAT MUST'VE STUNG!
BAM!

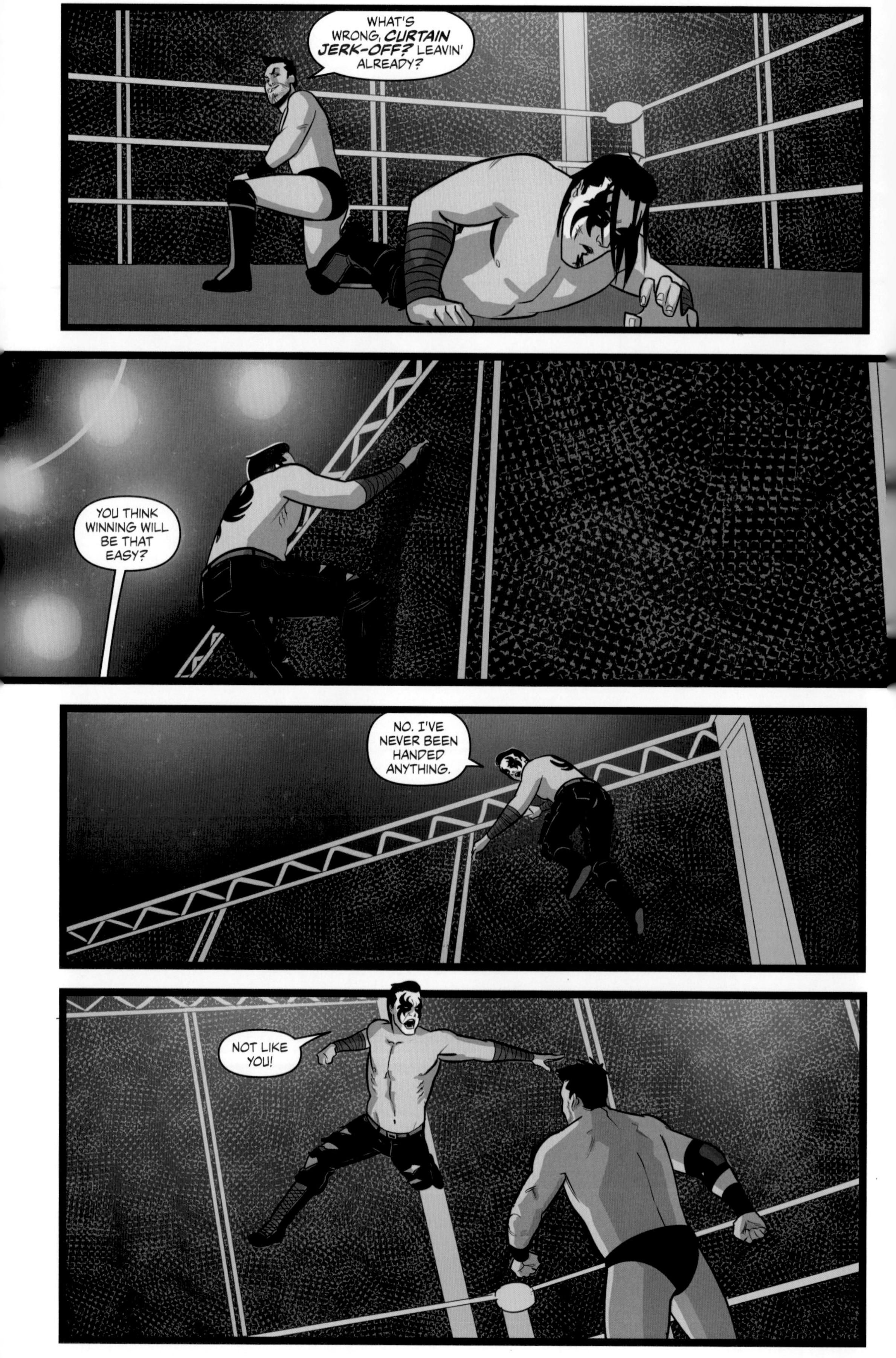
WHAT'S WRONG, CURTAIN JERK-OFF? LEAVIN' ALREADY?
YOU THINK WINNING WILL BE THAT EASY?
NO. I'VE NEVER BEEN HANDED ANYTHING.
NOT LIKE YOU!

ASTONISHING! I HOPE EVERYONE HAS A COMFORTABLE SEAT.
POW!
YEAH!!!
BECAUSE I HAVE A FEELING...
BOO!
...WE'RE JUST GETTING STARTED!
WHOA!!!
INCREDIBLE! BOTH MEN FALL TO THE MAT IN EXHAUSTION. WHO WILL RISE FIRST?
CRASH!
THIS IS AWESOME!
CLAP
CLAP
CLAP

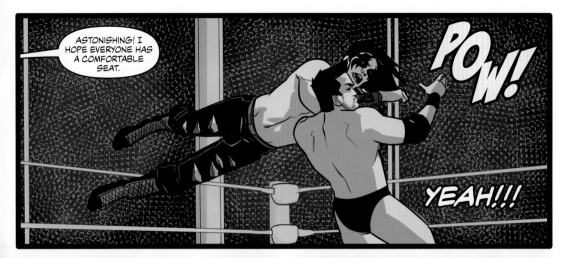

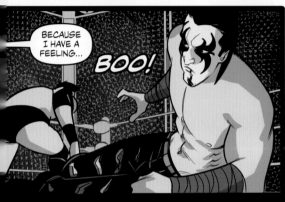

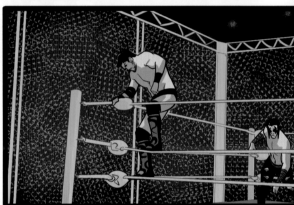

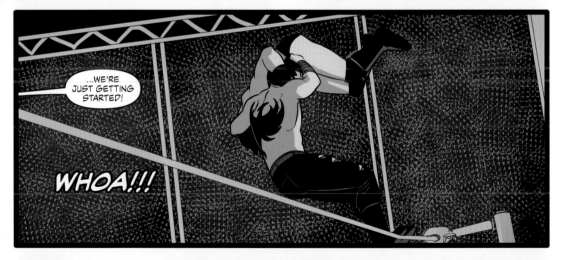

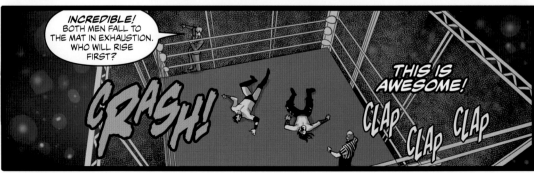

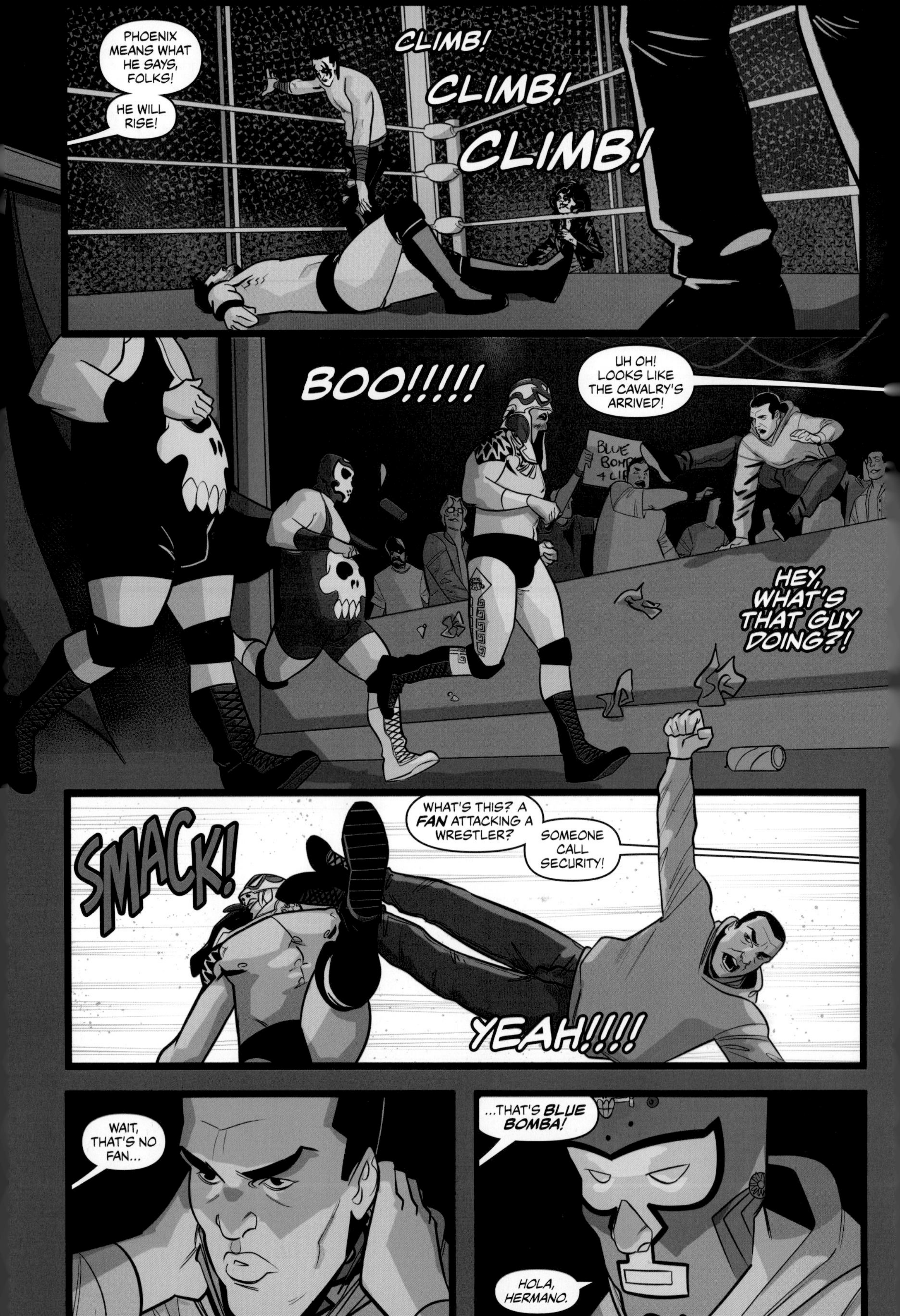
PHOENIX MEANS WHAT HE SAYS, FOLKS!
HE WILL RISE!
CLIMB!
CLIMB!
CLIMB!
BOO!!!!!
UH OH! LOOKS LIKE THE CAVALRY'S ARRIVED!
BLUE BOMB 4 LI
HEY, WHAT'S THAT GUY DOING?!
SMACK!
WHAT'S THIS? A FAN ATTACKING A WRESTLER?
SOMEONE CALL SECURITY!
YEAH!!!!
WAIT, THAT'S NO FAN...
...THAT'S BLUE BOMBA!
HOLA, HERMANO.

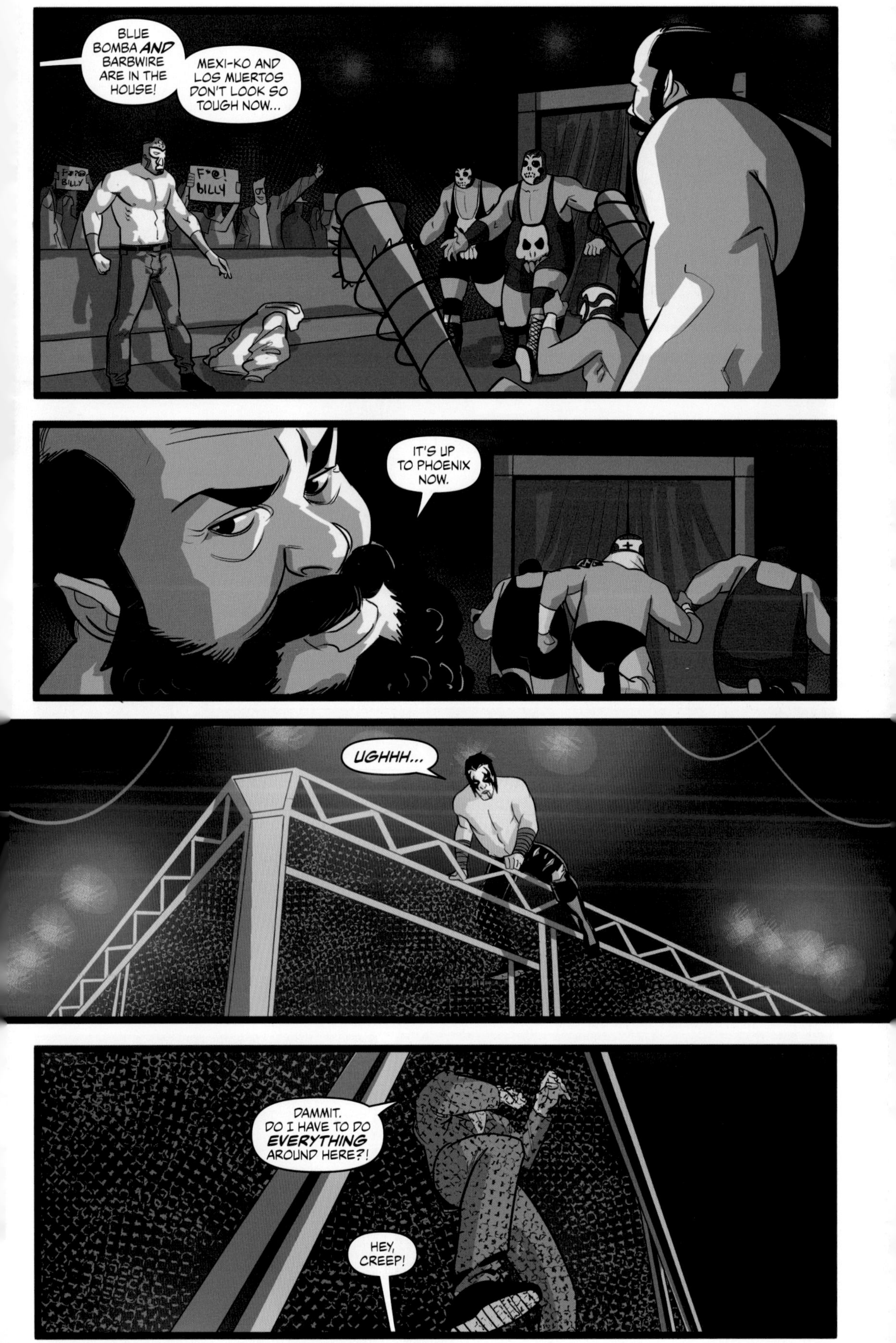
BLUE BOMBA AND BARBWIRE ARE IN THE HOUSE!
MEXI-KO AND LOS MUERTOS DON'T LOOK SO TOUGH NOW...
F*@! BILLY
IT'S UP TO PHOENIX NOW.
UGHHH...
DAMMIT. DO I HAVE TO DO EVERYTHING AROUND HERE?!
HEY, CREEP!

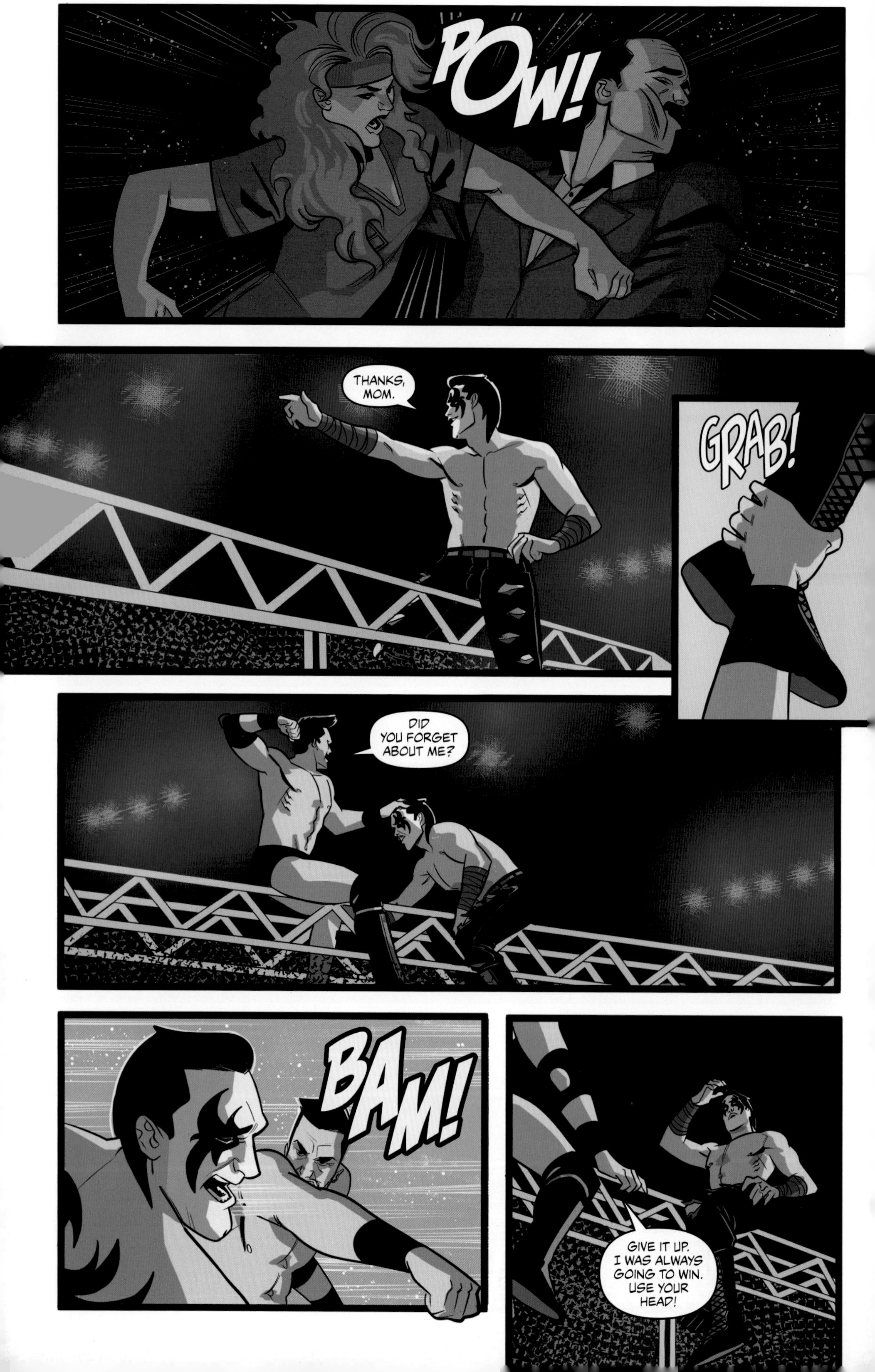
POW!
THANKS, MOM.
GRAB!
DID YOU FORGET ABOUT ME?
BAM!
GIVE IT UP. I WAS ALWAYS GOING TO WIN. USE YOUR HEAD!

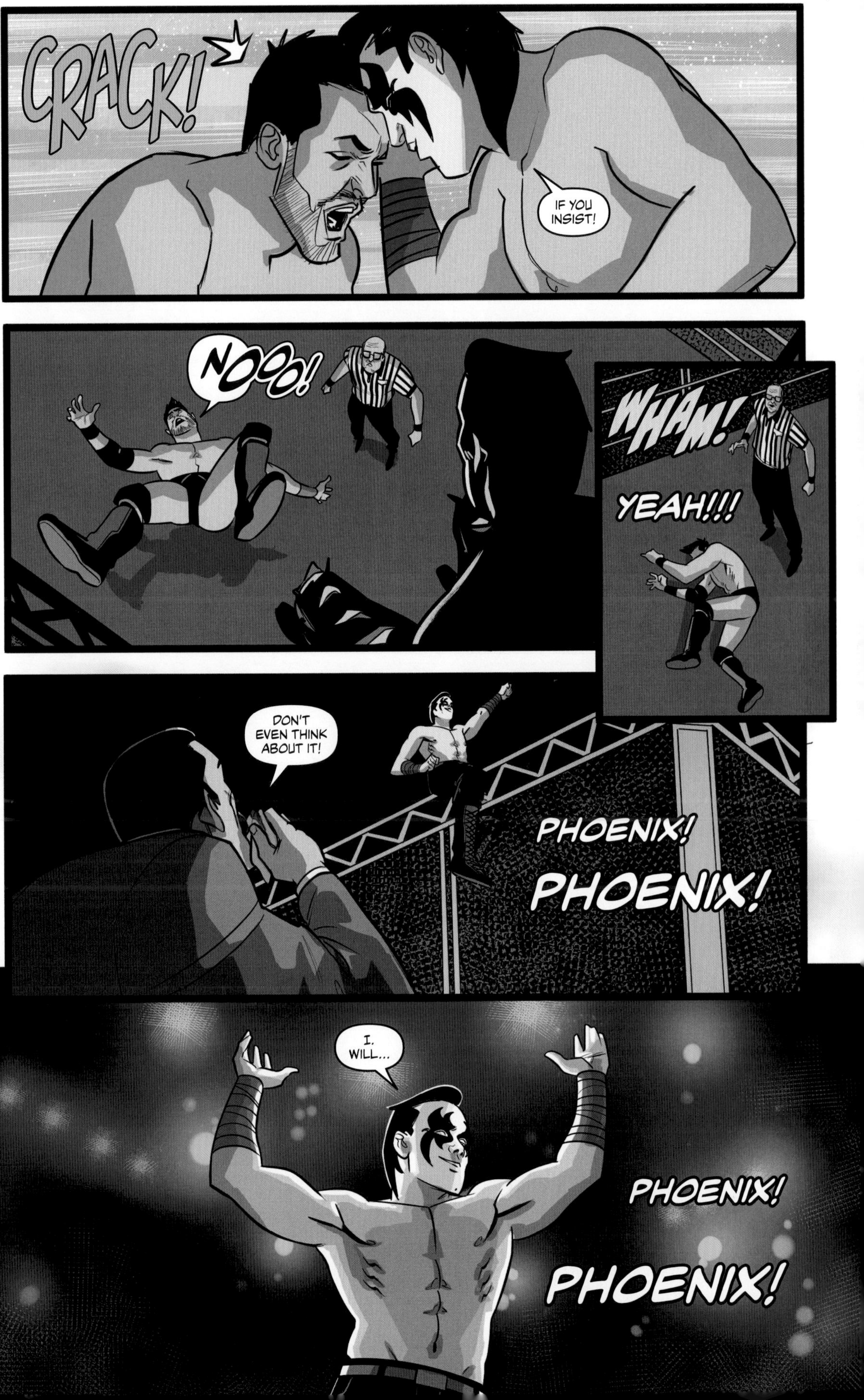
CRACK!
IF YOU INSIST!
NOOO!
WHAM!
YEAH!!!
DON'T EVEN THINK ABOUT IT!
PHOENIX!
PHOENIX!
I. WILL...
PHOENIX!
PHOENIX!

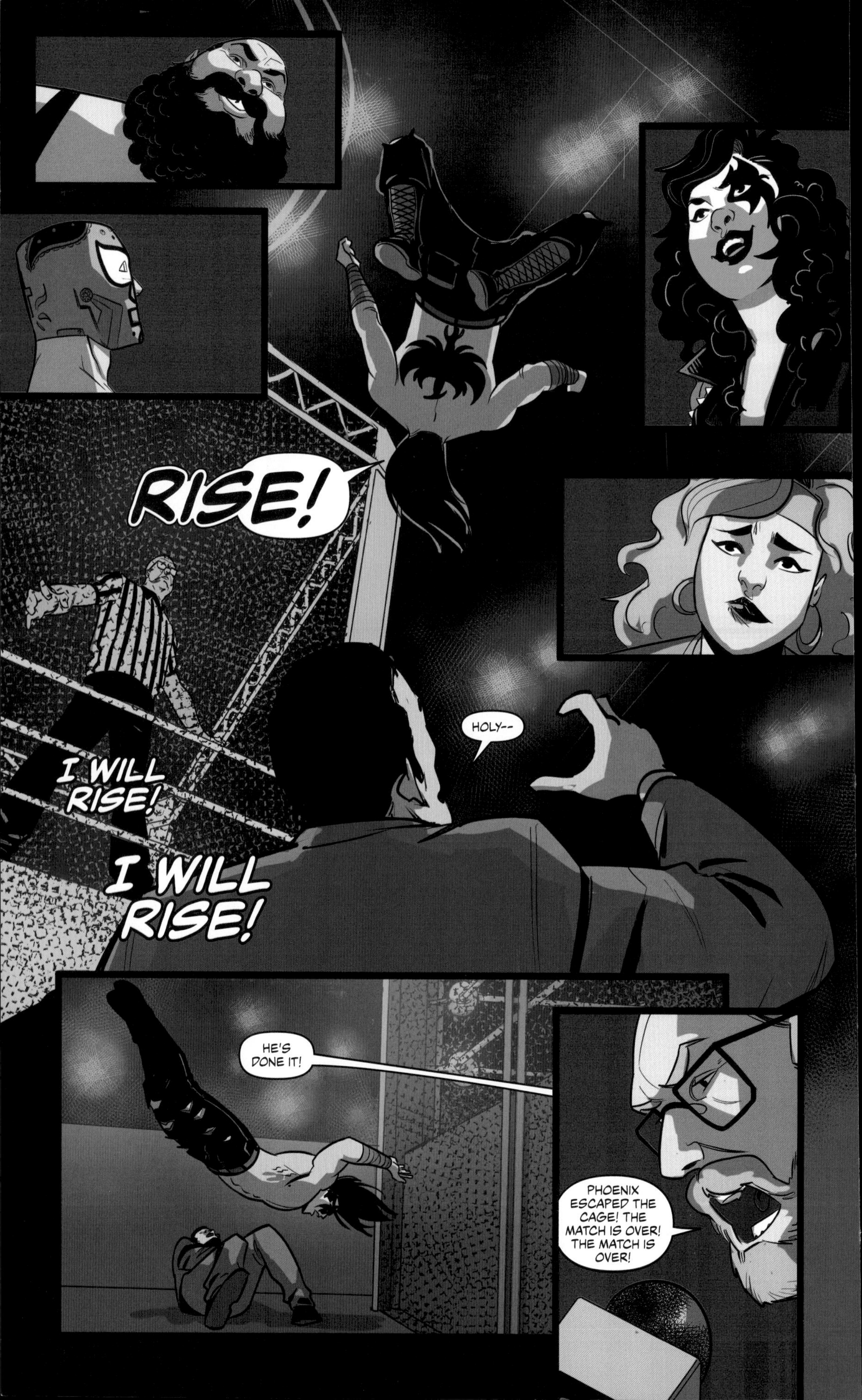
RISE!
I WILL RISE!
I WILL RISE!
HOLY--
HE'S DONE IT!
PHOENIX ESCAPED THE CAGE! THE MATCH IS OVER! THE MATCH IS OVER!

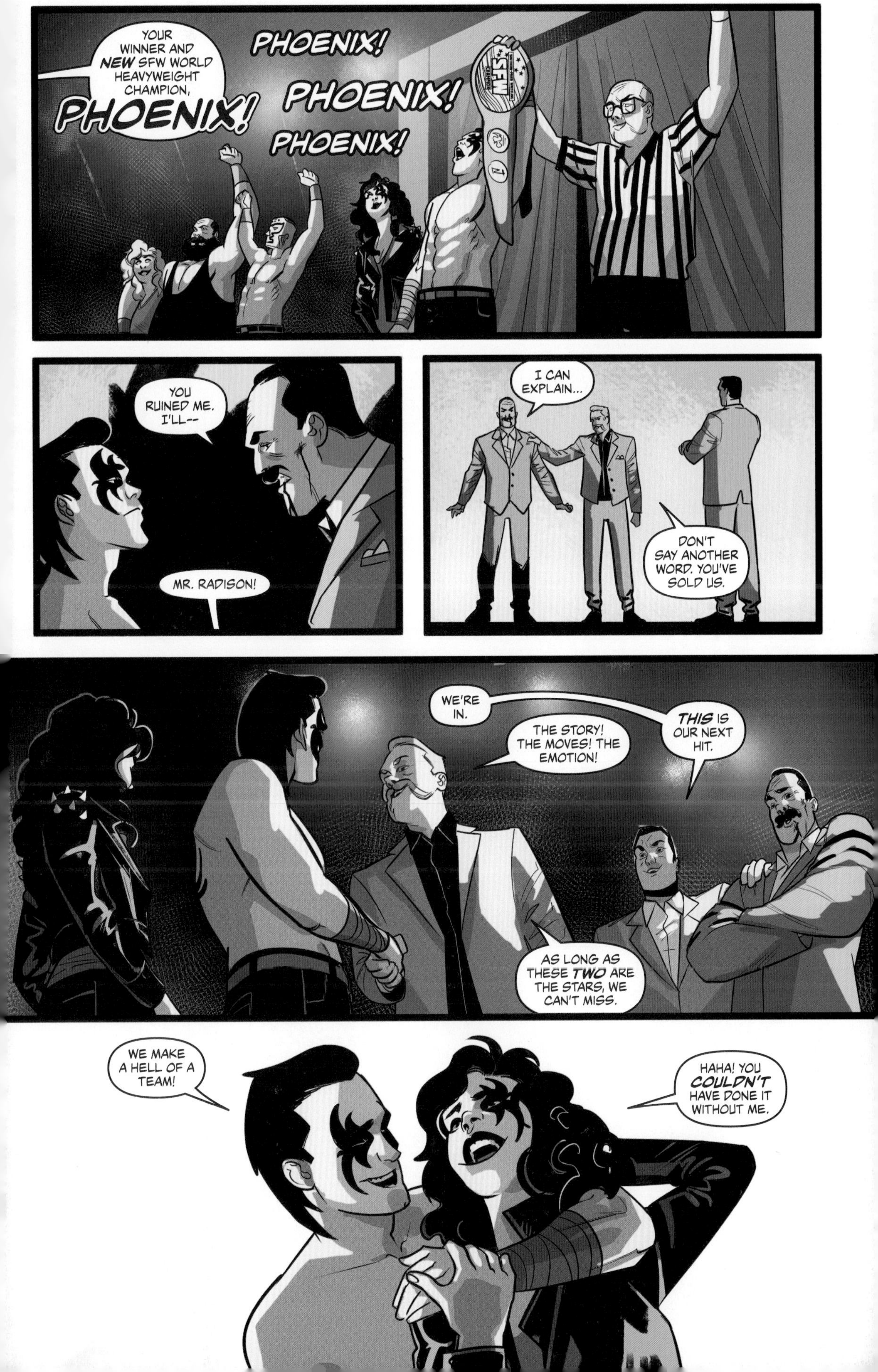

YOUR WINNER AND NEW SFW WORLD HEAVYWEIGHT CHAMPION, PHOENIX!
PHOENIX!
PHOENIX!
PHOENIX!
SFW
YOU RUINED ME. I'LL--
MR. RADISON!
I CAN EXPLAIN...
DON'T SAY ANOTHER WORD. YOU'VE SOLD US.
WE'RE IN.
THE STORY! THE MOVES! THE EMOTION!
THIS IS OUR NEXT HIT.
AS LONG AS THESE TWO ARE THE STARS, WE CAN'T MISS.
WE MAKE A HELL OF A TEAM!
HAHA! YOU COULDN'T HAVE DONE IT WITHOUT ME.

MONTHS LATER. AFW LEAGUE OFFICES.

LOOKS LIKE HE DIDN'T TAKE YOUR *ADVICE.*

NO, HE DID NOT.

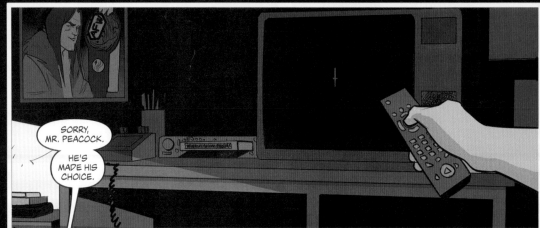

SORRY, MR. PEACOCK.

HE'S MADE HIS CHOICE.

IF PHOENIX DOESN'T WANT TO ACCEPT ME AS HIS *FATHER,* THEN HE'LL HAVE NO CHOICE BUT TO ACCEPT ME AS THE *COMPETITION.*

NO ONE MESSES WITH *BUDDY PEACOCK* AND GETS AWAY WITH IT!

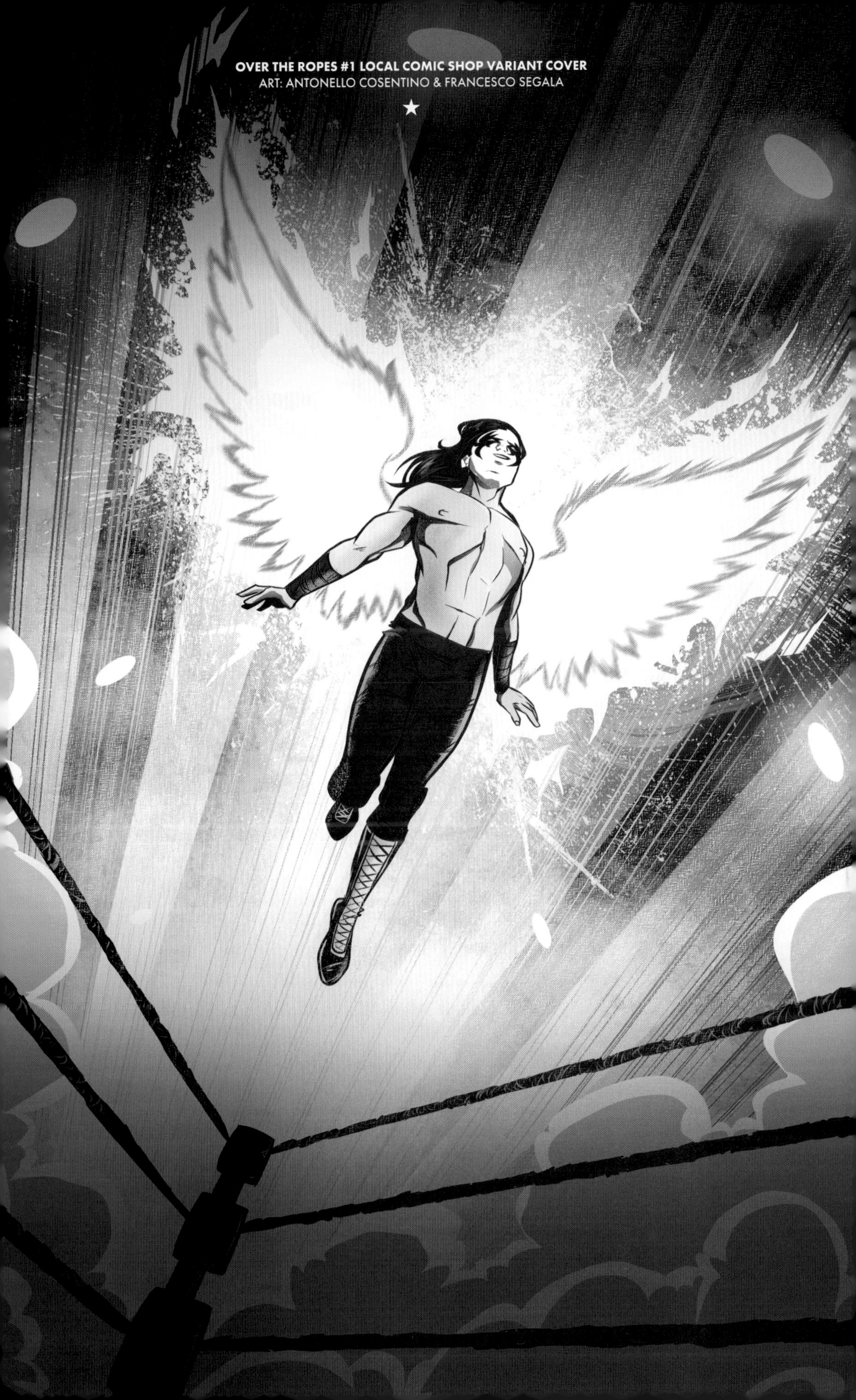

OVER THE ROPES #1 LOCAL COMIC SHOP VARIANT COVER
ART: ANTONELLO COSENTINO & FRANCESCO SEGALA

OVER THE ROPES #1 PRIDELAND COLLECTIBLES VARIANT COVER
ART: ANTONELLO COSENTINO & FRANCESCO SEGALA

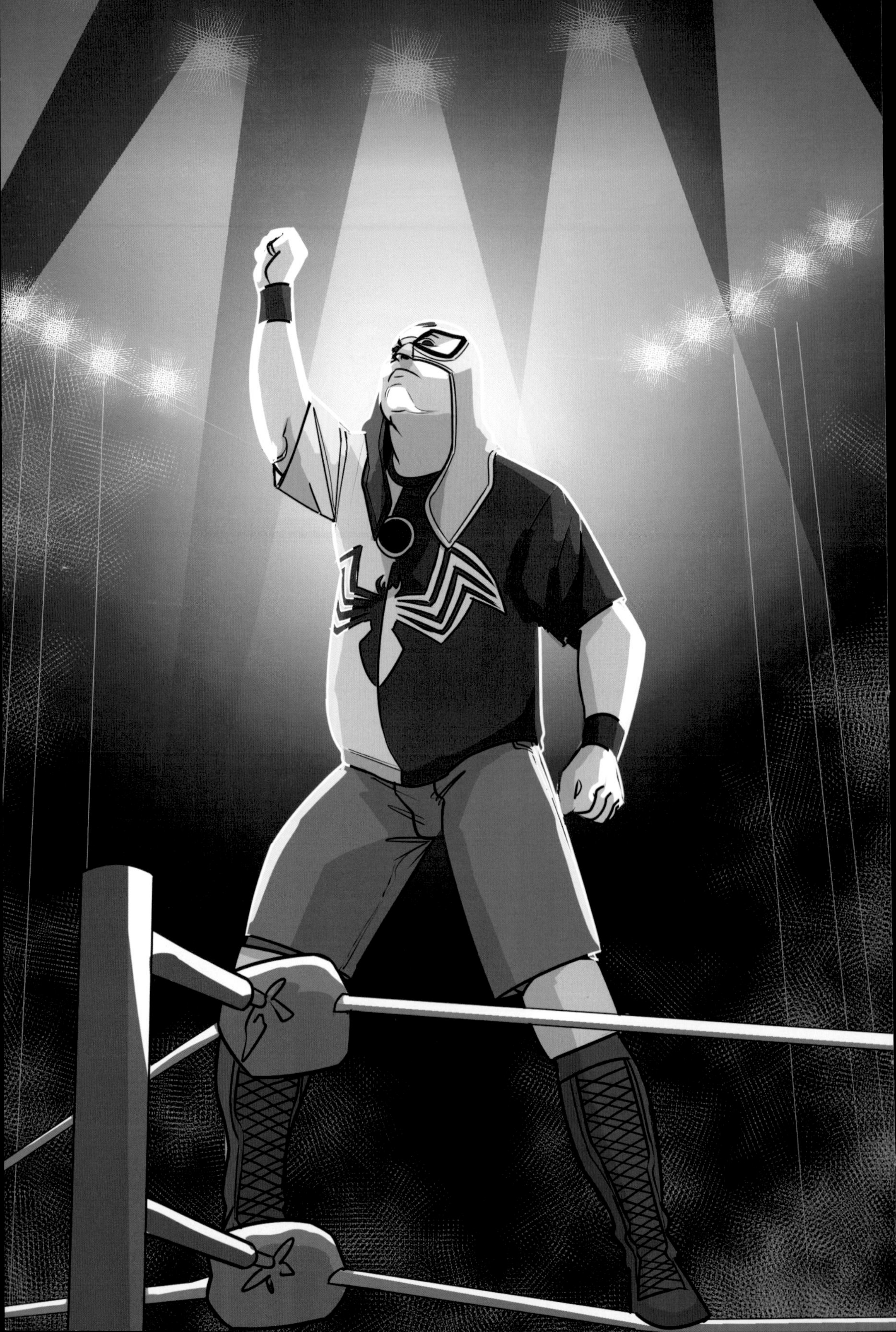

OVER THE ROPES #1 ONE STOP SHOP VARIANT COVER
ART: ALYSA AVERY & JONATHAN PRADA

★

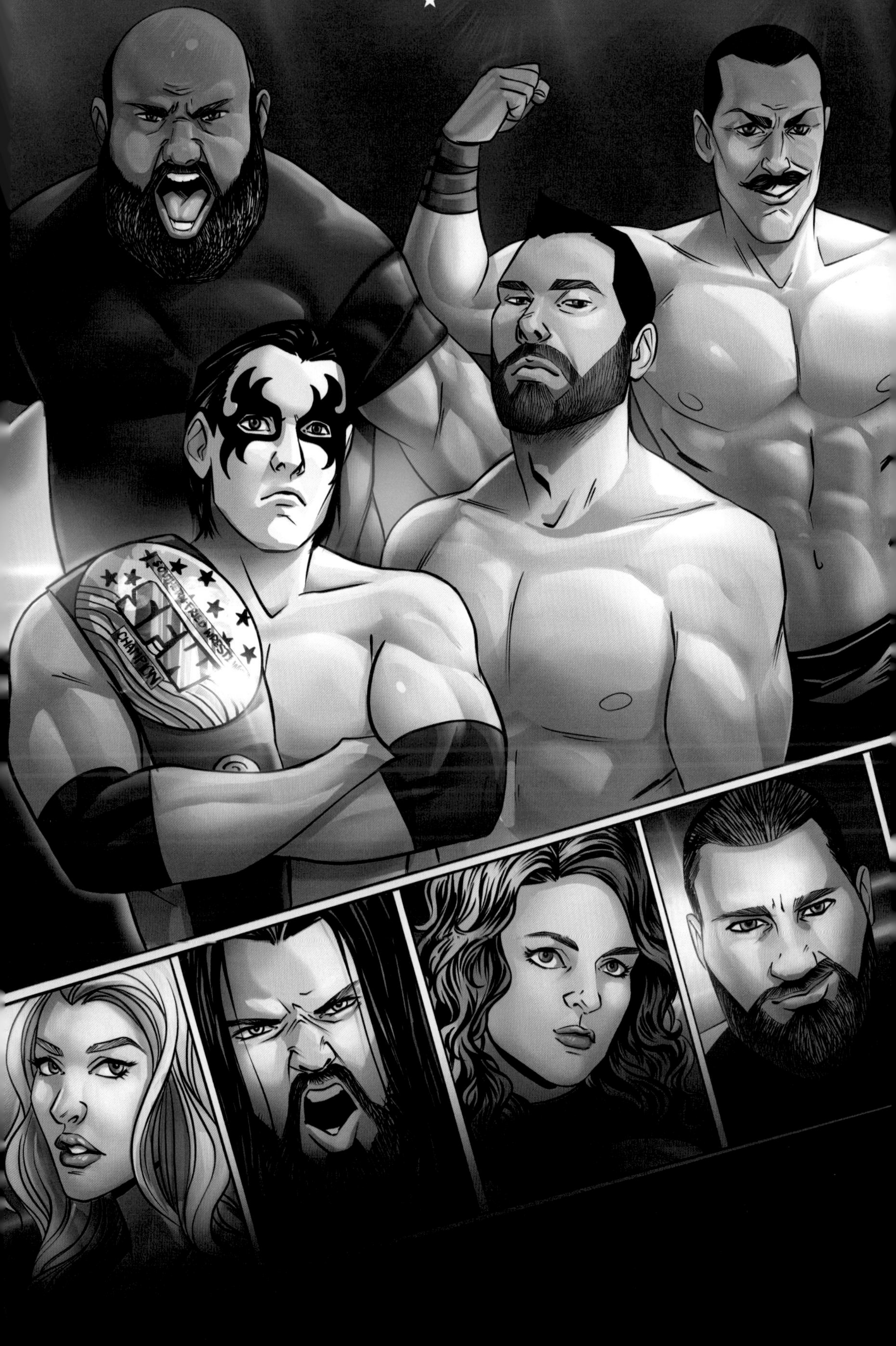
CHAMPION

OVER THE ROPES #1 CBSI VARIANT COVER
ART: ANTONELLO COSENTINO & FRANCESCO SEGALA

★

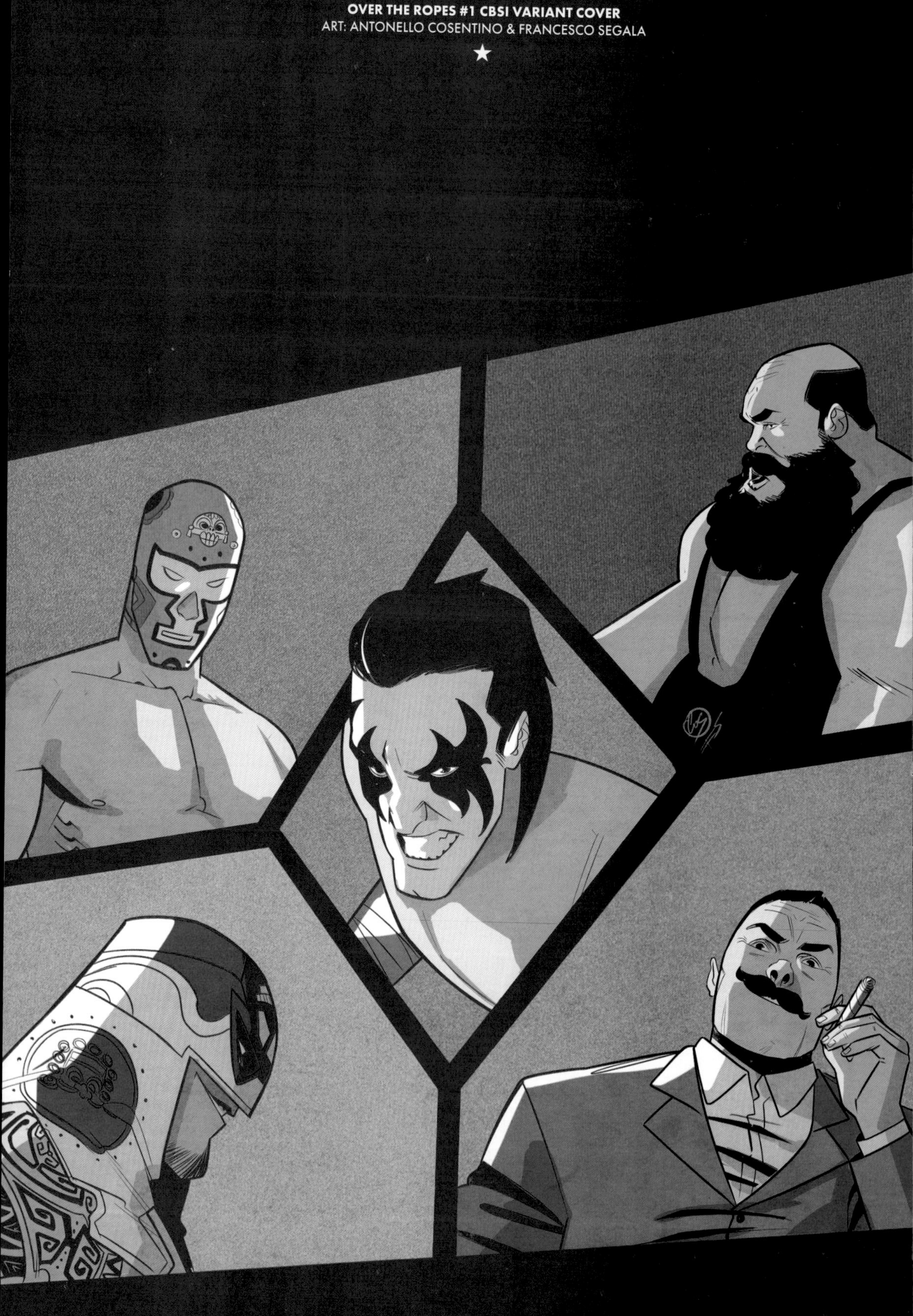

OVER THE ROPES #2 PRIDELAND COLLECTIBLES VARIANT COVER
ART: ANTONELLO COSENTINO & FRANCESCO SEGALA

★

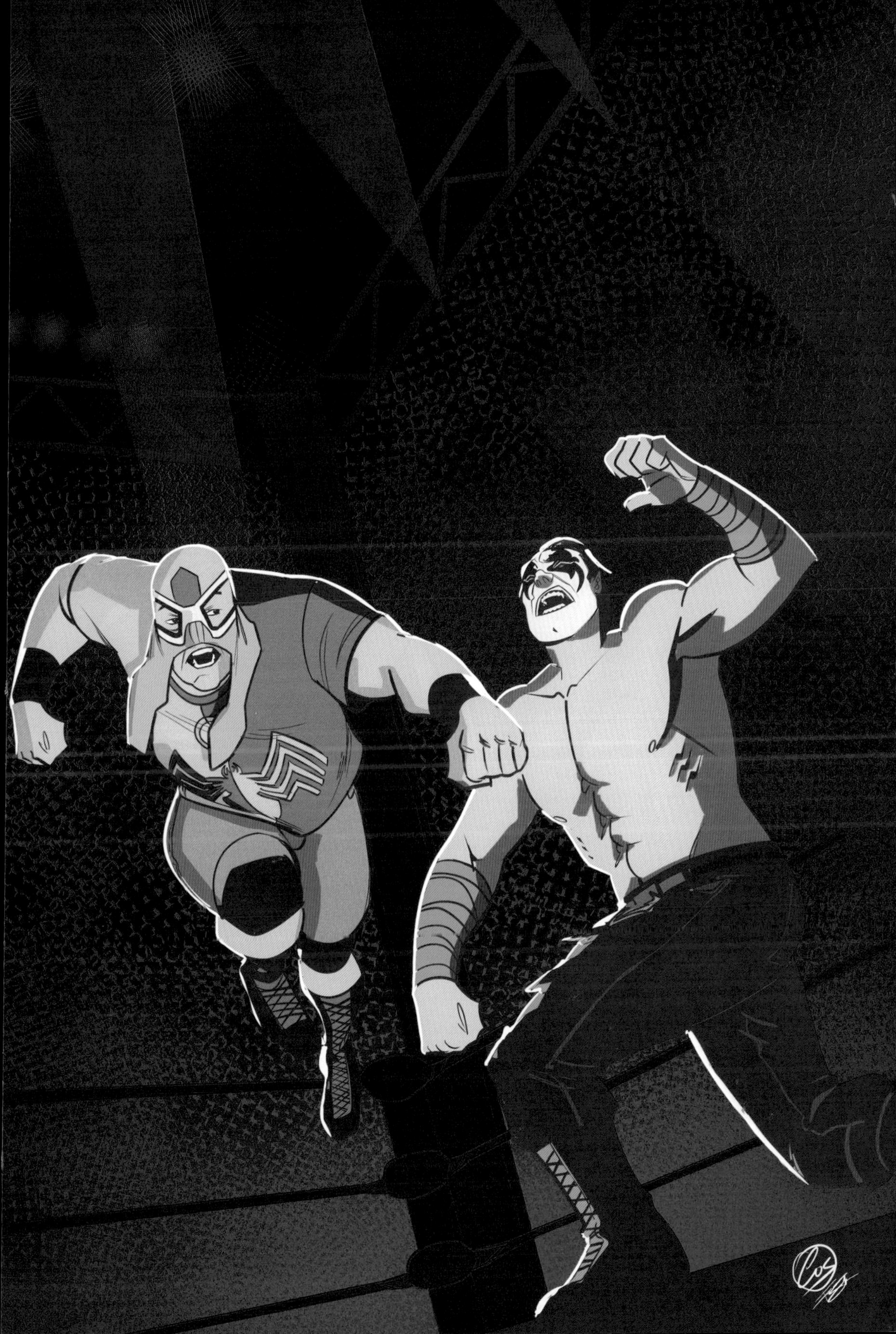

OVER THE ROPES #3 PRIDELAND COLLECTIBLES VARIANT COVER
ART: ANTONELLO COSENTINO & FRANCESCO SEGALA

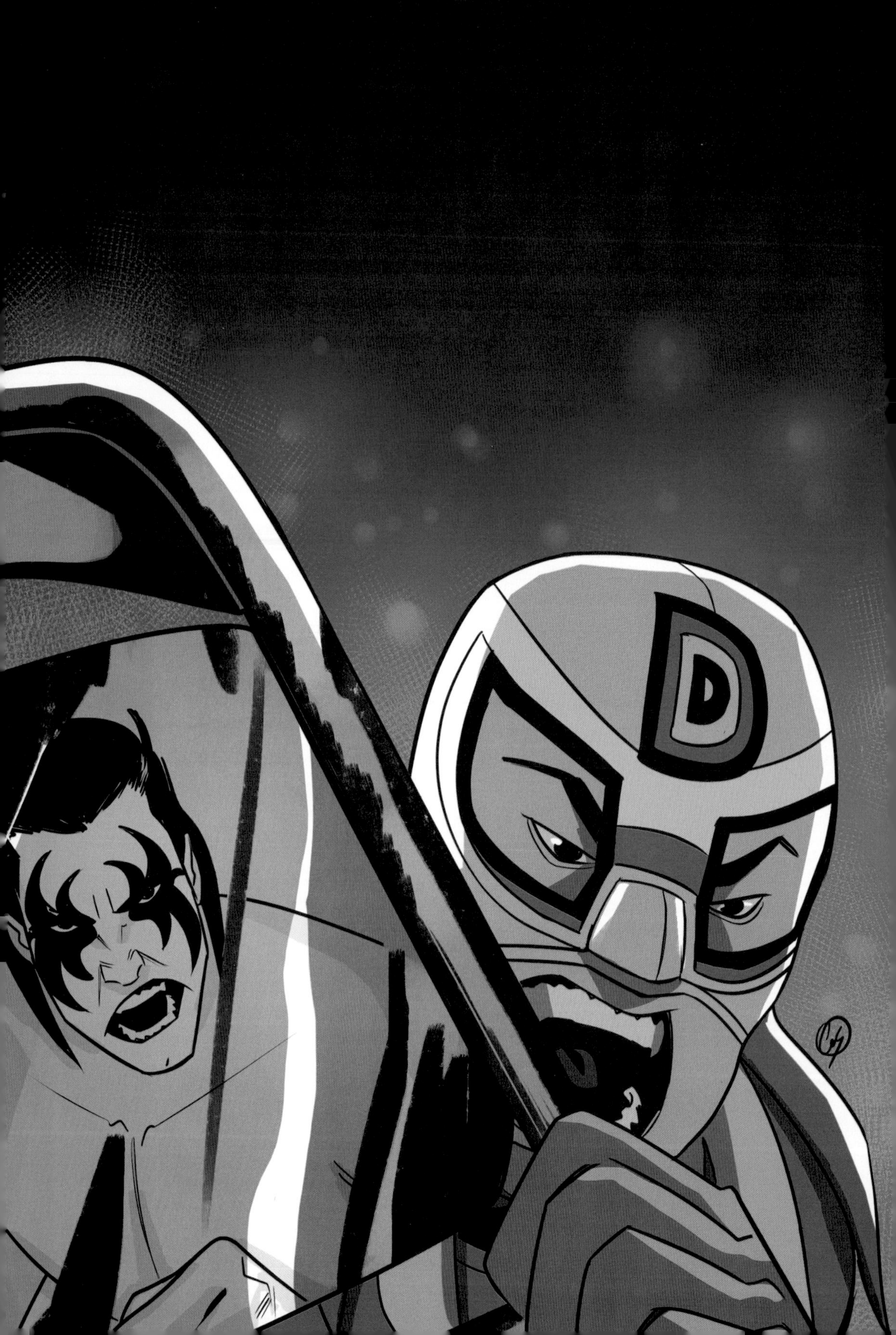

OVER THE ROPES #3 PRIDE AND COLLECTIBLES VARIANT COVER
ART: ANTONELLO COSENTINO & FRANCESCO SEGALA

★

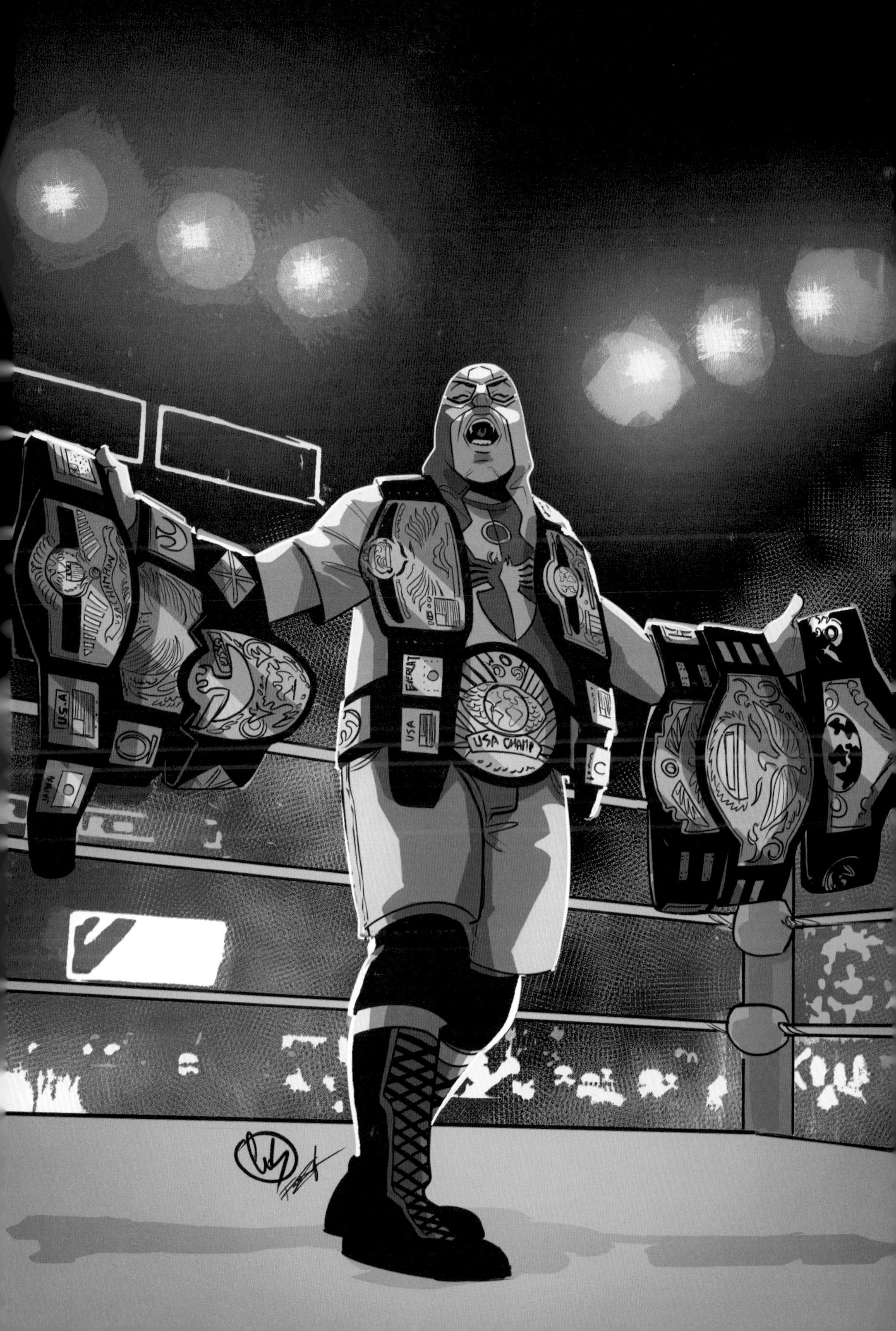
USA CHAMP
U.S.A
USA
JAPAN

OVER THE ROPES #4 INK COVER
ART: ANTONELLO COSENTINO

★

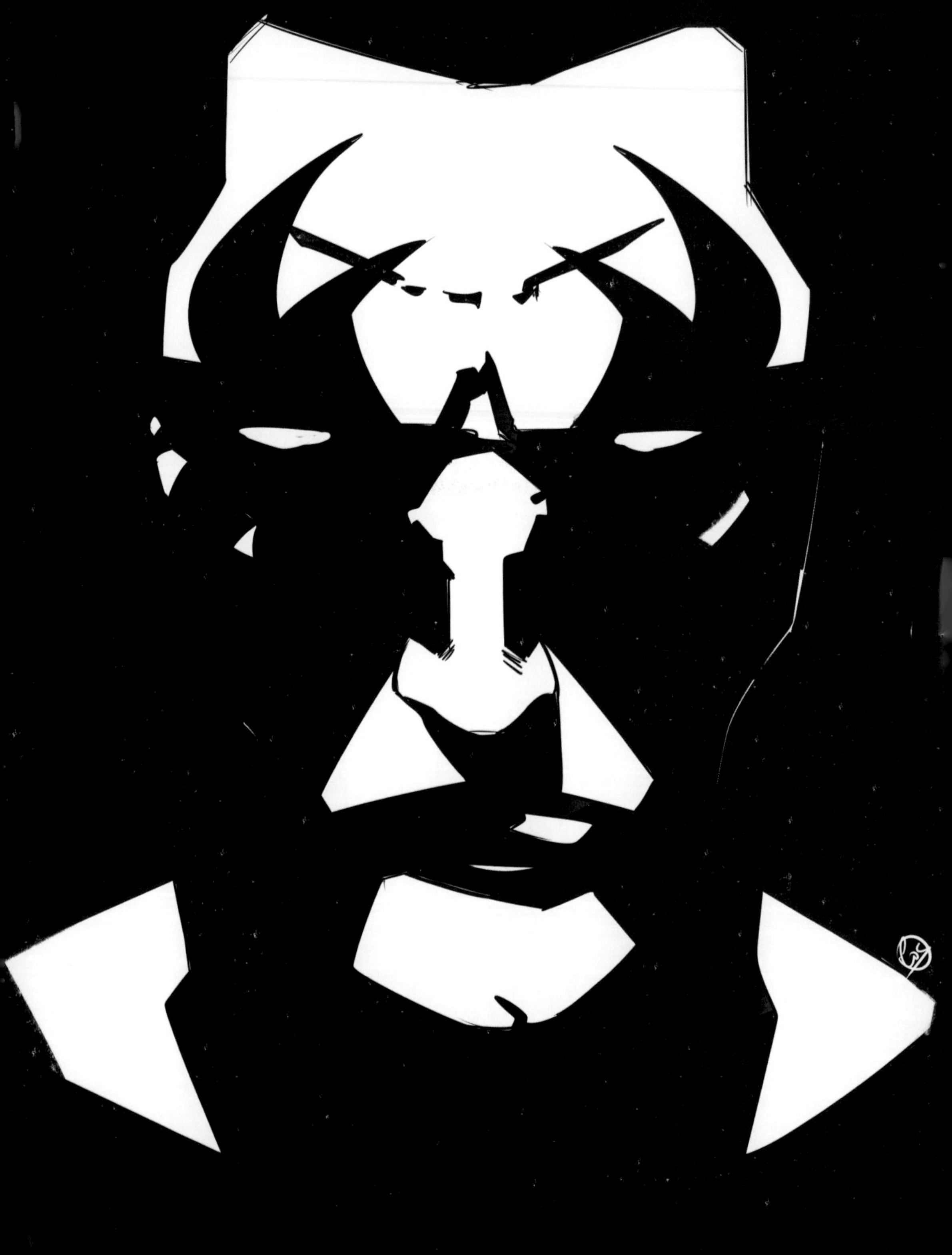

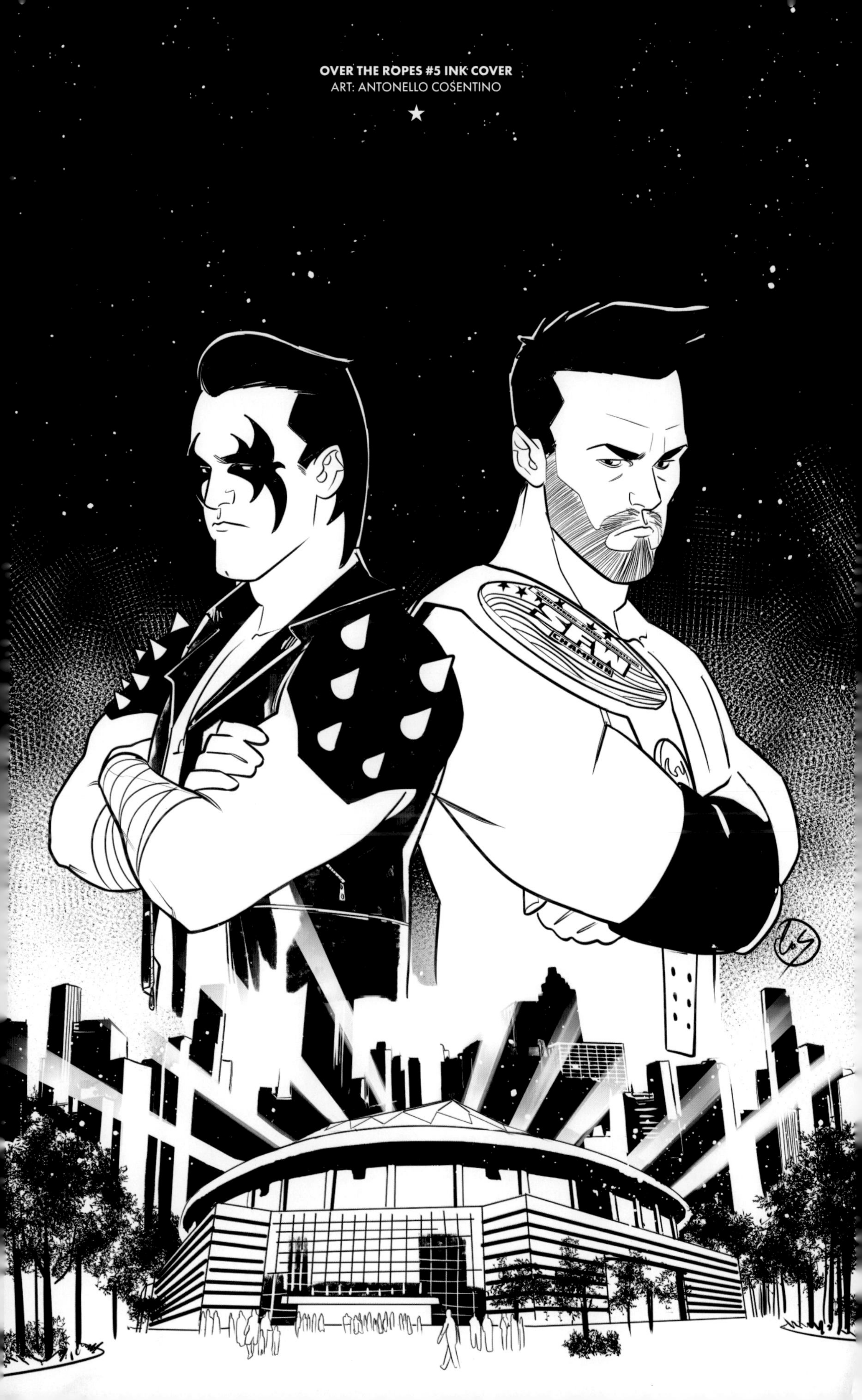
SFW
CHAMPION

OVER THE ROPES #5 INK COVER
ART: ANTONELLO COSENTINO

JAY "THE STINGER" SANDLIN

AS A LIFELONG WRESTLING AND COMIC BOOK FAN, JAY WAS THE PERFECT WRITER FOR THIS UNDERDOG STORY. IF YOU WANT TO LEARN MORE ABOUT HIM AND HIS OTHER BOOKS, HEAD OVER TO JAYSANDLIN.COM.

CREA

FRANCESCO ★ "BACKBREAKER" SEGALA

BORN IN ROME IN 1990, FRANCESCO IS A PART OF PANOPTICON STUDIO. HIS PREVIOUS WORK INCLUDES SUCH TITLES AS: ROCKO'S MODERN AFTERLIFE, FIREFLY, AND BUFFY.

ANTONELLO "BONECRUSHER" COSENTINO

ANTONELLO IS FROM TERMINI IMERESE, ITALY. AS A MEMBER OF EHM AUTOPRODUZIONI, HE HAS DONE INCREDIBLE WORK ON BOOKS LIKE: COSPLAY KILLER, THE BLACKENING, MARASSA, AND STRONGHOLD.

★ ★ ★ ★ ★ ★ ★ ★

TORS ★

JUSTIN "THE LUNCHBOX" ★ BIRCH

JUSTIN BIRCH IS A RINGO AWARD NOMINATED LETTERER BORN AND RAISED IN THE HILLS OF WEST VIRGINIA, WHERE HE LIVES WITH HIS LOVING WIFE, DAUGHTER, AND THEIR DOG, KIRBY.

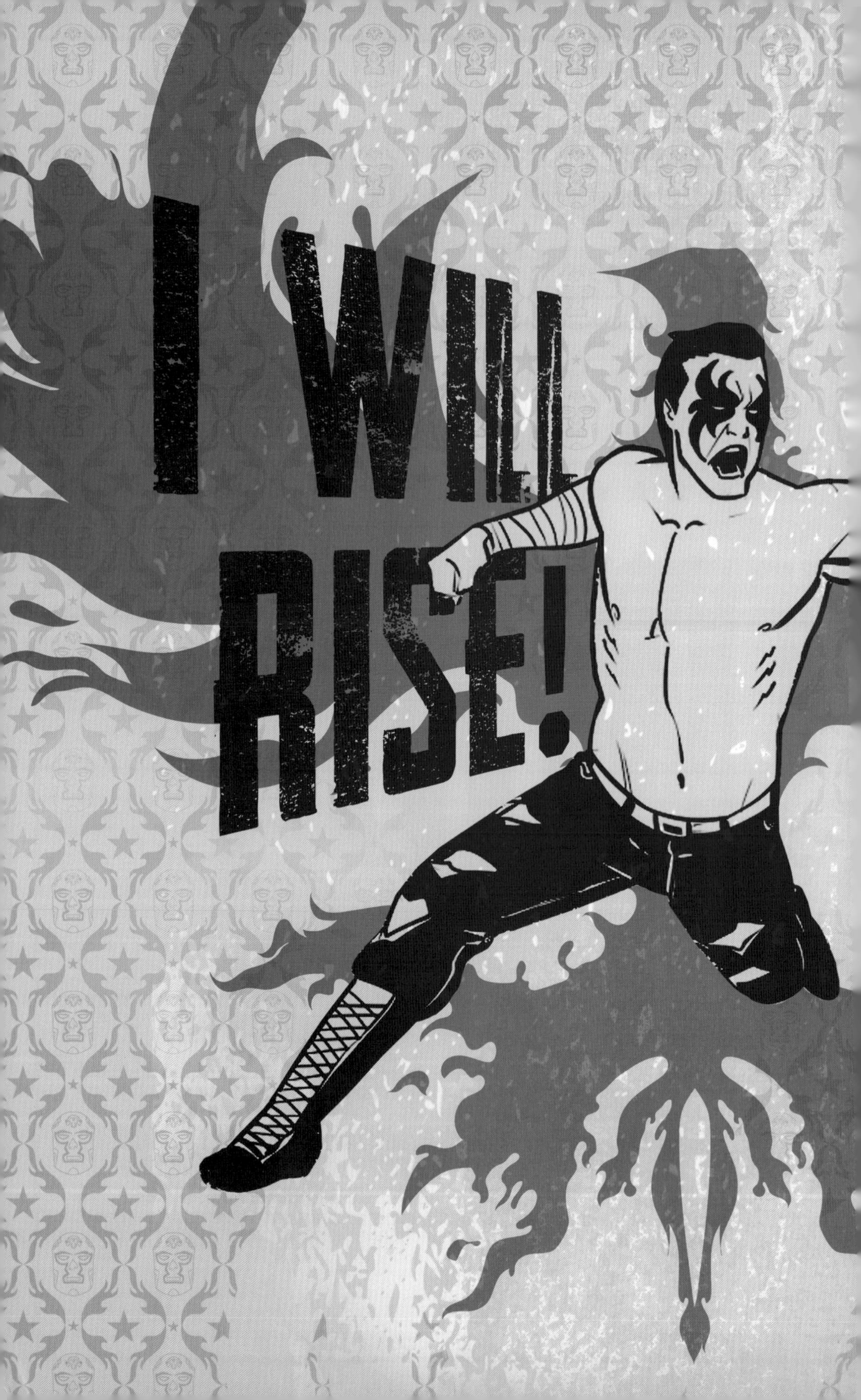
I WILL RISE!

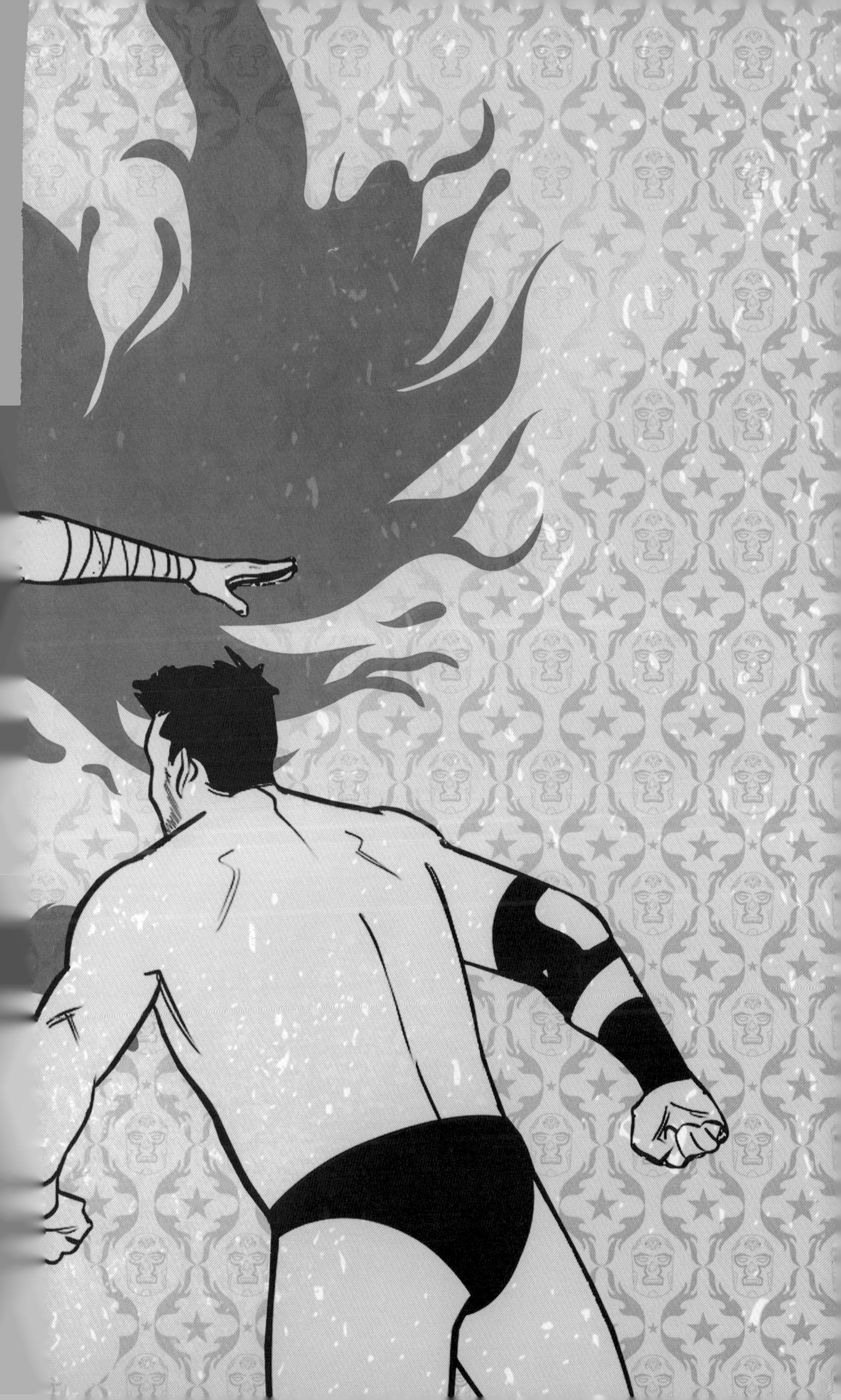

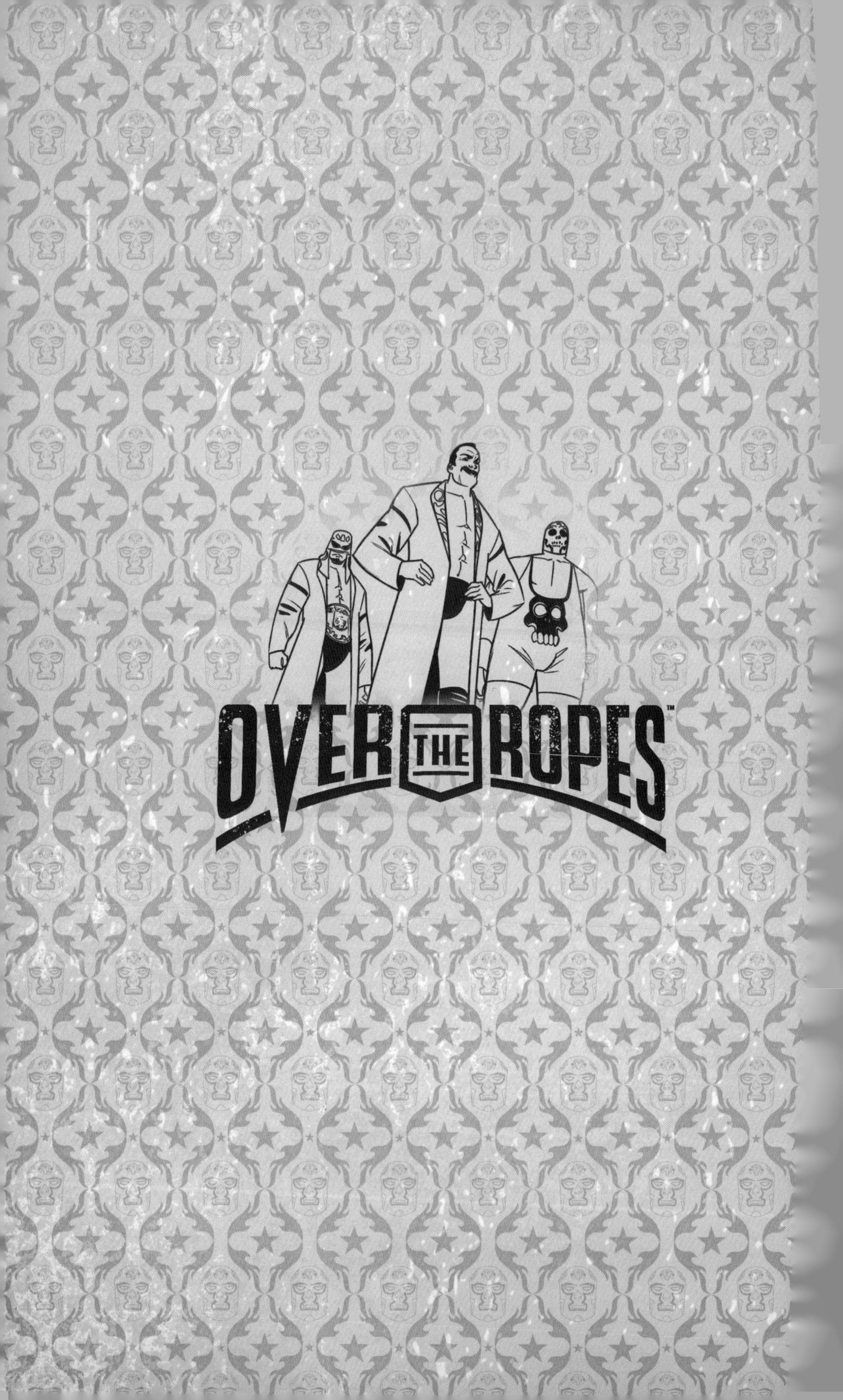

OVER THE ROPES™